RUSSIA'S GREAT MODERN PIANISTS

PAGANINIANA PUBLICATIONS, INC.
Box 27, Neptune, N. J. 07753.

BY DR. MARK ZILBERQUIT

For My Mother.

CONTENTS

Note: There is no significance to the order in which the artists' chapters appear. They are merely in the sequence in which the editor was able to complete them. The editor is also responsible for most of the captions and for the inevitable inconsistency in the spelling of many foreign names.

Dr.
Mark
Zilberquit

Foreword

If a person is entitled to judge how correctly he has chosen his profession, I can say without hesitation: my calling, my life's work is the piano.

Love for and commitment to piano art must have been inherited by me from my dear teachers, and first of all, from my mother — a pianist-pedagogue (a former pupil of professor Nadezhda V. Tchegodayieva, who had been Scriabin's student) who devoted over half a century to piano.

One of the pianists whose interview is included in this series of books, in reply to the question as to whether he teaches, said: "It is impossible to worship two gods at a time." Such an answer is, generally speaking, understandable, but as far as I am concerned, it is unacceptable. For me there exists one indivisible god — the piano. With equal fervor, I play the piano myself and teach my pupils. If time permits. I give solo concerts and deliver lectures to students on the history and methods of piano art, write books and articles about the piano, endeavor to research into the laws of piano performance and generalize the experience of the most outstanding of its representatives.

This series is devoted to Soviet performance — a most vivid and original phenomenon in contemporary art. It deals with the stars of Soviet piano playing. However, it should be kept in mind that in order to make them sparkle with all the might of their talent and mastery, a certain tradition was needed, the tradition that has been created by the work of many musicians, performers and pedagogue-pianists.

This series of books contains essays on Emil Gilels and Sviatoslav Richter – the titans of the contemporary art of piano performance. They have been reckoned among the greatest performers in the world for a long time and they have solidly established their reputation as such, so that they stand apart from the cohort of other Soviet pianists.

With eight eminent artists of the middle and young generations – Lazar Berman, Dimitri Baschkirov, Eliso Virsaladze, Nikolai Petrov, Vladimir Krainev, Gregory Sokolov, Andrei Gavrilov and Mikhail Pletnyov, I had the privilege of many detailed discussions of our craft (with some of them I am connected by bonds of many years of friendship and professional relations). Our discussions resulted in the essays-interviews that comprise this series.

During my meetings and talks with the pianists, we touched upon a great number of various problems. In some cases the opinions of my interlocutors coincided, in others their answers proved diametrically opposed. Probably there will be the same reaction on the part of the readers of this series. But this is only natural, because one of the main and most attractive peculiarities of the art of musical interpretation is the inimitability and uniqueness of every single talented artist-pianist, and, secondly, because musical performance is an art as alive and changeable as life itself.

Lazar Berman

Lazar Berman was born February 26, 1930, in Leningrad. He had not yet reached the age of two when he began the study of the piano. His very first teacher was his mother Anna Makhover, a former pupil of the famous Russian pianist Isabella Vengerova (one of Vengerova's pupils was later Gary Graffman). Her exceptionally serious attitude to his studies, her uncompromising approach towards them from his early childhood, her indubitable pedagogical talent – all that helped to reveal the rare gift of the boy at an early age.

The three-and-a-half year old Berman became the pupil of Samary Savshinsky, a noted pedagogue-methodologist, professor of the Leningrad Conservatory. However, Lazar Berman's mother invariably remained his home tutor.

Lyalik Berman's debut took place in Moscow when he was seven. He played at the All-Union Festival of young talents, where he performed a number of Mozart's and Chopin's pieces and even a mazurka of his own composition.

In 1939 the Bermans moved to Moscow and Lazar became the pupil of the outstanding pedagogue, performer and musical editor Alexander Goldenweiser. Under his tutelage Berman studied for 18 years. Goldenweiser, who was very fond of his pupil, took great interest in his artistic accomplishments.

The last years of Lazar Berman's studies were marked by his successful performances at three international competitions. He was the winner of the World Youth and Student Festival in Berlin (1951), he was awarded the fifth prize at the Queen Elisabeth Competition in Brussels (1956) and the third prize at the Liszt Competition in Budapest (1956).

Lazar Berman. Besides being one of the world's greatest pianists and the unquestioned champion of Liszt, he is a warm, lovable character and wins audiences immediately.

Since the 1950's Lazar Berman has pursued an active concert career. Though the pianist had always been a success with the public, for many years he was not popular with the critics. But in the 1970's there was "an explosion" of interest in Berman's performance. First he skyrocketed to success in Italy. And soon after that he was "discovered" by America. After his triumphant tour of the USA in 1976, he was acclaimed one of the greatest contemporary pianists in the world. Berman performs under such outstanding conductors as Bernstein, Maazel, Ormandy, Mazur, Barenboim; von Karajan, Abbado and Giulini made recordings with him. The pianist's records become bestsellers.

Lazar Berman is the head of a very united and diligent musical family. His wife Valentina teaches piano at the college of the Moscow Conservatory. And Pavlik, his son, who was twelve on his last birthday, is a gifted little violinist selflessly devoted to his instrument. He plays on a most rare 3/4 size Amati from the State Collection. His participation is absolutely indispensable in all the concerts of the Central Music School (CMS) of the Moscow Conservatory, where Lazar and Valentina Berman once studied. In this he follows his father's traditions whose performance had always adorned all the school and student concerts.

★   ★   ★

We first met with Lazar Berman in the late 1960's during our joint summer vacation in Estonia at one of the small resorts on the Baltic seashore. Much later, after his triumphant tours in Europe and America, I happened to write about him in one of the newspapers. I remember that Moscow was somewhat bewildered—Berman, of whom a "final" rather moderate opinion seemed to have been formed, became a number one sensation overnight . . .

And here we are sitting with Lazar Berman in his cozy Moscow apartment. The noted pianist eagerly accepted my suggestion that we have a discussion of some problems concerning piano performanceship. He willingly shared the reminiscences of his childhood, the years of his studies, his teachers, colleagues, interesting impressions and observations.

At the Bermans' home, from the left: Mrs. Lazar Berman,
Dr. Zilberquit, Berman and Mrs. Mark Zilberquit.

Speaking of himself, of his craft, Lazar Berman never posed as a
mentor. His manner is unassuming, he often spices his comments
with wisecracks.

Half a century of selfless devotion to art, to the piano. Fifty years
of back-breaking work at the instrument, tours, hundreds of concerts. Yes, today when Berman's name is among those of the best
pianists in the world, many people forget the "thorns" he had to
push through. But he himself will never forget them . . . In his life
there has been everything: lack of understanding, non-recognition,
one-sided, narrow appraisal of the critics who had slapped the label
of a "mere virtuoso" on him and stubbornly refused to see that the
Lazar Berman of the 70's-80's was by no means the same as the
Lyalik Berman of the 40's-50's.

However, no matter how his creative life was developing he always remained a selfless toiler of the piano, an artist for whom devotion to his beloved instrument, the imperative need to work with it was above success.

And this hard work at the piano began for Berman in early childhood. We may say with confidence that very few musicians had spent their early years in such endless practicing at the instrument as Lazar Berman.

Lazar "Lyalik" Berman at the age of seven. His mother dressed him like a child prodigy complete with long hair, velvet suit and large white bow tie.

We speak of the first steps the famous pianist made at the instrument:

LB: I began to study the piano at an age I do not even remember. It was my mother who took charge of my studies. Hardly was I able to sit at the instrument when she decisively put everything else aside as unimportant and started our studies. Throughout all the years of my pupilage there never was anything more important for her than my studies of the piano. The well-being of the family was my father's concern. I was hardly two years old when my mother began to stretch my hands, that is, the sinews between the fingers.

MZ: Did your mother consider that an obligatory exercise for beginners?

LB: Not only for beginners. I am now past fifty, but every day before sitting down at the piano I stretch my hands like that. I stretch every finger until I hear a click. That is the signal. The finger is ready to play.

MZ: Don't you think it dangerous? Can't you hurt your finger that way?

LB: I am careful. Of course you should know your stretch limit.

MZ: Does it mean that your mother began to teach you music not with music as such?

LB: Absolutely. First of all there was the preparation for the studies. However, at about the age of three I could already participate in the Festival of young talents in Leningrad. We were auditioned by quite an authoritative board which after the audition decreed, "the child Berman should be assigned to a pedagogue." That was how I became Samary Savshinsky's pupil.

MZ: Professor Savshinsky is famous today as the author of an interesting book, *The Pianist and His Work*. He was an experienced methodologist. What is his contribution to your career?

LB: I was Savshinsky's pupil for about five years. But as a matter of fact my mother carried out the major work with me. I usually came to the lessons with well-prepared material. As my mother was constantly at my side I memorized all the pieces practically "from her hands," learned everything by ear, and until I was eight I hardly knew the notes at all.

Samary Savshinsky really loved his little pupil dearly and was proud of him. After several months of his teaching Berman, he wrote in the newspaper *Leningrad Pravda*: "Today in the Leningrad Conservatory began the public tests . . . of a group of young musicians. The youngest of those being examined is Lyalya Berman, four years and nine months old. The boy fluently performs the compositions of Bach, Tchaikovsky and other composers."

MZ: How many hours did you spend at the instrument daily?

LB: Even in early childhood the daily quota established by Mother was about four or five hours. And on top of everything during all these hours Mother was sitting at my side. That was the way it went for 12 or 13 years till I gradually began practicing by myself. I've got to admit that Mother was quite despotic. But I

Alexander Goldenweiser, a world class musician, teacher and writer . . . . and Berman's mentor.

guess it only did me good. Because, unlike my son who is eager to practice on his violin from morning till night, I worked listessly to say the least. Without her despotism I think I wouldn't have achieved any outstanding results. However, this kind of practicing involuntarily suppressed my own initiative. I followed her instructions automatically. It must have resulted in my getting somewhat "mechanized," doing many things unconsciously.

MZ: What did your mother pay primary attention to in your studies?

LB: The major emphasis was laid on the development of the technical command. And with this end in view Mother offered me a great number of various exercises. My hand is not very big, and to tell you the truth, it's not very strong. I have always managed things owing to the dexterity imparted to me by my mother by means of certain exercises. One of her favorite exercises was "skips." Every day I sat down at the piano and played.

MZ: Was it of any help to you later?

LB: Definitely. For example, when performing the Liszt *Etude, Wild Chase*. I must confess that at one time there were even anecdotes about the way I played this exercise. As rumor had it, Mother made me dart to the instrument and play the necessary chord at a running jump.

MZ: I don't think your technical development consisted only in exercises.

LB: Of course not. Besides exercises I played scales a lot, but I played them mostly in an unusual manner. You know, the spirit of defiance, the desire to do everything against the rules is so typical of children. So I invented my own way of working at scales. I played the scales with the wrong fingering. For instance, I learned all the scales with the C-Major fingering or some with only two fingers, then with only three, etc. Certainly, with such fingering any high-quality performance of the scales couldn't be expected. However, gradually the traditionally difficult passages in some

Berman and Alexander Goldenweiser during their Conservatory days. Berman still "lives off" the repertoire he learned from Goldenweiser.

15

The post-graduate class of Goldenweiser. Berman is standing in the back, almost in the center. To the right of Goldenweiser are two legends, Professors Samuel Feinberg and Gregory Ginsburg. To the left, seated, is Leah Moiseyevna Levinson, ". . . a woman with a young soul capable of understanding the state of your creative spirit, of enjoying your success."

Berman with Emil Gilels during the 1956 Budapest Competition.

compositions began to come out well. Extremely inconvenient combinations did not seem difficult to me any longer. Yet there was a negative point to it. I ceased thinking of convenient fingering altogether, playing absolutely higgledy-piggledy.

MZ: What compositions did you play by the end of your studies with Savshinsky?

LB: I was already playing rather complicated pieces, including the first movement of the Beethoven *Third Concerto* with which I appeared before my future teacher Alexander Borisovich Goldenweiser in Moscow. My mother decided that I was to go on with my studies there. I must say that by that time my progress with the piano had somewhat turned my head, I had acquired the ways of a child prodigy which was ironically commented upon in one of the newspapers at the time. The point was that usually on coming to a concert I made directly for the main hall without paying any attention to the ticket-collectors. Once a ticket-collector tried to stop me and I said arrogantly to her, "Don't you know who I am? I'm Lyalik Berman!" Mother even dressed me as a child prodigy—a velvet suit with knickerbockers, mother-of-pearl buttons, and a white silk bow under my chin.

MZ: So, being such a "prodigy fully armed" both musically and psychologically, you got into Goldenweiser's class.

Goldenweiser is one of the pillars of the Russian and the Soviet piano school. A lot of works have been written about his pedagogical principles. But you must have had very rich experience in associating with him. What did he give you as a musician, as an artist, as a person?

LB: You may judge for yourself. I came to his class as a boy and I finished my studies with him as a mature musician. The nearly twenty years that I worked under Goldenweiser's supervision generally proved to be decisive for me. In fact, I did not have any other pedagogue. What am I obliged to my teacher for? Goldenweiser infused his pupils with musical culture based on very profound and correct reading of the composer's text. And what can be more important than to cultivate in a pupil a competent, truly creative approach to the composer's text? Because revealing the message is just the thing that means making music, at least in the stage of learning. I could say a lot more about his creative method, about some of his pedagogical advice. But I'll

18

point out only one more thing: Goldenweiser molded us as personalities by setting the example of selfless service to our art. He taught us to be faithful to our duty, to music. Goldenweiser paternally loved his pupils and took care of them in every way possible. Being aware that our family was financially hard up, he helped us. Once a month in the teaching department of the Conservatory I received an envelope with money.

MZ: Did you really have no other teacher than Goldenweiser?

LB: As soon as the war broke out our school was evacuated. In spite of the grave situation at the fronts, the State took care of us so that our studies should not be interrupted. The pupils were

Lazar Berman after winning the third prize at the 1956 Budapest Competition. To his right is the winner of the Competition, Lev Vlasenko.

evacuated together with their families and pedagogues. As Goldenweiser could not leave Moscow, for two years I studied with the marvelous musician Theodore Gutmann. It was with him, for example, that I went through the Liszt etudes and other pieces.

MZ: Who were your idols among the pianists in the years of your studies?

LB: At the time of my pupilage outstanding foreign musicians were rare guests in our country. Moreover, recording was not very well developed either. So, actually, I am the "child" of the native musical culture. And I did my best not to miss any of the concerts of the celebrated Soviet musicians.

It was Vladimir Sofronitsky who was a god to me. He captivated me by his mysteriousness, his singularity. What, in my opinion, unites Sofronitsky, Judina, Gould and Michelangeli? It is their unique, singular interpretation. One can imitate Richter, even Horowitz, but these four are inimitable.

MZ: You've mentioned Maria Judina.

LB: Judina was also a god, but an alien god, not mine. And of course these were our two titans, Richter and Gilels.

Sviatoslav Richter amazed me by his spontaneity. I emphasize — the spontaneity of Richter's art of the 40's-50's is a unique phenomenon in pianism. For instance, today nothing is heard of spontaneity. And Emil Gilels has always been a mentor for me. I have always felt and still feel taken over by the wonder of Gilels' unique tone. Undoubtedly Richter and Gilels inspired me as magnificent virtuosos by their technique. The more so, as at that time I already had my own considerable technical achievements. In this respect everything was even too good, I would say.

MZ: What do you mean by "too good"?

A famous caricature of Richter, who is so dexterous at the piano that it seems that he plays with more than two hands.

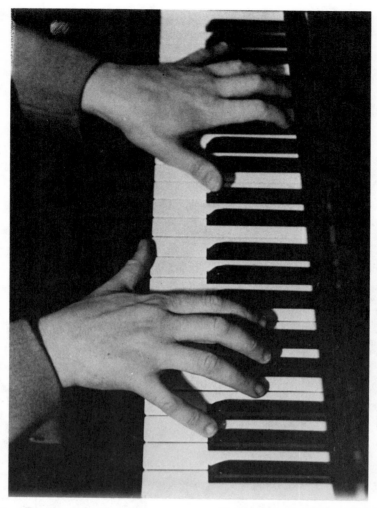

Lazar Berman's hands are comparatively small, with slim fingers that fit nicely between the black keys.

Lazar Berman playing a concert in the Great Hall of the Moscow Conservatory. This hall always overwhelms him since it was here that he first heard all the great masters.

LB: During all my school and Conservatory years I played scales a lot (occasionally I play them at present time too, only not regularly). And probably I got a little too engrossed in the technical aspect for which I was justly reproached at the time. In those years I was even jokingly nicknamed "Bermachine." [It is a pun, as in Russian "Bormachine" means a dentist's drill.]

MZ: How many hours a day did you spend at the instrument in the Conservatory years?

LB: I think not less than six or seven hours a day. In other words, apart from the lectures, I practiced the rest of the day.

MZ: Do you consider yourself a virtuoso by nature or was your legendary technique developed in the endless hours of practicing?

LB: Undoubtedly I consider myself to be a "grown" virtuoso, because I had no innate gift for that whatsoever. I mean first of all the peculiarities of the hand. I always frankly admit that there is no strength in my hand; my fingers are not long, my hand is not slim. Generally speaking, my hands do not seem to be meant for playing the piano, and they are shaped like a woman's. Have you seen the

hands of Rachmaninoff, Horowitz, Emil Gilels? Those are real pianist's hands! And what have I got?

MZ: Your example is another proof of how much can be achieved by persistent toil over many years. However, I think that even if you had not been gripped in the vise of the endless hours of practice at the time of your studies and your development had taken another course, sooner or later it would have brought you to the performance Olympus all the same. Talent cannot be replaced by any toil.

LB: You may be right.

MZ: As long as we are on the subject of virtuosity, I'd like to touch upon a number of problems in connection with piano technique.

LB: I'd gladly share my views on piano technique with you and even divulge some of my "secrets." But I want to warn you that I

"The most horrible thing for me, what I fear the most and do my best to avoid by all means, is that life should make me mechanized . . . .

did not take a direct route in piano performance. I guess I sometimes achieved the desired results by means of not the most rational devices. They were good for me, but in speaking of them I don't claim them to be universal. Let's take, for instance, octave technique. It is common knowledge that, as a rule, as preparatory foundation for octaves, we first employ special exercises, then come simple études, etc. With me it was quite different. When we dealt with the octaves for the first time, Goldenweiser gave me the following advice: take some études of Czerny op. 740 or the Bach two-part Inventions and play them in octaves. My greatest achievement was the performance of the étude of Clementi-Tausig F-minor. I played the whole left hand part in octaves. It is my own invention and I am very proud of it. I am absolutely sure that the pianist who can execute this étude in octaves accurately, in good

.... so that in spite of very extensive touring I can preserve the freshness of my musical emotions and inspire as well as entertain."

tempo, and without feeling any tiredness in the hand has achieved truly ideal octaves, as practically all the octave technical devices and formulas can be found in this étude: scales, arpeggio, skips, etc. Due to what factors have I managed that peculiar exercise? Some pianists play octaves owing to the configuration of their strong hands. I do it due to dexterity and inclusion of the whole body.

MZ: It is a very curious device, playing non-octave pieces in octaves. Only I do not quite agree with you that the Clementi étude involves all the octave formulas. For instance, there are no repetition octaves in it on which the second part of the Liszt *Sixth Rhapsody* (B dur) is based. By the way, have you ever played this composition?

LB: I have tried but it tires my hand.

The Clementi etude does not involve all the octave formulas. For instance, there are no repetition octaves in it on which the second part of the Liszt **Sixth Rhapsody** *is based.*

MZ: That's extremely interesting! You are a virtuoso of such high standing that nothing seems to be beyond your capability on the piano. Perhaps, if you really wanted to, you'd easily "catch up" on your repetitive octaves.

LB: The game is not worth the candle. I am not so fond of this music as to make an effort and take the trouble to do it. I hold that for the performance of this particular rhapsody the musician should possess one quality that I definitely lack—muscular strength of the hand. Its execution requires a very strongly built performer. And I have already mentioned that I play actually from almost every joint in my body. I did try but it tired my hand very soon. And I don't feel like working hard at music that doesn't stir me.

MZ: Your case of acquiring the octave technique without prac-

*"I tried to play the Liszt **Sixth** Rhapsody, but it tires my hand so much that I gave it up and rarely play it."*

ticing appropriate études is probably unique. But I don't think you will assert that it is possible to do without études in other types of technique as well.

LB: Of course, I won't. As for me, at one time I played almost all the instructive literature available: simple études of Czerny, then études of Cramer, Clementi-Tausig and all the fifty Czerny études op. 740. I believe every pianist ought to go through this.

MZ: Let us have a glimpse of how you worked at études.

LB: Very often, apart from the traditional ways, I used to play études in different keys. The whole point was to play the étude in another key with the original fingering.

MZ: The work on the Chopin and Liszt études is known to be the culmination in the virtuoso development of a young musician. And coming into contact with this music the performer can't help returning to it time and again. It would be interesting if you were to compare the Chopin études with those by Liszt.

"Every pianist ought to go through the 50 Czerny etudes of Opus 740."

LB: I believe Chopin's études are more difficult than Liszt's. Each Liszt étude is an image in itself that can be grasped and comprehended easier than the images of Chopin's études. In my opinion, Chopin's technique is more refined, more melodious. Every Chopin note is worth its weight in gold, so to say. Here you cannot profit by using the pedal. Besides, the Chopin études are more on finger technique than Liszt's, i.e., in the Liszt études formulas on octave and chord technique prevail.

And one more remark. In Chopin the instructive element, the technical formula is more obvious: there is the "chromatic" étude, "terza", "sesta", "octave" études, etc. It is more difficult to reveal their image-bearing sphere, as everything in them is highly concentrated. Liszt also has a certain formula but it is not so distinct as in Chopin's études. In the Liszt étude there may be several tasks. For instance, in *The Blizzard* it is tremolo and leaps.

MZ: You have made recordings of all the Liszt études, haven't you?

"I believe the Chopin etudes are more difficult than Liszt's."

LB: I have. And it was Sviatoslav Richter who inspired me to make those recordings. He played only eight études. I listened to them in concerts and was so astounded by the performance that I made up my mind to learn all twelve. Once I met Richter and asked, "Why do you play only eight études but not all the 12?" He answered, "Because I don't like the other four. I don't like this music." And among those four Richter spoke about there was also *Chasse Neige* which I greatly admire. I asked him in amazement, "Can you consider *Chasse Neige* to be bad music?" And I immediately began to hum a part of that piece."

"Don't you like it?"

"Yes, I do like this part," answered Richter, "but as to this one . . ." (and he hummed a part),

. . . "I don't like it at all."

MZ: Generally speaking, I can understand it. I don't think there is a single pianist who would like all the compositions of the Great Masters without any exception.

LB: I fully agree with you. For example, I have never played and will never play the Schumann *Toccata*, the Balakirev *Islamey*. As for the Liszt rhapsodies, with the exception of *The Pest Carnival*, I don't like them very much and I've recently turned down an offer to make recordings of all the Liszt rhapsodies.

MZ: At the beginning of our talk on technique you gave the octave études as the first example. And what about finger technique?

LB: In general, I prefer octave and chord technique. I feel more comfortable in it. This may be because I am myself a large man and I like everything large. The only exception is my wife—she is a mere slip of a woman.

So we come to finger technique. While mastering it I followed the traditional path on the one hand, working a lot at scales: on the other hand playing with "incorrect" fingering (deliberately!) I created additional difficulties for myself, and thus developed this type of technique more intensively to a certain extent.

MZ: You've mentioned the peculiarities of your hands. How did they affect the development of your finger technique?

LB: That's a very important question! As I've already pointed out, my hands are comparatively small and my fingers are slim, not fleshy. They rather easily slip between two adjacent black keys. It is convenient. However, my finger will not achieve much only by its mere strength. Therefore I always play with the entire arm, and as I've already stated, I manage owing to my dexterity, which is not innate but acquired, developed dexterity.

MZ: And if we dismiss the factor of the peculiarities of a particular pianist's hand, what are your considerations concerning finger technique development?

LB: I always compare the pianist's technique with that of a ballet dancer or a sportsman. By this I mean that flexibility of every joint is vital. Undoubtedly, it is of the utmost importance! Note how ballet dancers work at the bar, how football players warm up before a match. By means of their exercises, they stretch and make every joint work. All this is indispensable. That is why it is so vital to start studying at an early age when all the joints and sinews are extremely pliable. It was not without reason that my mother wouldn't shove my fingers. She got at the root of it! She may have started too early, but the course as such was correct. Only with flexible sinews and pliable joints can good finger technique be developed.

MZ: Well, as you repeatedly say that you've got an "inconvenient" hand, it must have been just because of the stretching of the joints and the flexibility thus acquired, and the elasticity of the hand that you could succeed in overcoming the technical difficulties of the finger technique. Isn't that the way it was?

LB: Precisely! I employed certain exercises with this end in view.

What do I achieve in this way? With my comparatively small hand, I have a rather big extension. Not everyone can stretch his fingers like that. For instance, I can stretch my forefinger and middlefinger to an octave.

MZ: Let's turn to another problem that has been troubling pianist-pedagogues for ages. In what tempo should a student play scales, études and complicated technical passages?

LB: It is also difficult for me to say anything edifying concerning this problem. At present, I hold that pieces on technique should be learned slowly. So to say, in a tempo that would allow, on the one hand, for the preservation of movement in the compositions and, on the other hand, for fixing one's attention and checking every note. This is what a man who is past fifty tells you now. But when a youngster, I played everything in an incredibly quick tempo. It was quite involuntary. I simply couldn't help it. My fingers played faster than my consciousness could control their playing. Goldenweiser could not do anything about it. He kept saying it would pass and I'd get over it. And my teacher proved to be right. By the way, the same thing was true of Gilels and Horowitz.

Lazar Berman and Carlo Maria Giulini.

MZ: We've touched upon the "childish" aspect of the finger technique problem. And now a few words about the adult side of the matter. In their practice, pianists may encounter hardships that hamper the use of the desired finger technique; for instance, in the case of "difficult" instruments.

LB: You are absolutely right. It is almost impossible to execute perfectly compositions on finger technique on bad instruments. In octave and chord technique on a difficult instrument one can find a way out by using the pedal, at times even due to the general noise . . . I hope my colleagues forgive my saying so! For the episodes on finger technique to come out well, the keyboard must be very even, the piano should be of excellent quality. That is why I avoid playing pieces on finger technique on bad instruments. What do I mean by a very good, even an ideal grand piano? It is an instrument on which I can play as if only with my fingers with my hand in the natural position and without pressing the keys too hard, so to say, "to the bottom," profiting by double repetition. For me, an ideal piano is one that plays, as I usually put it, by itself, so to say, that responds to every movement of your hand, an instrument that you can play as if by mere touch.

MZ: It is common knowledge that sometimes a difficult technical problem can be solved due to a device not pertaining directly to the given difficulty. For example, can the position of the pianist's body be of any help in overcoming purely finger technique difficulties?

LB: The pianist's body is always to a certain degree involved in the process of playing, even when it seems to the audience that the performer is sitting motionless at the instrument. Thus, to a certain extent the body is also involved in overcoming finger technique difficulties, no matter how paradoxical this may sound. I'll give you a most illustrative example as to how the correct position of the body helped me to solve a complicated problem of finger technique. In the Prokofiev *Sonata No. 8* (the coda of the first movement) there is a passage that is played in the upper part of the keyboard, somewhere in the three-line and four-line octave. I had been playing this composition for a long time, but every time, before that particular point, I felt uncertain. Sometimes I "skidded" at this point and I practically made a hash of it. To make a long story short, I was never sure whether this passage would

Lazar Berman rehearsing with the Philadelphia Orchestra under the baton of the venerable Eugene Ormandy.

come out well or not. Such was the case till the previous season when after an interval I renewed my work on this composition. And suddenly I had a brainwave: on reaching this tricky point I moved my body sharply to the right and at once the difficulty was eliminated. Similar things have happened while playing passages on octave and chord technique when the correct position of the body relative to the hands instantaneously eliminates the technical difficulty.

MZ: When dealing with technical problems we cannot help but discuss fingering. You've already mentioned the fingering experiments of the years of your pupilage. I believe you now give preference to the rational fingering.

LB: Certainly I do.

MZ: Then please tell us of your fingering principles.

LB: Several years ago I had an offer from the American publishing house "Schirmer" to edit my repertoire. I made an experiment and edited the Liszt *Sonata B-minor* in this fashion. But it was not published, as the publishers wanted to issue a whole series of my editions, but I was bored. I didn't go on with this work because I consider editor's fingering nonsense, unnecessary coercion of the future performer. It might be even a kind of misinformation for him. Fingering is an extremely intimate question. I've arrived at this conclusion quite recently. There are as many hands as there are people, and there are as many types of fingering as there are hands. Of course, one can write down his fingering just for the sake of interest. But to my mind, it cannot be of any real benefit, especially when big concert pieces are being edited,

Lazar Berman and Daniel Barenboim.

because those who are already performing them do not need it. I consider fingering to be highly individual. As a rule, when I begin working on a piece I first of all establish my fingering and only then do I look at what is written in the score. Sometimes my variant coincides, but at times I simply cannot play the fingering that is marked.

MZ: From your modest editing experience you've come to the conclusion that marking fingering in the score is inexpedient for advanced pianists. It is a moot point. Every pianist has his own fingering discoveries which, if made public, could save many of his colleagues, even quite mature ones, the trouble of "inventing the bicycle." For example, in the Klindworth edition of the Chopin Ballad (bars NN 130-131) there is seemingly quite natural, but in fact inconvenient fingering:

As soon as you change it putting the thumb under after every fourth finger, the inconvenience is immediately eliminated. I think this is very useful for every pianist to know.

LB: You are probably right.

MZ: Fingering recommendations are more important for students. Do you find such recommendations also inexpedient for students of the piano?

LB: You should not draw an analogy with editing, because while editing you are dealing with an anonymous musician. I'll edit the piece and someone at the other end of the planet will buy the score and begin studying the composition. If there is an actual student in front of me with whom I could discuss the fingering, that's quite another matter. I offer him a variant I consider convenient and ask if it is convenient for him. Suppose it is not. And I say, "Let's drop it and think of something else." And together we'll search for some interesting fingering that is suitable just for him.

MZ: As we are gradually touching upon the basic elements of pianism, it is high time we discussed the problems of tone production and sound quality. You mentioned that you had in a large measure to solve this problem of acquiring beautiful tone by yourself. How did it happen?

Lazar Bermon and Jacques Leiser, his American manager.

LB: That is true, I mainly solved it myself, and by the most primitive means at that. For instance, I began listening to the recordings of the Italian singers, thus trying to grasp the mystery of "bel canto," the secret of beautiful tone.

MZ: It is by no means such a primitive method. Anton Rubinstein also advised doing the same thing. However, you could have learned piano "bel canto" from pianists as well. It is well known that as for the beauty of the tone, the majority of the musicians of your generation idolized Konstantin Igumnov.

LB: Right you are, though for me the ideal tone was not that of Igumnov, but the inimitable sound of Heinrich Neuhaus. I would go to his concerts trying to comprehend how he managed it. I also tried to perceive the secret of Sofronitsky's beautiful tone. I didn't miss a single one of his concerts, and I often went not simply to listen to music but with a concrete end in view—to grasp the mystery of the beautiful sound I did not possess at that time. Eventually I did master it though, of course not only by virtue of listening to singers and pianists. I began to pay special attention to this matter. I no longer permitted myself to play just for the sake of playing, that is with colorless, meaningless sounds.

MZ: Beautiful sound on the piano as is well known is inseparable from the pedal. So let's tackle the problem of the pedal now.

LB: To know how to play with the pedal means to know how to play without the pedal. Those were the "pedal" precepts of my teacher Goldenweiser.

MZ: Goldenweiser's idea was upheld by other musicians. Gieseking is known to have recorded the Mozart Sonatas without pedal. But why deprive the piano sound of the diversified shades of color that the pedal gives it? Even while playing Mozart? The more so, as Mozart himself had willingly employed the knee lever operating the insulating mechanism. So you stick to Goldenweiser's point of view, don't you?

LB: Not now of course. But when I was his pupil, it was only natural that I reckoned with his advice and recommendations. But now I do employ the pedal, and rather intensively at that. At times I was even criticized for overdoing it. In particular, it was mentioned in some American critical articles.

Lazar Berman talks with the author, Dr. Mark Zilberquit.
**"Twice I was on the verge of giving up playing altogther.
For four years when I studied at school I was not allowed to
perform at a single open concert."**

Generally speaking, the main functions of the pedal, I think are
the following: pedalling adds a very special new coloring to cantilena music and provides a solid bass foundation for the whole
design of the composition. Incidentally I frequently employ the
third pedal as well (the latest example is the recording of the Prokofiev Suite).

MZ: We have discussed the problems of the technical realization
of a piece—fingering, tone production, pedal, but somewhat
abstractly. This is quite right as these aspects are valuable in
themselves and we pianists and pedagogues are aware of this.
However, we also know that they are all inseparable from the composer's conception, from the composer's text.

LB: Yes, of course, the composer's text is the very basis of
everything, the fundamental starting point in the work of a per-

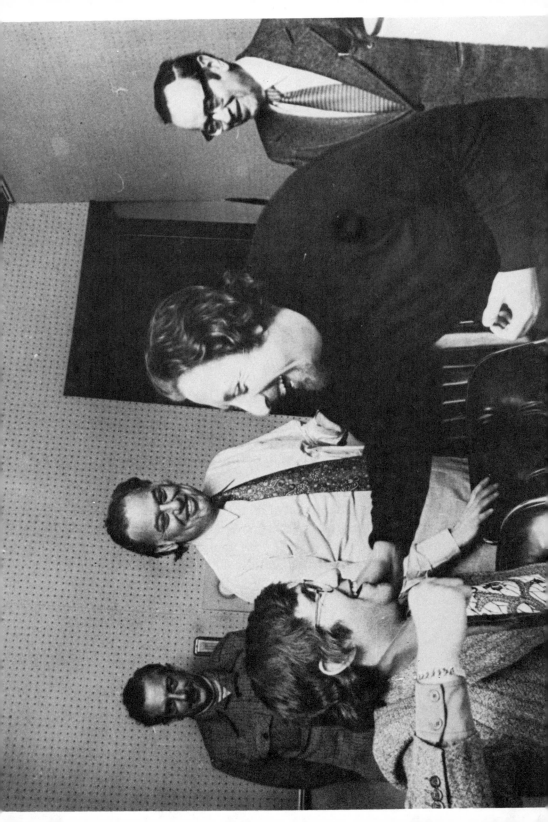

former. I only wanted to make it clear that I don't identify the notion of the composer's "concept" with the composer's "text". The former is a broader notion. To grasp its meaning, it is not enough to study the urtext, no matter how thoroughly. I always tell everyone that a musician should know history. How can you perform a composition, say of the second half of the 18th century, without knowing what important historic events took place in the author's native land at the time, what the major cultural-historic problems of the epoch were? To continue. I cannot understand pianists who, having played the Beethoven sonatas for years, never took the trouble to open the volume of the composer's letters, to study them thoroughly, thus attempting to gain an insight into the composer's world. Composers were people just like us. They strolled along the streets, their problems, sorrows and joys were inseparable from real life, their epoch. And it is essential that the musician understand this.

MZ: You are absolutely right. This is often the reason for our disappointment at the performance of some young pianists, "newly-fledged" laureates. Their spiritual world, their knowledge and comprehension of the essence of the music they play, their interpretation of the composer's style is much narrower, much poorer than their pianistic capabilities. They can play very smoothly, in very quick tempo, but they don't grasp the spiritual value of the music they are performing.

LB: There is no denying that. It was not by chance that, speaking of my teacher, I emphasized his instilling in his pupils a strict and creative attitude to the text as one of his most important merits. It was particularly that accurate and intelligent approach which led me to sensational discoveries in such a popular and well-known composition as the Tchaikovsky *First Concerto*. I did not simply study the text that is commonly used by all the pianists, but I carefully studied the rough draft of Tchaikovsky's notes for the manuscript of this composition. As a result I discovered a lot of

Lazar Berman, during one of his American tours, entertains with a selection from his huge repertoire of extremely funny stories.

discrepancies between the original and the present-day tradition of its performance. Literally speaking, I felt ill when studying the manuscript of the composition. And I am glad I managed to restore the author's original conception. Here is another example of confirming how different can be the conceptions of the "composer's text" (in this case a traditionally accepted variant, performed hundreds of times) and the "composer's conception" that could be revealed only by means of special research.

MZ: At the same time the very expression of "following" the composer's text, of "adherence" to the composer's text is also rather relative. Let's compare Sviatoslav Richter's and Vladimir Horowitz's interpretations of the Schumann *Toccata* that you do not like. The difference is dramatic, although both pianists are faithful to the composer, each in his own way. I think there was also a great difference between the interpretations of the celebrated "Chopinists" of different generations—Josef Hofmann, Alfred Cortot, Artur Rubinstein—and all of them must have differed from that of Chopin. They must have differed in volume of tone, rubato and, of course, tempo.

LB: As far as the tempo is concerned, it is in general a very complicated problem, and very disputable at that. At least, for me it is a moot point.

MZ: That is quite understandable: the tempo in the Bach compositions is a most serious problem in itself, not to speak of tempo in general.

LB: I'm not going to point out any composer in particular, though in speaking of the tempo I mean the composers of the past. Through my own experience I am closer to the music of the past than to contemporary music. For example, let's take Liszt's tempo. Liszt's pupils are believed to have played his compositions to him and to have heard him play them. It means they knew his tempos precisely and could pass their knowledge on to their own pupils, and the latter to theirs and thus, owing to this live tradition, they have come down to our days.

Lazar Berman with Kurt Waldheim, who gave a reception in his honor with other distinguished guests.

Lazar Berman considers himself a very lucky man. He has a lovable, adoring wife who bore him a musical genius as a son. At ten years of age the young Berman was already playing virtuoso violin concerti, and everyone who is associated with the boy, whose name is Pavel (Pavlik), considers him to be a rare genius with huge potential.

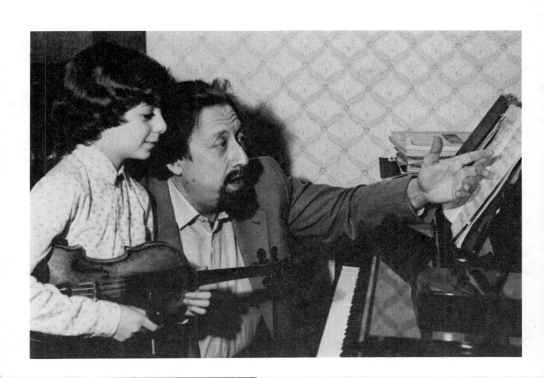

Such an opinion does exist. I do not share it. In this connection I always remember the children's game "the telephone," when words whispered from one person to another are so distorted as to be absolutely unrecognizable in the end. Throughout the centuries there have been so many changes in the way of life that the Liszt tempos must inevitably have been distorted as well. And I mean distorted in both ways—they've become slower and faster.

MZ: I am not sure it could be called "distortion." The fascination and the value of the art of performance lies in the fact that each generation offers its own "reading" of the composition, its contemporary interpretation, that is, from generation to generation the interpretation is somewhat altered.

LB: That's just the point! And not only from generation to generation. I was infatuated with Vladimir Horowitz's interpretation of *The Mephisto Waltz*—he doesn't play it fast at all. He is an old pianist belonging to the old generation, yet he plays it in a new way, not as he played it decades ago. Therefore he cannot be even called an old pianist. He cannot be spoken of as a great master of the past. He is a great master of the present or perhaps even the future. And such a seemingly disputable interpretation of this composition as his is probably more in compliance with the composer's conception.

There is one more point referring to tempos and related to the composer's instruction. We say that nowadays "allegro" is one thing and it used to be different. Nor is "presto" the same now. What I mean is that if you look at the composer's instructions it is not so much the tempos as such which are of paramount importance, as the correlation between them. Here one can hit the mark, get precisely at the core of the composer's intention when the latter indicates certain changes of tempo. This should be followed strictly. To my mind this is extremely important.

Besides, the problem of tempos is connected with many attendant circumstances, such as, for instance, peculiarities of the instrument.

MZ: Does this mean that if you come into a concert hall with a mediocre instrument you change the tempo while adapting yourself to that instrument?

LB: Sometimes I do. If the instrument does not respond to me, does not sound clear, there is nothing to do but slow down the tem-

Lazar Berman made his American debut with the New Jersey Symphony Orchestra under Thomas Michalak. The concert was a huge success and was helpful in putting both Michalak, a Polish immigrant violinist-conductor, and Berman "on the map."

47

Lazar Berman rehearsing Tchaikovsky's First Piano Con-certo with Herbert von Karajan.

po. And this is what comes of it: for instance, I don't find my recording of the Prokofiev *Eighth Sonata* made by Deutsche Grammophon quite to my satisfaction. The reason was that I played the finale more reservedly than I found necessary simply because I could not play in the tempo I was used to on that piano. It was difficult for me to play on that instrument. Everything came out somewhat messy. But it is essential that the entire texture be well heard, the melodious nature of even the most difficult and complex passages be revealed. But if I played in my usual tempo on that piano I should have failed to reveal the melodious nature of the composition.

MZ: While speaking of the years of your studies you said that you used to practice a lot. What is the regime of your daily practice now?

LB: I must say that I am not satisfied with my practicing primarily because I haven't yet learned how to organize it well. Though I've achieved certain results, I am still displeased with myself.

MZ: But to speak more specifically, how do you usually arrange your practice? For instance, do you start with a warming up as before?

LB: Now my warming-up is minimum; I just play a few Chopin etudes and that's about all.

MZ: Do you play them in fast tempo?

LB: No, slowly. It is not so important to play in tempo; the main thing is to play in slow time. Then I play some scales or exercises to stretch the fingers.

MZ: Do you do that every day?

LB: I try to do it every day. At present such warming up lasts for some 20-30 minutes, because actually the fingers are constantly at work. A more intensive warm-up is rather of greater importance before a concert.

MZ: Maestro, will you please dwell on how your idea of the composition you are going to perform is usually formed, how its interpretation comes into being?

LB: I have the following principle. If the composition is familiar to me, I start studying it at once. If it is absolutely unfamiliar, or I don't know it well, I prefer, if possible, to listen to its recording. Because for me it is very important to comprehend, to hear the whole of it. So I proceed, not from the parts to the whole, but from the whole to the parts when working at a composition. To my mind it is necessary for

"Now my warming up is a minimum; I just play a few Chopin etudes and that's about it."

realization of the composer's conception. The particulars should be subjugated to the tasks of the whole. That is why it is so important for me to see how it all looks on the whole in order to grasp the form. And it is easier for me when I listen to the recording of a new piece. If I more or less know the composition, I never listen to anyone's interpretation before creating my own. The interpretation of a musical piece, like the foetus of a living organism, is formed gradually, while you are playing it over and over. It comes to life and little by little turns into a whole completed individual thing that is your own.

MZ: So the schedule of your daily practice is absolutely spontaneous, isn't it?

Pavlik Berman playing his first major recital at the Conservatory. It was a huge success and immediately pushed him into the limelight.

The warm bond existing between Lazar and Pavel Berman is beautiful.

LB: Generally speaking it is. Today I have been playing only a Mozart sonata all day long. I feel I cannot play anything else. Yesterday it was the same. And the day before yesterday I played Rachmaninoff's *Rhapsody on a Theme of Paganini* all day.

MZ: Are you going to play it somewhere in the near future?

LB: No, I simply learn it because I haven't performed it before. I use my spare time while there are no concerts in order to learn some new pieces.

I commence the work on a new piece in a special way. My wife calls it my "passive regimen of work." I make no attempt to

Berman is a rare type of perfectionist . . . one that is not too common in the Soviet Union. Here he is trying the piano in the Great Hall of the Conservatory.

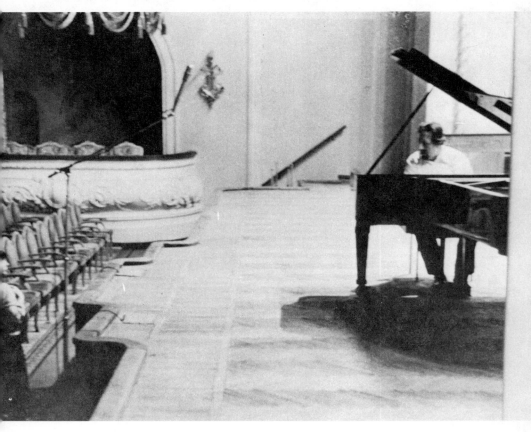

remember it. I simply play it. I can never tell beforehand when it will have been learned. This moment comes unexpectedly, like the flower buds swell gradually and all of a sudden they break into leaf and practically in a day or two we see the leaves blossoming out. A similar latent ripening occurs in me, but I haven't the slightest idea of how it develops. In my case it is the saddest period because I don't like to learn new things. I don't enjoy it in the least until the piece comes out well. In the meantime, I simply play the piece and I repeat it. I usually try to play in slow tempo.

MZ: Please describe how you enlarge your repertoire. For in-

His wife moves all about the Hall, sitting in different chairs and positions, advising Berman how his sound changes from one position to the other.

THE WHITE HOUSE

WASHINGTON

December 9, 1977

To Lazar Berman

Thank you for sending me your
recent recording of Rachmaninoff's
Piano Concerto No. 3 and your latest
recording of the Years of Pilgrimage
of Franz Liszt.

I appreciate your thoughtfulness in
providing these albums and look forward to hearing them.

You were kind to write such a warm
letter upon leaving the United States
at the conclusion of your concert
tour. I am grateful for your words
of goodwill.

Sincerely,

Jimmy Carter

Mr. Lazar Berman
155 West 68th Street
New York, New York 10023

A letter from President Jimmy Carter.

"I once tried to record all the Rachmaninoff *Preludes*.
I realized that half of the 24 *Preludes* left me unmoved and I
just couldn't do the job."

stance, do you strive to learn and perform the whole cycle of compositions if you are already playing part of them?

LB: The choice of every new composition is a creative act in itself. And as in any creative process, it is the search that leads to success, and it is not always an easy one. Here is an example that may be the answer to your question.

Once I received a letter from the Rachmaninoff Society which at one time existed in Odessa. It was soon after my recording of Rachmaninoff's *Musical Moments* came out. The head of the Society wrote on behalf of music lovers that almost every sitting of the Society began with an audition of one of the *Musical Moments*. He wrote that they thought no one played Rachmaninoff as well as I did and therefore they asked me to record all the Rachmaninoff *Preludes*. I was all for doing it there and then (people were asking me for it); I received the permission of the firm "Melodia" and settled down to work with zeal. But I soon discovered that more than half of those 24 preludes left me unmoved. I tried hard to somehow make myself do it but it is the same as living with a wife you don't love. I just couldn't do it. To make a long story short, I gave up the offer.

MZ: Does this mean that in the choice of repertoire you are guided only by what you like or dislike? Shouldn't a pianist also proceed from considerations of enlightening people? As long as the composer found it possible to include the pieces you dislike into the cycle, perhaps you ought not to exclude them but perform them along with those you admire.

LB: I prefer not to force myself to do it.

MZ: For several decades you've been concertizing as a solo pianist. Could you share the impressions of the creative activities you've devoted your whole life to?

LB: Of course, it is very tempting to be a concertizing musician. But at the same time it is torture, at least it is for me. I know musicians who do not suffer from that, but I hate a nomadic life even if I am on tour in the best cities and if I put up at the best hotels. For me, the day when I leave home is the bitterest day in my life, no matter where I am going. The only consolation for me is the fact that I'm leaving for a short period of time. So, psychologically, I don't feel happy when on tour.

Berman practicing.

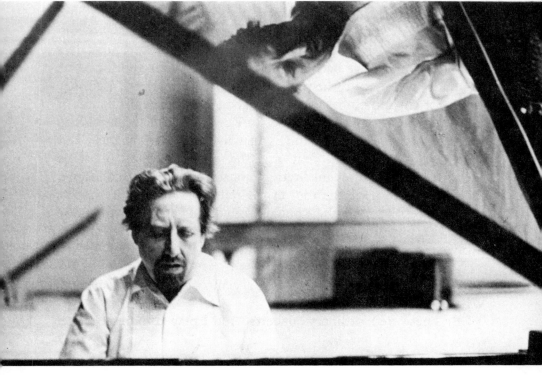

MZ: Proceeding from your experience as a soloist, what advice and recommendations can you give to performers seeking the career of solo playing?

LB: Firstly, a soloist-performer should like the nomadic life; he should enjoy going to airports, changing hotels, or at least, not find it all trying. Secondly, I believe that a person who wants to become a soloist must love people. I don't understand performers who play solely for themselves. I think that prominent musicians, and musicians in general, ought to respect those for whom they are playing. That is what I try never to forget. I always think that I must give pleasure to people by what I am doing, by my playing. This is what one must concentrate on, but not on the fear that usually afflicts us lest something should not come out well.

MZ: I know your artistic biography rather well, I know you've encountered hardships, there have been difficult periods in your life, in your art. There have been failures. But in the end you were "still in the saddle."

LB: True, there have been failures as there usually are in everyone's life. But the trick is not to be afraid of failures. You've got to turn any failure to your advantage, so to say; you must be able to discover the reason for it and to realize what should be done to avoid its repetition in the future. This is what I'd like to advise the young. And one more thing. You should never refuse to consult other musicians; you should remain a pupil forever, no matter how famous you have become as a performer. It is important, it is absolutely necessary to help one another, be it a friend, a former teacher or any other noted or simply good musician. As a matter of fact, there are various kinds of failures. I differentiate them into two categories. The first kind is usually caused by chance. But there are also failures that are the natural result of some phenomenon. But after meditation, consulting an older colleague, one manages to trace the root of the failure, its cause. As Caesar said, "Successes imbue the Romans with daring and failures imbue them with fortitude." These are very wise words and they should always be remembered by us performers too.

MZ: You must have won world acclaim after certain concerts. Where and how did they occur?

LB: These were ordinary concerts. And I played there no better

Recording with Claudio Abbado. Abbado was born in Milan on June 26, 1933 and studied conducting with Swarowsky in Vienna. In 1958 he won the Koussevitzky conducting prize and in 1963 he took the Mitropoulos prize.

Berman is no conductor, but he shows Daniel Barenboim certain points he wants to stress. Barenboim, besides being a fine conductor, is a great pianist in his own right.

than at other concerts. There was nothing special about them. I simply played where I was listened to. It was in Italy.

MZ: And how did your American triumph start?

LB: It was a concert that I don't find special from the creative point of view. I played in my usual way. On the contrary, it occurred under most unpleasant circumstances. It was not in a hall but outside in a covered stadium. My performance left much to be desired. I could have played much better. I was ominously nervous and at the beginning I was very much constrained. My nervousness gradually subsided in the course of my playing. These are not the concerts I consider to be my highlights.

In this connection I remember another episode in 1955 when I played the Rachmaninoff *Third Concerto* for the second time in my life. It was in Leningrad. I had played it the first time very badly in Riga—I was dreadfully nervous! On arriving in Leningrad, I began to feel nervous again because I was going to play with one of the best orchestras of the time under Kurt Sanderling. We sat down to rehearse. I had a feeling of constraint all the time at the thought of the major orchestra I was to participate with. I was crushed by the orchestra's authority, its high standing. I was twenty-five, and it was the first time I was playing with such a marvelous orchestra. I cannot say that I had been a complete failure in Riga; everything

E. Altman, great Soviet cellist, Lazar Berman and musicologist Dr. Herbert R. Axelrod prior to impromptu trios at the author's home.

was more or less all right, but somewhat uncertain, smudged, some things were made a hash of. So I was awfully displeased with myself. But the rehearsal with Sanderling was quite proper. Everything came out well. I remember the concertmaster patronizingly patted my shoulder as if to say "well done," and I left for the artists' room. Suddenly Sanderling entered and said, "Please tell me why you are so much afraid of us? It is you who should dictate to us, play the solo, but instead you play somewhat carefully, timidly." When he finished speaking I suddenly flew into a passion which is not typical of me. I rarely become angry at all. I came to the final rehearsal with only one thought in mind: "Now I'll show you!" And I started playing in an entirely different manner. I could

Lazar Berman with the author, Dr. Mark Zilberquit.

actually feel the members of the orchestra collect themselves and "fall into line" playing under my lead. We played the concerto in one breath after which the orchestra gave me a great ovation. The concert itself was no less successful. I was in ecstasy. The musicians who heard me then still recall this performance. It was a blending of a first-class orchestra, an inspired conductor and an inspired soloist. We kindled each other. I remember that when I was playing the last part, tears were streaming down my cheeks. I was in a semi-hysterical state. When the final chord sounded, everyone in the hall got up to their feet. I'd say that never again have I experienced a greater joy than at that performance.

MZ: That is a thrilling story. I would like to point out one thing that sounded like a secondary detail but is tremendously important for a performer: I mean nervousness. More than once you have mentioned being nervous during a performance. How do you manage to overcome your nervousness so that it does not interfere with your playing?

LB: For me, the most unpleasant part is not the concert itself but the preparation for it. As a matter of fact, at a concert I play with equal vigor in any hall, in any place and for any audience. Every time I do my best, whether I am playing for the children of the town of Asbury Park or for the enlightened music lovers of the city of New York. Of late I find that I am almost calm at my performance. But when I was younger, I was frightfully nervous. I remember that at the concerts my right foot kept jumping on the pedal because of my nervousness. It was at the time when my hands were rushing ahead of my mind. Therefore I often "swerved." I could not pull myself together, had no control over myself. As far as the nervousness before the concert is concerned, it depends on where I am to play.

MZ: Certainly the stage dictates its own laws. And at times it happens that no matter how experienced the performer or how thoroughly he has been preparing himself for the atmosphere of the concert, unexpected things of various kinds can crop up. They may seem to be trifles and yet they can utterly ruin the preconceived interpretation. But sometimes incidents may occur that are far from trifling and they can throw the performer entirely off his balance, upset his equanimity. Isn't that so?

LB: Absolutely. For instance, what the incident in Milan cost me! At that time I did not yet enjoy international popularity. Therefore any success was of importance to me. I knew that the success of a performer to a great extent depended on the review of the most popular newspaper in Milan, Italy. It is widely read throughout the country as is the *New York Times* in America. And just as in *The New York Times* Harold Schonberg has been and still remains the leading figure, in Milan Franco Abiatti was such a leading critic. His opinion determined whether a performer was a success or a failure in Italy. Never in my life have I met Schonberg, nor had I ever met Abiatti. They do not like to meet performers. Naturally I was anxious to see what the man on whom so much depended looked like. So when I stepped out onto the stage of the Milan Conservatory named after Verdi, I saw that the house was

During a party in Moscow, Lazar Berman sat down at a small piano and played with fingers, hands and arms.

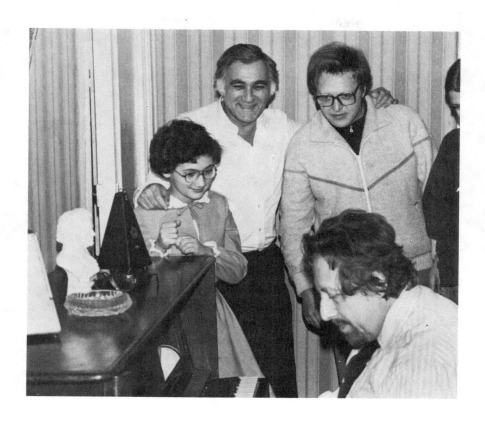

The "clowning around," while it looked very funny, didn't sound bad at all, and Berman continued playing some very difficult music for quite a while.

almost full, and in the very first row there was a middle-aged very stout gentleman and the seats next to him were vacant. I immediately jumped to the conclusion that the gentleman was Franco Abiatti. I began with the Schumann *Sonata*. As a rule I never let myself get distracted and cast glances into the audience. But this was a special case and I simply couldn't help glancing at him from time to time. And suddenly I saw that the man was sitting with his head hanging very low. "Thank God!" I thought, "he is carried away. Now I'll add fuel to the fire!" And I started playing with even more fervor. But while playing some soft episode in the sec-

*The photo above, depicting Berman in serious concentra-
tion, plus the photo on the facing page, shows Berman as
Jacques Leiser describes him: "A beautiful human being."*

ond movement I suddenly heard somebody snoring. Snoring loudly! I stole a sidelong glance at the audience. How horrible! Franco
Abiatti is sound asleep at my concert! It is a complete failure!
Tomorrow it will be in all the papers! Well, I mournfully finished
the Schumann *Sonata* and began the Liszt *Dante Sonata*. When I
played pianissimo he was still sleeping—fortissimo, still sleeping!
Hardly had I finished when he started applauding enthusiastically.
I made my bows and a special bow to him. I went back stage awfully upset and told my impresario that Franco Abiatti had been fast
asleep throughout my performance. "But it was Bolla, not Abiatti,"
my impresario consoled me. "What Bolla?" "Don't you know
Bolla?"-he seemed amazed. "How could I know Bolla if this was
only the third time that I have been in Milan?" It turned out that
the man was a concert fan, an engineer by profession and on coming to a concert he immediately drowsed off and slept till the very

end of the concert, with short intervals for the applause. Everybody knew it, was accustomed to it and paid no attention to him at all. But how anxious I had been!

MZ: It's unlikely that the amusing incident you described when speaking about nervousness was the only one in your artistic biography. Have there been any during your American tour?

LB: Yes, I remember, for instance, such a funny episode. The point is that for me a concert is not entirely a pleasure. It is hard work. I approach it as a difficult task. But in America, they like the performer to smile the moment he appears on the stage. It seemed strange to me. The pianist steps out onto the stage. He is about to create something . . . Frankly speaking, what is there to smile at? And there I was, playing in Boston. After the concert I received a standing ovation. I came out to take my bows. Of course, I was dead tired and didn't feel like smiling at all. And suddenly I saw a lady in the first row point to her mouth with her fingers. I couldn't

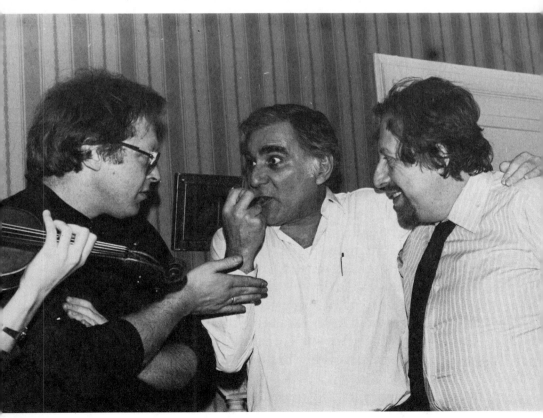

imagine what she meant by it. I came out time and time again and she still stretched her lips with her fingers. I began pondering over what it could mean. And suddenly I recollected that my wife often pointed to my beard to brush away the crumbs after I had eaten because I really eat carelessly. So it occurred to me that there might be some crumbs in my beard after the sandwich I had eaten and that the lady was hinting that I must shake the crumbs off my beard. So I took out a handkerchief and began rubbing my lips and beard vigorously. When I came out on the stage again the irrepressible lady kept on pointing at her mouth as before. I couldn't make head nor tail of it. Only the next day did it dawn upon me that she simply demanded that I should smile.

MZ: Have you any spare time for a hobby outside of your profession, like collecting something?

LB: I cannot say that I go in for it seriously, yet I do collect stamps. I am interested in a certain theme — the history of World War II. It so happened that the years of my early adolescence coincided with that most tragic event in the twentieth century. And it left its mark on me as I was 11-15 years old, that delicate, sensitive time in a child's life. Everything connected with the war stuck in my memory. I bought and still buy books with photos about the war. At times, while resting I look through my modest collection and recall those years of the evacuation. I remember how we slept on the floor or three of us together in one cold bed, how we practiced in chilly unheated rooms with our coats on and felt boots (valenki) on our feet, and with gloves in which there were holes specially made for our fingers. I also remember that in the evening we used to place a small bottle of kerosene with a little wick in it near the music stand (to economize on electricity).

In general I often think of the war. Sometimes I step out onto the stage of some splendid concert hall, I look at the well-fed and well-dressed audience and in my mind's eye I see the wounded in hospitals where I had performed as a boy, to whom as to this or any other audience I did my best to bring pleasure and joy with my art.

As a representative of one of the most peaceful professions in the world I desire that never again should people be menaced with war . . .

MZ: There is a saying "When cannons speak the Muses are silent." But one may paraphrase it: "When Muses speak cannons are silent." So may the Muses speak forever!

Tikhon Khrennikov

Tikhon Khrennikov was born in the small Central Russian town of Yelets on June 10, 1913. Although the large family he comes from had no professional musicians among their ancestry, the boy exhibited a bent for music in fairly early childhood, starting to take piano lessons when he was nine. Shortly after, he began to write music. Among his childhood efforts were piano pieces — marches, waltzes, studies.

Moving to Moscow at 16, the youth studied music professionally at the Gnesin Secondary Music School, after which he went on to the Moscow Conservatoire, where he studied under Vissarion Shebalin (composition) and Heinrich Neuhaus (piano).

Khrennikov recorded his first major accomplishment as a composer and pianist in 1933, when he performed his First Piano Concerto. Since then he has been successfully at work in a wide variety of musical genres comprising ten operas, ballets, symphonies, operettas, vocal pieces and a wealth of music for stage and screen.

The composer has made a notable contribution to the development of the instrumental concerto genre. To date, Khrennikov has three piano concertos, two violin concertos and one cello concerto to his credit.

His piano concertos reveal two aspects of his talent — those of a composer and of a performer. Khrennikov possesses bright pianistic abilities and complete mastery of the keyboard, and has given many performances of his concertos which evoked the enthusiastic comments of the world press.

Tikhon Khrennikov with his daughter Natasha. Circa 1945.

Following one of his recitals, the *Philadelphia Inquirer* reported that the composer had exhibited a monumental technique and keen attention to sonic subtleties thus enhancing the impression left by his music. Echoing the statement, another press report described the guest performer as a superb interpreter of his music who had displayed perfect mastery of the piano, a gripping power of attack and inexhaustible resources of vitality.

Since 1948, Khrennikov has been at the head of the USSR Union of Composers, which brings together more than 2,200 composers and musicologists. In addition, he has been devoting a great deal of time to his responsibilities as a leading public figure of the Soviet musical community. As chairman of the Organizing Committee of the International Tchaikovsky Competition, Khrennikov has done much for the advancement of the art of musical performance.

Khrennikov is an Honorary Member of the Italian Tiberian Academy (1976), a Corresponding Member of the GDR Academy of Arts (1978) and Chairman of the USSR National Musical Council.

Tikhon Khrennikov with the outstanding Soviet ballerina Maya Plisetskaya, who also happens to be Mrs. Rodion Shchedrin.

Khrennikov addressing the Congress of Composers of the USSR. In the background, from the left, are Shostakovich, Shaporin and Khachaturian.

Obtaining an interview with Khrennikov was found to be a challenge: his degree of preoccupation is simply incredible. Our first interview had to be adjourned and re-instituted since the composer was completing his Third Piano Concerto as well as music for another in his long series of films. Another obstacle was his permanent and immense public responsibilities. As a matter of fact, for more than 30 years—ever since he assumed chairmanship of the USSR Union of Composers, Khrennikov has been living, as it were, two parallel lives. One is purely creative—the extremely intense life of a composer, pianist and educator (Khrennikov has for many years been professor of composition at the Moscow Conservatoire). The other is the life of a public figure and statesman with a daily load of wide-ranging problems to be tackled.

When we did meet in Khrennikov's spacious but cozy flat, settling down in his workroom for our repeatedly postponed interview, we were constantly interrupted by telephone calls: even at home Khrennikov is troubled with various work problems and requests, all of which receive their due share of consideration and personal participation.

As I listened to Khrennikov respond to what must have been a request, I recalled one of his fellow-composers saying many years ago: "Khrennikov is a man of extraordinary kindness, responsiveness and moral generosity. The latter quality leaves a distinct mark on his music. His simplicity of expression and openness of feelings lend his pieces some specific warmth of tonality and captivating lyricism, which never fails to fascinate audiences."

Finally, the telephone conversation ended and and we proceeded with the conversation.

Alone with this major musician, I felt tempted to discuss a great many musical problems with him. However, my specific purpose, dictated by the content of the present book, led me to confine myself to purely pianistic questions.

I began by requesting him to tell me how music had entered his life.

Two great living Soviet composers, Tikhon Khrennikov and Rodion Shchedrin.

Tikhon Khrennikov accompanying G. Dudarev.

TK: I was my parents' tenth child. My elder brothers and sisters were already in school and scarcely had I turned six when of my own accord I joined them there. It was precisely in school that my musical abilities came into notice: among other things, I had taught myself to strum on the guitar and I zestfully sang, displaying purity of voice.

MK: Who was your first piano teacher?

TK: Following my ninth birthday my parents, who strove to give all their children an education, bought some fair quality piano and invited a teacher for me. He was Joseph Queton, a Czech by nationality and an alumnus of the Moscow Conservatoire. Shortly, however, I switched to Vladimir Agarkov, who, in addition to having an excellent command of the piano (he had graduated from the class of Konstantin Igumnov), wrote music.

MZ: How old were you when you became interested in composition?

TK: My early attempts at melody-making came before I learned to play the piano. I tried to play by ear on the guitar. However, the example of Agarkov, who, as I said, wrote music, was a great inspiration to me and soon I began to try my hand at composition. My first piece recorded on note paper was a piano study. My composing efforts were welcomed by my teacher. His support, on the one hand, and my own enthusiasm, on the other, induced me to devote more and more time and effort to music writing. That was how I produced marches, waltzes, romances, and other piano pieces.

MZ: How long did you work under Agarkov?

TK: I regret to say it was a short period. Soon after our classes began, Agarkov left Yelets. Then for some time I took lessons from another very good teacher, Anna Vargunina, a well-educated woman and an enthusiastic educator.

Khrennikov as a composer, soloist and actor playing a soldier as he sings and accompanies himself in the movie **The Train is Rolling to the East.**

A group of composers on the construction site of the Belomor-Baltiysky canal. Khrennikov is standing in front. Circa 1930.

MZ: When did you resolve to become a professional musician, and how?

TK: In the winter of 1927, I came to Moscow with a thick folder of pieces I had composed. Mikhail Gnesin, who received me, was a remarkable musician, composer and educator. He gave me an audition, and he said that I should seriously devote myself to music in the future, but meanwhile to finish school. Following Gnesin's advice, I returned to Yelets, completed my school course and, in another two years, in the autumn of 1929, finally settled in Moscow, entering the Gnesin Music School.

MZ: Who were your teachers in the Gnesin School?

TK: I was extremely lucky with my teachers. My composition master was Mikhail Gnesin himself and I studied counterpoint and fugue under Heinrich Litinsky and piano under Efraim Gelman. Incidentally, it was in the Gnesin School that I made major progress in piano playing. The knowledge and skills I acquired there sustained me even in the Conservatoire.

MZ: What were your first impressions of Moscow?

TK: It is easy to realize that for a provincial youth who was avidly imbibing whatever pertained to art, Moscow's theatrical performances, museums, exhibitions, concerts, were nothing short of a stupendous experience. Among the powerful impressions I received were my attendance at the concerts that were being given by pianists of the day. Of course, in the early 1930's Moscow did not offer the wealth of piano concerts comparable to the present. However, each pianist was a personality. In those days I exhibited a particular awakening of interest in the piano. After hearing the concerts of those inspired keyboard artists, I passionately felt like mastering the instrument myself.

MZ: Which of the pianists lent you particular inspiration?

Tikhon Khrennikov promised himself that "if he made it" he would do everything possible to help less fortunate children to find their way in the musical world. He is still supporting children's musical activities.

Klara (Clara) Khrennikova, wife of Tikhon. Circa 1930.

TK: In those days, the piano scene was dominated by distinguished personalities such as Alexander Goldenweiser, Konstantin Igumnov, Samuel Feinberg, Heinrich Neuhaus, who was my future piano professor in the Conservatoire. Of the younger masters, sparkling virtuosity was displayed by Grigori Ginzburg. Two years before I came to Moscow a triumph in a Chopin Competition (the first to be held with the participation of Soviet performers) was scored by Lev Oborin. I have clear memories of how I first chanced upon him in Moscow. When I entered the Gnesin School I did not have a piano of my own and had to use a hired one. Once when I came to the rental office in order to make my monthly payment, there were two people present—a clerk and a fairly handsome young man who, as I understood, was there on identical business. When asked what his name was, the man said: "Oborin." Apparently hearing the name for the first time, the clerk asked him to repeat it. I felt like tearing him to shreds. **Oborin!** I had heard about his spectacular success back in Yelets, where, using my poor crystal receiver, I had caught a program in which he had played and had never dreamed of ever meeting him!

Tikhon Khrennikov with his mother.

Tikhon Khrennikov with his sister Nadezhda.

MZ: Was your First Piano Concerto, marked Op. 1, really your maiden composing effort?

TK: Except for the pieces which I wrote like all students of composition, it really was my first serious composition.

MZ: Why did you opt for the concerto genre?

TK: My powerful source of inspiration were concertos by Tchaikovsky and Rachmaninov, especially the latter. Rachmaninov's *First Concerto*, a vivid, melodious work, was also marked Op. 1. Apart from that, in the concerto genre, a pianist can show both his qualities as a soloist and his ability for ensemble playing. And the performance of a concerto itself is graced by some element of festivity. All these factors must have conspired to incline me toward my choice.

MZ: In the almost 50 years which have passed since you wrote your *First Concerto* it has been played on many occasions by pianists of many countries. How did it gain world recognition?

TK: In 1935 I was invited to perform my concerto in a major art festival in Leningrad. This markedly representative musical forum attracted musicians and other personalities in the arts from many countries. My work immediately received an international recognition, being reviewed in several countries simultaneously. Some of the reviews, in addition to purely informative data regarding the concert, contained individual evaluative elements.

Tikhon Khrennikov was born in Yelets on June 10, 1913. He was the "boy who made good" from the town—and he never forgot it, either. He played many concerts in Yelets and was finally awarded a diploma making him an honorary citizen of the city of Yelets. He is shown here after the ceremony.

Tikhon Khrennikov with his brother Mitrophan.

One of the witnesses described the stir which swept over this young musician before he presented himself to the public who had gathered for the premiere. "The young composer and pianist was so agitated that he could not bring himself to appear on the stage. Alexander Melik-Pashayev (a noted Soviet orchestra leader who did the conducting that day) literally had to push him out. However, things went well. A brilliant execution of his concerto made Khrennikov a big success."

Here is another pertinent statement published in the leading Soviet musical magazine *Sovietskaya muzyka:* "An undeniably vivid and otherwise talented work, Khrennikov's concerto became the peak of the festival." Closing the review, the magazine said: "The author's execution revealed all advantages of a 'master's eye'—creative freedom, elasticity, confidence. As a pianist, Khren-

Tikhon Khrennikov with Elena Fabianovna Gnesina. They had a close life-time friendship.

The house in Yelets where the pianist spent his childhood.

nikov, in spite of the smallness of his hand, skillfully curbs all difficulties and technical caprices of his concerto.''

I reminded the composer about the article, asking him how the work was received by his Conservatoire professor, Heinrich Neuhaus.

TK: Neuhaus supported me as long as I worked on the concerto, expressing his positive attitude to the work on many subsequent occasions as well.

MZ: How was your First Concerto received by other pianists?

TK: Before I performed it in Leningrad, I had played my concerto in Moscow with the remarkable conductor Georg Sebastian, who was then working in the Soviet Union and later in France. The Moscow concert was also attended by Neuhaus's teacher Leopold Godowski, who was then also staying in our country. Neuhaus, not without pride, invited Godowski to listen to his pupil's work. (Incidentally, Godowski heard it again in the Leningrad Festival). This Polish pianist had very warm words to say about my concerto and me. Back in Europe, he also spoke highly of my work and even made appropriate press statements. I scarcely have to say that it was a great honor for me to receive the high appreciation of one of the foremost performers of all times.

MZ: How did your creative career develop in the years which directly followed the creation of this piano concerto?

TK: Primarily a composer, and a young one at that time, I proceeded to turn to other genres. Almost simultaneously with my piano concerto I worked on my First Symphony, which had its premiere in 1935. Parallel with that, I made my debut as a theatrical composer. The success of my works inspired me to broaden my scope in genre terms. At last my innermost dream came true: I wrote my maiden opera, *In the Storm*. I also started work for the films. Incidentally, the writing of screen music aroused my enthusiasm to the extent of crowding out work in some other musical genres for a while. Because the pictures to which I contributed were completely musical, work on them was as interesting as it was complex. After I became first Secretary of the USSR Union of Composers in 1949, I found myself having much

Berlin, Germany. May, 1945. Near the Reichstag with a group of Soviet soldiers. Tikhon Khrennikov is in the center, and to his right is Matvei Blantner, author of the well-known Katyusha.

Besides his musical duties, Khrennikov has a huge 12-hour-a-day administrative job, among other things, entertaining people like Dr. Herbert R. Axelrod (center) and Rodion Shchedrin.

less time left for composing. All these factors kept me away from the piano. Nor did I give public performances of my concerto.

MZ: Was your concerto played by others in those years?

TK: Yes. Beginning in the 1930s—shortly after it made its appearance—my First Piano Concerto had been increasingly entering pianists' repertoire.

MZ: And you never played it yourself since?

TK: I was invited to perform it again in the late 1950s, and I consented. After a terribly long break I went back to the piano in an effort to regain my mostly lost performing fitness. It will be recalled that concert pianists make it a point never to miss a single day's practice. Aware of how difficult it is to recover lost ground, some rule out breaks even in their brief summer holidays. You can imagine how tough I found the going after more than 20 years of scarcely any exercise (at times I had accompanied concert performers of my romances but that was nowhere near what was necessary). However, I did succeed in regaining my technique and went back to frequent performances of my First Concerto—in Bulgaria, Czechoslovakia, Japan and other countries. The success of my first piano work and a desire to renew my repertoire prompted me to write my Second Concerto, which was completed and introduced in 1972.

The music critics and audiences gave a remarkably warm welcome to Khrennikov's new work. "The Second Concerto," wrote the magazine *Muzykalnaya zhizn*, "is both a profoundly mature work and one that powerfully breathes youth. Its stormy

Tikhon Khrennikov hard at work. His most difficult task is finding the time to write the beautiful music for which he is so famous.

Berlin, Germany. May, 1945. Tikhon Khrennikov with the composer Matvei Blantner near the Brandenburg Gate. Khrennikov was at the front lines entertaining the troops when the war ended.

As a Deputy, Tikhon Khrennikov must maintain contact with the people he represents.

Tikhon Khrennikov with the playwright Alexei Faiko, author of the libretti for Khrennikov's operas In Storm *and* **Mother.**

seething of forces, vigor, downright youthful temperament are captivating. A sensation of genuine life fills literally each of its notes and each of its shades.''

Khrennikov's *Second Concerto* rapidly earned extensive international recognition. Substantial contributing factors were the author's own performances held in different countries.

TK: My new piano concerto was a truly resounding success. I played it in Britain, France and practically all the Socialist countries. It was given an extremely warm reception in Spain, where I played it in Barcelona and Seville. I will never forget my performance of the Second Concerto in Italy. In Rome alone I played it on three successive evenings each time to a packed audience.

MZ: As far as I remember, your new work was an enormous success in the United States as well?

Tikhon Khrennikov and Aram Khachaturian; two views.

TK: Yes. As a member of a Soviet musical delegation which also included Yevgeni Svetlanov, Leonid and Pavel Kogan, I was invited to concerts dedicated to the bicentennary celebration of the American Revolution in Philadelphia. For two consecutive days I gave open-stage performances of my concerto to audiences of 17,000. The concerts of all the three Soviet musicians aroused an immense general interest. Pavel Kogan, who performed my violin concerto, and Leonid Kogan, who played a concerto by Dmitri Shostakovich, were given as rousing a welcome as I was.

MZ: As far as I know, your 1976 performance in Philadelphia was not your first visit to the United States?

TK: I first travelled to America in 1959 in a delegation which also included Dmitri Shostakovich and Dmitri Kabalevsky. My *First Symphony* was then played. Our concerts began in Boston, where I heard what perhaps was the best performance of my symphony by the famous Boston Symphony Orchestra, which was then at the zenith of its mastery and fame. In those days its leader was Charles Munch, a truly great conductor. Incidentally, he spoke very highly about my work, which has held a firm place in his repertoire. Together with the Boston Symphony Munch travelled all across America and included my symphony in all his programs. In Philadelphia it has been known ever since it was introduced there by Leopold Stokowsky in the 1930's. In 1959, I heard my symphony as interpreted by Eugene Ormandy. In 1961 I was invited to a music festival in Los Angeles. During that tour on which I was accompanied by Kara Karayev, my Second Symphony and Violin Concerto were performed with Igor Bezrodny as soloist.

MZ: While your First and Second Piano Concertos are separated by a time span something like 40 years, your Second and Third ones are only 10 years apart, aren't they?

TK: Yes. By the beginning of the 1980's I had really completed my *Third Piano Concerto*. Though I hate to challenge my own tradition, I will introduce it myself as I did its predecessors.

MZ: It is on record that the composer's performance of his own work has some specific value both to the public and to the work's own fate. Whoever listened to works by Rachmaninoff and Prokofiev as interpreted by their composers justly thought themselves lucky. Similarly, it is great luck that audiences will be able to listen to your new composition as interpreted by you. But, as we know,

PHILADELPHIA ORCHESTRA

CARNEGIE HALL

SEVENTH CONCERT

TUESDAY EVENING, FEBRUARY 16, 1937
at 8.45

EUGENE ORMANDY, Conducting

KHRENNIKOV .... **Symphony**

    I. Allegro non troppo
    II. Adagio
    III. Allegro molto

(First Performance in New York)

STRAVINSKY .... **Suite "The Fire Bird"**

    I. Introduction
    II. The Fire Bird and Her Dance
    III. Dance of the Princesses
    IIII. Kastchei's Infernal Dance
    V. Berceuse
    VI. Finale

MOUSSORGSKY   **"Pictures at an Exhibition"**
(Orchestrated by Lucien Cailliet)

    Promenade
    I. Gnomus
    Promenade
    II. "Il vecchio Castello"
    Promenade
    III. Tuilleries. Dispute d'enfants après jeux
    IIII. Bydlo
    Promenade
    V. Ballet de poussins dans leurs coques
    VI. Samuel Goldenberg und Schmuyle
    VII. "Limoges. Le Marche"
    VIII. Catacombae. Sepulcrum Romanum
    Con mortuis in lingua mortua
    IX. La cabane sur des pattes de poule
    X. La grande porte de Kiev

(First New York Performance of this Orchestration)

ALFRED REGINALD ALLEN, Manager
LOUIS A. MATTSON, Assistant Manager
GIRARD TRUST COMPANY BUILDING, PHILADELPHIA

Khrennikov Symphony Heard

Ormandy Presents Young Russian's Work in Philadelphia Orchestra Concert.

By W. J. HENDERSON.

The Philadelphia Orchestra, Eugene Ormandy conducting, gave a concert of the first order last evening in Carnegie Hall. The high level was attained firstly by the introduction of a new symphony written by a young man who entered the Moscow Conservatory in 1932 and wrote his opus 1 in that and the following year; and secondly, by the virtuoso playing of the orchestra.

The symphony (of course, without key designation) is the opus 4 of Tikhon Khrennikov, still under 20, and it is without question the most promising work which has come out of Russia in recent years. This must be said with the music of Shostakovitch still fresh in the memory.

This composition is in three movements, allegro, adagio and finale. The thematic material of the opening and closing sections of the finale assume the guise of the absent scherzo, though the movement as a whole will not quite answer to such a classification. The basic first theme of the first movement reveals to us at once Khrennikov's trends in the direction of vivacious utterance. He knows the language of the advanced school, but speaks it naturally and straightforwardly. The announcement of the theme by a bassoon discloses itself as one of those melodic broken lines which the modernists have made a feature of their music.

The second principal theme is a finely sustained catilena. There are several subsidiary motives, which are employed with great skill in the development of the movement. But in spite of a really masterly handling of polytonality, which is only an occasional and never obtrusive, and of a persistent ranging through the mazes of tonality, the impression, surviving after the close of the movement is one of power to conceive genuinely musical subjects and with them to rear a structure which combines architectural symmetry with strength and which possesses that somewhat intangible quality which for want of a precise term we call "atmosphere." One feels the presence of a musical mind imprinting upon one's own a message tensely and compactly framed. The movement has, moreover, considerable excellently written free counterpoint and individuality in instrumentation. It is not a flawless creation, it has some open spots through which its substance momentarily escapes and some thin shaky leaping along imperfectly made connections. But on the whole, it has form and easily discernible direction of progress.

The slow movement of a symphony is the bottomless pit for many composers, but not for this young, ardent and confident Russian. He sings a broad and cleanly lined melody which has the illusion of clinging closely to the harmonic foundations of the fathers. It is an

Tikhon Khrennikov with Nemirovich-Danchenko after the opening night of the opera **In Storm.**

your piano concertos are being performed by other pianists besides you. Which of them do you think is their best interpreter?

TK: I find it difficult to judge the foreign pianists. I seldom have heard them play my piano concertos. However, in our country my concertos are played on frequent occasions. For instance,   superb interpreter of my Second Concerto is Lazar Berman.

MZ: Is there any substantial difference between his interpretation and yours?

TK: As an artist of intense individuality, Berman, of course, has evolved his own conception and offers his own performance of my work. But, according to another tradition, a pianist who brings into the repertoire a concerto I have written first plays it to me. I try to keep from putting pressure on the performer but if something obviously conflicts with my conception of the work, I point it out to the pianist in the form of a desire. Incidentally, when I first heard my First Symphony as interpreted by Eugene Ormandy it sounded much slower than I felt it should. I said this to Ormandy, and he modified the speed accordingly.

Khrennikov with chess-playing friends Mikhail Botvinnik, Vasily Smyslov and Paul Keres after the 1948 World Championship Match held in Moscow.

MZ: Have you ever performed works other than yours?

TK: Once I set my sights on playing a program which would be made up of *Concerto Number One* by Shostakovich, the *Concerto* by Aram Khachaturian and my Second Concerto. I even prepared the program. However, my preoccupation foiled my plan. Thus, the fact that I play only my own concertos is not dictated by some creative principles but is simply due to lack of time for relevant preparations.

As I heard Khrennikov say what he did, I though that it would be interesting to listen to a modern composer interpret works by his colleagues. It is really a pity that his plan did not materialize.

It is equally remarkable that Khrennikov would like to perform mainly *concertos*. It is easy to see that of all instrumental genres he has particular affinity for that of a concerto. Incidentally, the com-

Khrennikov taking bows with Conductor Svetlanov on the stage of the Bolshoi Hall after the debut of his second Piano Concerto.

Dmitri Kabalevsky, Dmitri Shostakovich and Tikhon Khrennikov discussing problems of musical life.

poser has achieved very interesting creative results here. Highly indicative is his *Second Piano Concerto*. Paying tribute to tradition, Khrennikov, unlike many other modern composers, revives the principle of soloist-orchestra competition (a favorite device of Mozart!). On the other hand, he introduces an obvious element of innovation: the composer uses fairly long solo episodes (for instance, the opening 66-bar *moderato*) which affords a broad disclosure of the pianist's solo potential.

Nevertheless, the fact that all that Khrennikov writes for the piano are concertos naturally led me to ask him another question.

MZ: Thus, as a piano composer you have written three concertos. Why have you confined yourself to one piano genre? Or, more specifically, why, being blessed with the rare gift of a melodist—you are a composer of extremely popular songs and music for films and theatrical performances—don't you create preludes or, more broadly, miniatures?

TK: It is precisely my long and coveted dream to write more piano works. I remember Shostakovich saying to me after I had written my *Second Concerto*: "You simply must write for the piano. Among other things, you should create concert solo pieces." I can feel it myself and I hope some day my dream will be brought to fruition.

MZ: Now that we have discussed your creative endeavor and a number of general problems pertaining to the piano art, we will, if you don't mind, touch on another question. Do you feel that in recent times composers have exhibited some coolness to the piano? At times one can hear that the piano is incapable of reflecting the complex problems of our time. This is why it has been countered by various chamber orchestras and even some instruments which came into being in the 20th Century.

TK: I know that some composers go for recently invented electronic music and other experimental musical media. To my mind, however, the key reason for this phenomenon—you were quite right in observing that the interest in the piano has somewhat abated—lies elsewhere. A look at the work of major piano com-

Khrennikov with Mikhail Khomitzer, one of the best performers of Khrennikov's **Cello Concerto.**

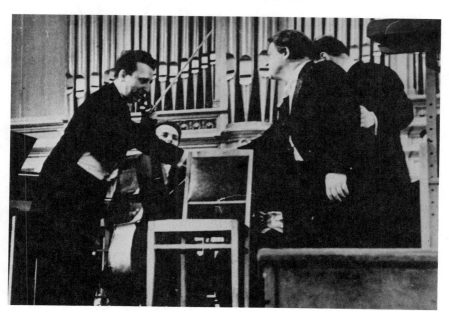

Klara and Tikhon Khrennikov with the well-known conductor Samuel Samosud.

Tikhon Khrennikov with the famous composer Yuri Shaporin.

Above: Tikhon Khrennikov with Efrem Zimbalist in Moscow. Top, facing page: Warm relations always connected Khrennikov with his elder colleague Sergei Prokofiev. Bottom, facing page: Khrennikov with producer Ilya Rappoport, author of the stage version of **Much Ado About Nothing** *shown at the Vakhtangov Theater.*

Sitting on the jury of the Tchaikovsky Competition with Leonid Kogan.

posers immediately shows that each of them has evolved his own identity, his own style and his own attitude to the instrument. It is a great problem to invent something new. Let us recall one specific moment in the history of the pianistic art. It would appear that after Scriabin, Debussy, Ravel and Rachmaninoff it was difficult, if not impossible, to find new colors and media of expression in the piano sound. However, Prokofiev demonstrated that the piano potential was far from exhausted. And he did succeed in shaping his own attitude to the instrument.

MZ: Your creative endeavor spans more than 50 years. You have witnessed the evolution of modern piano art. What do you think will be the hallmark of the piano works of the immediate future?

TK: It would be risky to forecast the ways to be followed by piano art. We know that, contrary to forecasts, a major composer creates his own style, offering his own interpretation of the piano. However, it seems that a piano composer who creates significant works cannot ignore traditions. I will give you a pertinent example.

Representatives of the Dagestan community meeting with Deputy Khrennikov. On the left is the well-known poet Rasul Gamzatov. Below: Khrennikov plays for his daughter Natasha. They are still very close friends.

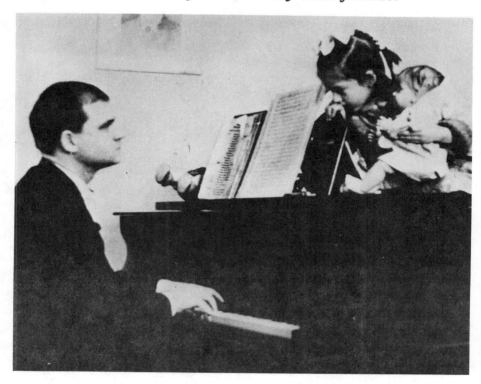

Above and facing page: Tikhon Khrennikov with the pianist of the world, Artur Rubinstein.

In my estimation, the greatest 20th-century piano composer is Prokofiev. But no matter how great an innovator he was—this is an unassailable fact—his style distinctly reveals his organic link with the leading composers of the past both in terms of genres and forms. Most important, loyal to the tradition of both Western European and Russian music, he was undeviatingly loyal to melodiousness, which underlies even his most complex works. Thus, I see prospects for the piano art in the observation of tradition fertilized by a true talent rather than in experimentation.

MZ: What specific composing techniques do you think should form a necessary or at least substantial element of a major piano work?

TK: I assume that an intensely fertile field for creative quest is formed by a fusion of the best that has been invented by romantic and post-romantic composers with a substantial element of polyphony; this would by no means exclude the melodic principle. For instance, the legacy of Prokofiev or Shostakovich graphically shows that each composer can find his own niche in the art of the piano without losing his identity by following this healthy princi-

A famous meeting of Khrennikov with Leopold Stokowski. Stokowski introduced many Khrennikov works to American audiences.

Top, facing page: A group of Soviet composers before their concert in Rome. From the left: Karen Khatchaturian, Rodion Shchedrin, Tikhon Khrennikov, Arno Babadzjanian and Andrei Eshpai. Bottom, facing page: Khrennikov meeting with Zoltan Kodaly in Moscow.

ple. This is why these two composers are justly held to be successors to the best traditions of many distinguished masters of the past. This is why I also strive to be guided in my concertos by the same principle, attaching such great importance, among other things, to polyphony.

MZ: Your *First Concerto* and, still more, your *Second* constitute an organic combination of the polyphonic style with the homophonic-harmonic. All signs show that you have had good schooling in polyphony. To which of your teachers do you owe it?

TK: I was really given a thorough grounding in polyphony by Professor Heinrich Litinsky, a composer and our leading master of polyphony. Incidentally, among his pupils also was Aram Khachaturian. We received an excellent schooling in his class. I

Khrennikov with two of the world's greatest violinists: Ruggiero Ricci on the left and Leonid Kogan on the right.

Khrennikov with an old friend, Roy Harris, after the presentation of one of Harris' works.

have in mind not so much the composing skill as a mode of musical thinking. My use of polyphonic devices and frequent resorting to a combination of homophonic-harmonic techniques with polyphonic are not the result of a rational choice but a natural expression of my mode of musical thinking, of my feelings and frames of mind. You are right in saying that this combination is a hallmark of my piano style. It is distinct enough in my *First Concerto* and was carried a step further in my *Second.* In my *Third Concerto* the combination of these two principles is there as well, the entire work having a manifestly melodic basis.

Klara and Tikhon Khrennikov with conductor Vasily Nebolsin, one of the best interpreters of Khrennikov's Second Symphony.

Top, facing page: Klara and Tikhon Khrennikov with the well-known Soviet writer Konstantin Fedin and his wife. Bottom, facing page: Khrennikov with the composer Kara Karaev before their flight to the USA in 1961.

Khrennikov has a tough task . . . deep down he is a great pianist . . . perhaps even deeper down he is a great composer . . . yet the world still proclaims him as perhaps the best music administrator in the arts.

MZ: Will you give some more details about your *Third Concerto?*

TK: I have already told you about my "kitchen." But of course the important thing is not the techniques the author employs in creating a work. Above all, I strove for my *Third Concerto* to be woven of beautiful, vivid, interesting music. I strove to make it a virtuoso concert work in the best sense of the word, interesting both to pianists and to audiences. And, as I said earlier, I wanted it to have a beautiful melodic basis. Of course, "the beautiful" in music and in art in general is an individual concept. Obviously, in my case, as in everyone else's, it is based on my individual sensations.

Another range of problems I encountered in my *Third Concerto* dealt with the musical fabric. After all, one danger is that of lapsing into the already tried and therefore the banal. Another one is an artificial urge for originality, which has never yielded good results

Khrennikov's patriotic themes have become very popular with many Eastern countries. This is the cover for his **In Storm,** *the Khrennikov opera shown in Bratislava, Czechoslovakia.*

either. Having to steer clear of these two dangers, I strove for some "golden mean." Whether I have succeeded only time will tell. In our time, I repeat, it is a great challenge to write original piano works that would exhibit the author's individual pattern of thought and emotion. Only major talents can measure up to the challenge. For instance, Stravinsky, as I see it, never resolved the problem of musical fabric in his piano works, any more than it was resolved in his piano pieces by another remarkably talented composer, Benjamin Britten. At any rate, his piano concerto leaves no impression, not even when it is performed by the outstanding pianist Sviatoslav Richter.

Khrennikov takes a bow with the actors after the debut of his comic opera Much Ado About . . . Hearts *presented in the Moscow Chamber Music Theater in 1972.*

Khrennikov with Igor Stravinsky in Moscow.

MZ: Which of the 20th-century composers, apart from Prokofiev and Shostakovich, are, in your opinion, major masters of the piano art?

TK: Above all, I should say this applies to Paul Hindemith, in whose piano works the vivid interesting element claims a large proportion of the music.

MZ: What material helps you get yourself back into performing shape following a prolonged interval?

TK: Among the time-tested expedients which help me fairly quickly regain "concert hands" are scales and the Brahms exercises, of which those based on double notes—thirds, sixths, octaves—are particularly good for me.

The official American portrait: Shostakovich, Kabalevsky, conductor Charles Munch, Khrennikov, Dankevich, Aaron Copland and Fikret Amirov.

MZ: What is the place of the piano in your composing process? In other words, do you compose music on the piano?

TK: I assume that composing should not be done on the instrument. Most important, the composer should hear his music with his inner ear and only then test it on the instrument. I create music lying on the sofa in the workroom in which we are sitting now. My eyes closed, musical thoughts, images and melodies come to me of their own accord. But, of course, passages and other compositional elements pertaining to the musical fabric can be developed and tested as to their sounding and facility of performances only on the piano. It is at the stage of instrument work that the composer can experimentally choose the best variant of many.

MZ: You have been chairman of the Organizing Committee of many of the Tchaikovsky competitions. What do you think of international performing competitions in general?

TK: In our day, nobody will deny the positive value of competitions. The general necessity of competitions is beyond any question. It is another matter that too many competitions of all possible kinds have crept into the musical scene, to date. It is difficult to imagine performing life without the Tchaikovsky competitions in Moscow, or the Jacques Thibaud and Marguerite Long contests in Paris, or the Queen Elisabeth competition in Brussels and many more. But then, rapidly multiplying, their number has reached dozens! And victory in one of the less significant competitions, which affords the winner his title and some degree of renown (let alone the material benefits) makes him feel that he can concertize before serious, exacting audiences. Regrettably, few of these winners grow into major artists. As a result, just a few years after victory in a competition, such a musician develops a gap between his ostensibly justified ambitions and his actual creative potential.

MZ: The majority of major composers exhibited a brilliant mastery of the piano or some other instrument. Take celebrated

A review of a Scandinavian performance of Natalia Conus' production of Khrennikov's ballet **Our Yard.**

Ballet i Þjóðleikhúsi:

Ys og þys út af engu

Tónlist: Tikhon Khrennikof
Dansar og leikstjórn: Natalja Konjús

A skírdag frumsýndi Þjóðleikhúsið ballettinn Ys og þys út af engu við mikla hrifningu viðstaddra — en áhöpp hafa orðið til þess, að sýningar voru ekki teknar upp aftur fyrr en nú um síðustu helgi.

Ballett þessi er nýr af nálinni. Hann var frumsýndur í fyrra í Stóra leikhúsinu í Moskvu, en tónlist Tikhons Khrennikofs hefur verið í smíðum í nokkra áratugi, allt frá því hann fyrst samdi leikhúsmúsik við þann

Til vinstri: Ásdís Magnúsdóttir og Þórarinn Baldvinsson.

gleðileik Shakespeares sem ballettinn er smíðaður um. Þrátt fyrir skamman aldur er ballettinn engan veginn nýtískulegur. Tónlistin er allt að því ógúðlega hefðbundin, en lætur vel í eyrum og er bersýnilega mjög vel „dansandi". Ballettmeistari Þjóðleikhússins, Natalja Konjús, samdi dansana. Aðferð hennar er svipuð og ýmissa sovéskra kóreografa annarra: Byggt er mestan part á klassískri hefð, en þar fyrir utan meira hugsað um þá leikrænu þætti sem stuðla að því að persónur með ábild og rétti verði til á sviðinu.

Útkoman varð skemmtileg sýning og skynsamleg. Skynsamleg vegna þess, að bæði tónlist og hinn gamansami andi leiksins, sem hélt í skefjum ljóðrænni angurværð (og tilfinningasemi) eru til þess fallin að laða að sér lítt ballettvana Íslendinga. Auk þess tekst Natalju Konjús, sem og á fyrri sýningu í vetur, að setja markið mátulega hátt fyrir íslenska dansflokkinn og gesti hans. Með

öðrum orðum: Menn hafa það ekki á tilfinningunni að veittur sé umtalsverður afsláttur frá kröfum til atvinnudansara. Og unnið hefur verið af því kappi, að áhorfendur sjá fyrir sér augljósar framfarir frá sýningu til sýningar.

Auður Bjarnadóttir og Maris Liepa, gestur frá Stóra leikhúsinu í Moskvu, fóru með aðalhlutverkin Hero og Claudio. Auður gekk ekki heil til leiks á frumsýningu, þurfti mjög að takmarka ýmsar tæknilegar raunir, og var það út af fyrir sig afrek hversu henni tókst að komast frá því með ágætum lýriskum þokka. Liepa er að sjálfsögðu þaulreyndur dansari og kraftmikill í sólónúmerum sínum — svo mjög að stundum varð sviðið helst til lítið fyrir hann. Hitt er svo ljóst að elskhugahlutverk sem hans er ekki alltof þakklátt, svo mjög sem það er jafnan reiknað aðalballerínunni til upphefðar

Ásdís Magnúsdóttir fór með hlutverk Beatríz og vann þar með sigur góðan með hressilegu fjöri, öryggi og skopvísi. Á móti

henni dansaði Þórarinn Baldvinsson og reði yfir sveiflu og þrótti sem ekki kallar á aðfinnslur. Samleikur þeirra Nönnu Ólafsdóttur og Bessa Bjarnasonar í hlutverkum Margrétar og Borachio var ágæti spaugilegur — Ballett á það á hættu að breytast í ópersónulega fimleika en Ásdísi og Nönnu tókst einmitt prýðilega að búa til manneskjur í þessari mjög svo skilorðsbundnu listgrein. Og Bessi Bjarnason bætti við enn einni sönnun um það, að hann er andskotanum útrúðabetri.

Leiksyndir Jóns Þórissonar voru fallega bjartar og léttar eins og við átti.

Verða nú ekki fleiri nöfn talin að sinni; sem betur fer eru þær framfarir, sem Ásdís Magnúsdóttir nannar með mestum tilþrifum, ekki bundnar við enn dansara eða tvo, það hefur verið gæfa dansflokksins og vera samstíga í bæði beinni og yfirfærðri merkingu. Vonandi verður atviratið velgengni Ys og þys út af engu ekki til að valda neinum truflunum í þeim efnum.

Arni Bergmann

Maris Liepa og Auður Bjarnadóttir í aðalhlutverkunum.

performers and improvisers such as Bach, Mozart, Beethoven, Chopin, Liszt, Rachmaninov and Prokofiev. Don't you think that one of the reasons for the present scarcity of important piano works is the practical disappearance of composer-pianists?

TK: You are absolutely right! Precisely because I believe that a composer must be a high-class performer, in my conservatoire I always try to cultivate in pupils a highly serious attitude to the piano. All students and post-graduates of my class exhibit a free

Xenia Erdeli (far left) congratulating Khrennikov after his performance with the Bolshoi.

Khrennikov with one of the best-known Soviet singers, Sergei Lemeshev, who often performs works of Khrennikov.

command of the piano. I always say to my pupils that a composer must enable himself to feel completely at home with the instrument. After all, some gifted students have written good music, but owing to their performing helplessness, cannot play it on the piano—a totally impermissible situation.

Regrettably, as far as I can see, the approach to the problem in the United States is somewhat different from mine. During one of my American tours, I visited a number of composer training centers. To our great surprise (I travelled with Dmitri Kabalevsky) we discovered that instrumental skill was obviously underestimated in the United States. It is on record that Berlioz, not being a master of the piano, was a fine guitar player. There were brilliant composer-violinists such as Wieniawski and Ysaye. In short, mastery of at least one instrument is simply a must for a composer. But, of course, the most useful instrument, which meets the greatest number of a musician's requirements, is the piano, which has long crowded out the organ as the king of musical instruments.

Nikolai Petrov

Nikolai Petrov was born April 14, 1943, in Moscow. He represents the third generation of the Petrovs' musical dynasty. His grandfather was a famous singer, the soloist of the Bolshoi; his grandmother was a pianist who had graduated from the Moscow Conservatory with honors (with a Gold Medal). Nikolai Petrov's parents are also musicians: his father is a cellist, laureate of a USSR Contest of violinists and cellists; his mother is a former pianist and ballerina.

The rare gift of Nikolai Petrov, his phenomenal ear for music and his potential as a virtuoso were displayed at a very early age. When he was two he used to play different melodies by ear, and when he was three his musical and general education began under the guidance of his grandmother: studying the piano, listening to music, learning foreign languages.

Like most musically gifted children, Nikolai Petrov entered the Central Music School of the Moscow Conservatory where his instructor was Tatyana Kestner, one of the most experienced pedagogues. In 1961, Nikolai Petrov entered the Moscow Conservatory in the class of the celebrated Soviet pianist and pedagogue Professor Yakov Zak. And only a year later he became one of the winners of the Van Cliburn International Contest in Fort Worth, Texas. Already at that time American critics noted in the 19-year old youngster the makings of a prominent musician. "He has everything—masterly technique, warmth and musicality—to make him a giant among pianists," wrote the *Christian Science Monitor*.

Two years passed and in 1964 Petrov earned another title of laureate having won the Silver Medal at the prestigious Queen Elisabeth Concours in Brussels. Though Petrov scored this victory when he was still a Conservatory student, the press noted his mature performance. "The talent of this fully-shaped musician is truly unique," observed *La Libre Belgique*. "One marvels at the magic of his technique, warm feeling and diversity of coloring."

Nikolai Petrov.

While visiting with Dr. Axelrod in Moscow, Petrov played some of the ORIGINAL *Liszt-Paganini* Variations . . . *the ones which were always considered too difficult to play. Petrov recorded them (a first!) and they will be issued by the* Musical Heritage Society *in North America.*

A typical Petrov poster . . . but this was for Vassily Petrov, the famous Russian bass and Nikolai's grandfather!

For the 200th Anniversary of the birth of Paganini, Petrov played all the Liszt-Paganini variations, plus other Paganini transcriptions.

Today Nikolai Petrov is an acclaimed soloist whose artistry is well-known to music lovers of more than 40 countries. His repertory is varied: he successfully performs a great deal of classical music, searches for and brings back to life undeservedly forgotten compositions of the past, and devotes much creative energy to performing Soviet contemporary music. Nikolai Petrov is one of the favorite pianists of Aram Khachaturian, Tikhon Khrennikov, Rodion Shchedrin and Andrei Eshpai, whose compositions he has performed more than once, often being their first interpreter.

Nikolai Petrov lives in a cozy house in the country not far from Moscow with his wife Larissa and their five-year-old daughter, who has already begun the study of the piano and will perhaps continue the glorious musical traditions of the Petrovs.

* * * *

Our talks with Petrov whom I've known for over twenty years began in his Moscow apartment (where he appears very seldom, preferring to live in the country) which is the family "nest" of the Petrovs. Once it belonged to the pianist's grandfather, Vasili Petrov, a wonderful singer, one of the first People's Artists of the Republic. Many outstanding artists representing Russian and Soviet culture used to come to that apartment—famous writers, actors, many celebrated musicians. Among them were the renowned composers and performers David Oistrakh, Alexander Goldenweiser, Lev Oborin and many others. In that benevolent atmosphere imbued with music and creative work, Nikolai Petrov's personality was molded.

And today next to the family portraits and weathered posters of Vasili Petrov, and the bass, there hang the colorful posters in different languages of his grandson Nikolai Petrov. The pianist started our conversation.

NP: It is no accident that these posters are here. They represent the programs of the most memorable concerts, especially significant to me. As a matter of fact, having followed the path that is the usual run of things for most contemporary pianists (I mean my studies, participation and victories in contests), I began my activities of a soloist making up my repertory in an ordinary way. If I set out to learn some compositions, at the moment I mastered them, I added them to those that I had been already performing. In fact I acted exactly like the majority of the young (as well as not young) performers. It had been my routine until I began to look upon the problem of the program content from an entirely different standpoint. I consider this to be perhaps one of the most important turning points in my career as an artist. These posters are, so to say, the evidence of an absolutely new approach to the repertory, of my new repertory "policy," if I may put it so.

MZ: For a high-class performer, the problem of the repertory is probably of primary importance. The kind of repertory a musician chooses characterizes the evolution of an artist-interpreter, his creative aspirations. The way you embark upon the subject of this problem shows how urgent it is for you. What does your nontraditional approach to the choice of repertory consist of?

NP: I believe that every program should have a certain "pivotal" message. In this respect a musician-performer ought to work at the program make-up somewhat like a playwright or a producer works at a theatre play; the program should have a plot, development, culmination and finale. At one time I played the following program: in the first part, the Beethoven *Sonata No. 29;* in the second part, the Prokofiev *Sonata No. 8.* Both compositions are of large scale but some important common points that would link them in one program are lacking. At present I wouldn't play such a program.

MZ: You've given an example of the program that does not satisfy you today. Then tell us of one or two programs that comply with your principles.

NP: With pleasure. The first program included compositions of Schumann and Debussy. In the stylistic sense, these pieces seem to have little in common. So what gave me the right to unite them in one program? The first part was the rendition of Schumann's compositions that had been lately rediscovered: *Exercises*—fifteen études in the form of free variations on a theme of Beethoven, and a vocal cycle, *A Poet's Love* (with Alexei Maslennikov); in the se-

Nikolai "Kolya" Petrov with his grandmother Yevgenia Petrova.

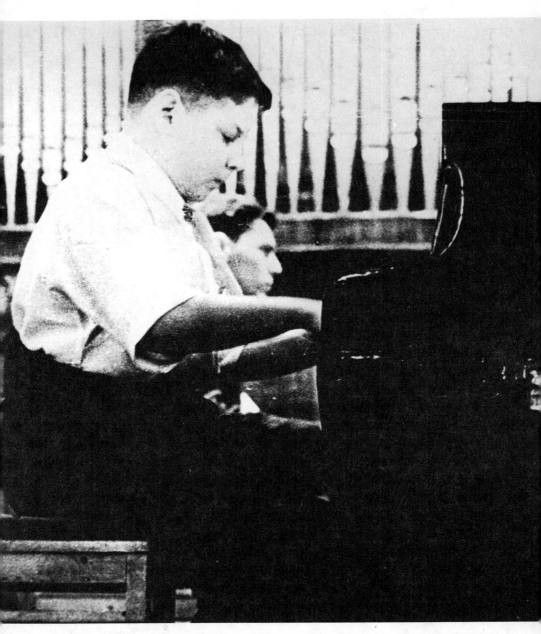

Nikolai Petrov's first performance at a school in the small hall of the Moscow Conservatory.

cond part, Debussy's *Six Etudes* and *The Island of Joy* were performed. But the conceptual link bridging the whole program was the inclusion in it of the Schumann *Six Canonic Etudes* written for a pedal piano which is no longer used in Debussy's arrangement for two pianos. The second program I'd like to mention was devoted to the 200th anniversary of Paganini. Paganini on the piano . . .

MZ: It is indeed a unique program. I doubt if anyone else in the world performs it.

NP: I can proudly say that I am still the only performer of this program. But maybe the essentials are not in that. Brahm's *Variations on a Theme of Paganini* is performed on the stage often enough. Schumann's pieces, op. 10, as far as I know, are practically never played in concerts. As for the composition of the contemporary composer Yuri Falik, *Dedication to Paganini*, it is written specially for that program. And finally, the first edition of the Paganini-Liszt études that had not been performed even by Liszt himself. In fact, they were executed for the first time in the season of 1980-1981, when I began performing this program. I do not claim these two programs to be standard. But they are given as an example to illustrate my words and it was a most fascinating experience for me to prepare and to perform them.

MZ: That's quite interesting. The problem of compiling a concert program opens up a special sphere of creative search for the performer, reveals his musical gusto, comprehension of contemporary tendencies in performance.

NP: To finish this topic I'll impart one more of my designs, which I hope to realize soon. I'd like to arrange a "Musical evening of keyboards." Imagine a stage with two organs, two pianos, a harpsichord and a celesta. In the first part of the concert, together with my friend Swedish organist Eric Lunquist, we'll perform the recently rediscovered *Six Organ Concertos* of Padre Antonio Soler for two organs (it will be the first recital both in the Soviet Union and in Sweden). In the second part we'll play Schumann's *Canonic Etudes* for two pianos, and a composition of the Soviet composer Yuri Falik.

MZ: I see also another aspect of the repertoire problem. Possessing the richest possible repertorial heritage in comparison with other instruments, pianists are far from anxious about it. Many wonderful compositions have been undeservedly forgotten. You mentioned your plans to play a monographic concert of Brahms' compositions and I recall his *Chorals* that are unfamiliar to pianists and to the public. But it is music of genius!

NP: Yes, you are quite right. Once I tried to analyze the repertory belonging to the most outstanding classical composers that was being performed and I came to a very sad conclusion: only a small part of what had been written by these composers actually was heard on the concert stage. The majority of pianists play the same compositions. For example, at the request of the Italians (I like very much to learn pieces to comply with some firm request) I learned the Saint-Saëns *Fifth Concerto*. And in many cities and towns where I played it, it was heard for the first time. Yes, for the very first time! And do we often hear the *First, Third and Fourth Concertos* of Saint-Saëns? This also is a very rare occurrence.

MZ: You said that you had followed the path traditional for most contemporary pianists. Please, tell us how it all started.

NP: My first teacher was my grandmother Yevgenia Petrova, formerly a fine pianist, the student of Professor Karl Kipp. When I was one year old (!) she began to play opera transcriptions to me. By the age of five or seven I knew practically all the popular opera music. My grandmother guided me even later, after I entered school.

MZ: Do you remember how the lessons of the piano progressed in the first years of your studies? What did your grandmother pay special attention to?

NP: According to the reminiscences of my relatives, I had extremely good hands for a small child and a brilliant ear for music (my parents liked to show me off to their guests, especially musicians: they would play various chords or some sound combinations at random on the piano and I guessed all the notes straight away). My grandmother was a well-educated woman and she was not only a piano teacher for me. She taught me solfeggio, elements of harmony, the French language. It was a complex education. And for several years at school I was still drawing on the store of knowledge I had absorbed from my grandmother.

MZ: So you came to school very well prepared; it must have impressed the examination board. Do you remember what you played at the entrance examination?

Nikolai Petrov with his mother, Irina Petrova, formerly a pianist and ballerina, now a playwright.

NP: I do not remember at all what I played. I only remember that at the examination, presided over by the most noted Moscow musicians, I felt quite emancipated, to say the least. On entering the classroom I made straight for the table and started shaking hands with the members of the board one after another. And in reply to the question of what I could do, I answered unhesitatingly: "Everything!"

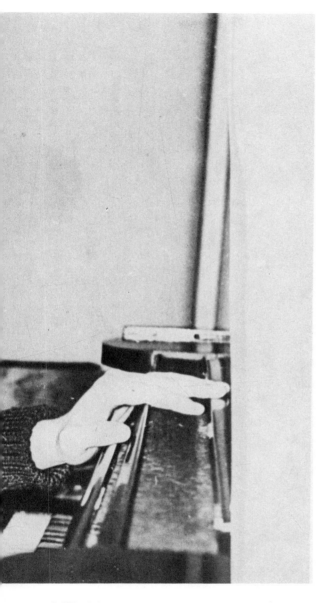

Nikolai Petrov is a serious musician and always has been.

MZ: I know that throughout all the ten years of your studies at the Central Music School your tutor was Tatyana Kestner, one of the most experienced Moscow pedagogues. How did your lessons with Tatyana Kestner go?

NP: At first at her lessons I just sat at the piano. But it did not take her long to establish contact with me. Tatyana Kestner is an outstanding children's pedagogue. She gives a great deal to young

musicians—practically until they achieve artistic maturity. Probably due to my large hands, which were well-suited for playing the piano, I was very soon ahead of the program. All the technical pieces came out well. And it is particularly this that takes up most of the time during the school years.

MZ: Does it mean that in your school years you did not in general practice much?

Nikolai Petrov with his Conservatory Professor Yakov Zak.

NP: I don't remember how many hours a day I used to practice. The essential thing was that, as I realized only later, my practicing was not efficient. I learned how to use the time rationally only in my very last years at school. I must confess that maybe owing to the characteristics of my hands I could never set an example of many hours of "heroic" deeds at the piano. For instance, many pianists spend a lot of time warming up before a concert or even

Three laureates of the famous Queen Elisabeth Competition in Brussels: Nikolai Petrov, Jean-Claude Van den Heiden and Yevgeny Mogilevsky.

before their usual daily practice. I may not touch the instrument for a whole month, but "restore" my form, so to say, "get in trim" in a day or two.

MZ: Did you go through a great deal of scales, études, exercises in your school years?

NP: Of course, like all the pupils, I played a lot of Czerny's études. As far as scales are concerned, I passed my examination scales and since then I have never played scales or exercises. In general I think that if a pianist needs to better his technique, undoubtedly, he has got to go through all these things. When he possesses innate, natural virtuosity, everything necessary for the normal technical development may be found in the repertory, in the music he is playing.

MZ: So with what repertory "outfit" did you leave school?

NP: By that time I was playing serious and complicated pieces, among them *Death Dance, Don Juan* of Mozart-Liszt, Prokofiev's *Second Sonata*.

Nikolai Petrov, Yakov Zak and Zak's assistant, Mikhail Mezhlumov.

Elisabeth, Queen of the Belgians, congratulates the winners, including our hero, Nikolai Petrov, upper right.

MZ: The age of 18 which you reached when you were graduating from the CMS is a period full of thorns for a young man, especially for a creative personality. Did you experience any disappointment, any crisis at that time which would have somehow affected your future? Or did everything go smoothly, "swimmingly"?

NP: You've just hit the nail on the head. The point is that I was awfully self-confident; I was absolutely sure that I played beautifully. When I was in the 10th grade an All-Russia and then an All-Union Contest of musicians and performers was held. I had

A caricature of Petrov, who "always had an eye open for a cigarette lighter," which he collected enthusiastically as a youngster.

Nikolai Petrov playing during his first American tour.

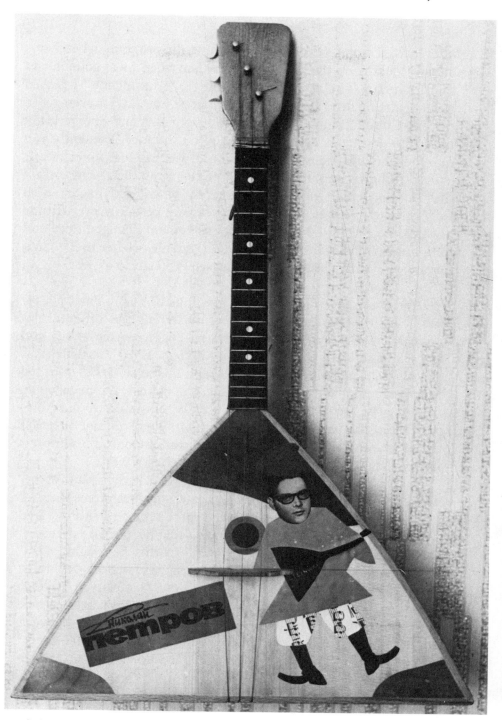

A balalaika that Petrov's friends decorated just for him.

not received scores yet or started learning the program, when I was already looking up the calendar for the day when I was going to get the first prize. The result was appallingly "triumphant." I passed as far as the finale of the All-Russia Contest but did not even get to the All-Union Competition. I played very fast and energetically but it did not make a great impression on the jury. Evidently you must toil before you spin! This failure was not lost upon me. It proved to be an important turning point in my life. I saw clearly that nothing could be achieved merely with good hands, with finger-flying passages and loud octaves. But certainly my attitude towards the piano and study of the instrument changed once and for all under the influence of my unforgettable teacher in the Conservatory and my post-graduate course, Professor Yakov Zak.

I remember the student musical evenings of Yakov Zak's master class, which I was lucky to attend. With all the different individuals (such wonderful musicians as Yevgeny Mogilevsky and Lhubov Timofejeva graduated from his class, Eliso Virsaladze was his post-graduate student) it made a solid impression that reflected the creative "signature" of Yakov Zak, the pianist, the pedagogue.

Judging by how the students usually clustered round their teacher and the way he mixed with them, great mutual affection between the students and the pedagogue was obvious. This impression of mine was confirmed by Nikolai Petrov's words.

NP: The first thing that comes to mind when I think of my teacher is that in his class there always reigned an atmosphere of warmth, friendship, benevolence, and mutual understanding. And the second thing of utmost importance is that his tutelage exceeded the limits of teaching the piano. It was Art that he taught.

MZ: Having entered Yakov Zak's class after school you must have been desirable material for him. Unique virtuosity, a brilliant general background—all that was a perfect basis for rearing a true artist. But there was a kind of "gap" between your merits—between your technique, and your musical achievements, wasn't there? How did Yakov Zak manage to establish the necessary balance between the two?

Nikolai Petrov.

146

Nikolai Petrov with Van Cliburn during Petrov's participation on the jury of the famous Van Cliburn Competition. On the facing page is Nikolai Petrov with Rodion Shchedrin. Petrov is one of the best interpreters of Shchedrin's works. The composer says that Petrov's hands are as if they were specifically created to play his music!

NP: Precisely. I became Yakov Zak's pupil as a not-bad "half-finished product," and he started to "polish" me. Very soon I realized that in Zak's class entirely different categories and values prevailed. The principal thing was that Zak taught me how to work. I understood that by practicing efficiently for three or four hours a day tremendous results could be achieved.

Nikolai Petrov and Aram Khatchaturian after Petrov played the Concerto-Rhapsody. *The inscription on the photo says:* "Dear Kolya! Your interpretation of my Concerto Rhapsody is that of a genius. Thank you. Aram Khatchaturian, Dec. 16, 1968."

MZ: Which of your teacher's recommendations concerning practicing habits proved of utmost importance for you?

NP: Zak taught me to practice softly and slowly, that is, he taught me the things I was not doing at all. Of course it is all individual. For instance, Sviatoslav Richter practices very loudly, repeating one or another episode an innumerable number of times.

Nikolai Petrov and his beautiful wife Larisa. On the facing page is another musical caricature of Petrov.

But for me it was Zak's method of practicing that proved effective. Besides, he taught me to read the composer's text competently and creatively.

MZ: The results became obvious immediately. Only a year later you found yourself among the winners of the Van Cliburn Contest in Texas.

NP: Really, soon after I entered the Conservatory, the terms of the contest in Texas were announced. In comparison with other competitions, the terms of the piano competition in Fort Worth were hideously difficult: there were special compositions and chamber music and an hour-long program of the performer's own choice.

MZ: How did your performance at the Van Cliburn Competition turn out?

Nikolai Petrov with his wife Larisa and his daughter Zhenya.

NP: I was quite a success at this Contest and was awarded the second prize. The winner was an American—Ralph Votapek. By the way, we were both scored an equal number of points in the finale, but the person who sponsored the first prize declared that he preferred it to be awarded to an American. So at the second voting the scale weighed in favor of Votapek.

Nineteen-year-old Nikolai Petrov was the youngest participant of the Contest. Yet, as early as that time the great perspectives of his gift were quite evident. "He has enormous pianistic potentialities, high temperament, vivid artistry," the famous pianist and pedagogue Lev Oborin, one of the jury, wrote at the time. "Of course he is still in the making but he is promising to turn into a very prominent artistic individual."

Twenty years have elapsed since then. Nikolai Petrov has already been on the jury of the Texas contest himself. So we dwelt on some urgent problems of a contemporary musical competition.

MZ: I recall one wise business manager who worked in the Philharmonic Society and on the radio and who was always besieged by the laureates of different competitions demanding concerts and broadcasting of their performances. Once, in a fit of temper, he said that it would do no harm to arrange a yearly "thin-

During the many interviews for this chapter, the Petrovs and Zilberquits became quite friendly. Here are both families.

ning out" of the laureates. Indeed, don't you think that there is a certain "overproduction" of laureates of musical competitions?

NP: If we turn to the history of any international competition, we'll immediately see that not all the laureates can stand the test of time, that is, become serious artists capable of original and interesting concertizing careers. This just reaffirms your remark about "overproduction" of laureates. There may be an infinite number of rewards—diplomas, bonuses, premiums, prizes. But the title of the laureate, to my mind, should be conferred only upon the most deserving, not more than three. Only in this way can we do away with the inflation of the title of "laureate" itself.

MZ: It is common knowledge that the main characteristic of any contest is its program. Don't you find the programs of some prestigious contests not perfect enough and instead of "discovering" a musician, an artist, they single out athlete-performers, "all-arounders"?

NP: I hold that inclusion into the programs of purely sporting elements, as, for instance, learning in the shortest possible period of time a most difficult concerto of doubtful worth as it was in Brussels, is absolutely unnecessary, superfluous, and meaningless. Let's imagine that there has appeared a pianist of Vladimir Horowitz's rank but he has had one demerit—it takes him long to learn a composition. As a result, at the Brussels Competition he will fail to get a prize, though he may stand head and shoulders above the winners. And mind, I'm telling you all this not as a contestant who bears a grudge against this competition—quite the opposite: I was the only one among the finalists who did play from memory that obligatory concerto learned within a week! And now I even don't remember the name of its author, not to speak of the music itself—in one ear and out the other.

MZ: In your opinion, which of the contemporary competitions offers a young musician the greatest opportunity for the successful beginning of a concert career?

NP: The Van Cliburn Contest is essentially different from others in its terms as it opens up a brilliant perspective to the first three laureates—the prize-winners. The tours of the U.S.A. and other countries scheduled for three years after victory in the Fort Worth Contest, performances with major American orchestras, tours around Europe, recordings and TV broadcasts are indeed a rare boon to a young pianist. So if the winner is truly talented, in three years' time everything goes swimmingly for him. He becomes a popular concertizing performer with a name famous with the public. However, we all know that the Moscow Tchaikovsky Competition and the Brussels competition are probably the most prestigious.

MZ: As a member of the jury of the Van Cliburn Contest, you must be familiar with the system of preparation of young American pianists for this competition. What are its advantages and disadvantages as compared to the system of preparation for competitions in the Soviet Union?

When Nikolai Petrov played a very intricate **waltz, Dr. Axelrod asked Mrs. Petrov to dance. Nikolai stopped playing immediately!**

NP: I happened to listen to many young pianists nurtured in the U.S.A. and other countries. In particular I acquainted myself with their achievements when I was on the jury of the Van Cliburn Contest. The introduction usually begins with the booklet that presents, for instance, such information as, "in 1960-1962 studied with Vladimir Horowitz; in 1962-1965, with Nadia Boulanger; in 1965-66, with Claudio Arrau; in 1966-68 was the probationer of . . ." And then it turns out that he is only some twenty years old, but in the years of his studies he managed to be under the tutelage of four or five different masters. Moreover, having taken one lesson from Horowitz, such a student already considers himself to be Horowitz's pupil and proclaims it from the housetop. Undoubtedly, someone really studies under his tutelage. But we know very well that any pedagogue starts with the attempt to find "common language" with his new pupil, introduces him to his particular methods, his "creative laboratory," and all this takes many months if not years. And as soon as such a contact is finally established, as soon as the pedagogue begins to feel that something comes of it, the student switches over to another teacher. What's the big idea?

In this respect I find our system splendid. Coached by one pedagogue, at school as a rule, a pupil gets everything from the rudiments and proceeds to achieve a certain degree of maturity. And then under the guidance of a maitre, a pedagogue-artist, the student goes through the whole orderly "training" of the highest degree of difficulty. So we know a musician as, for instance "Neuhaus' pupil," and this speaks for itself. Here it is simply impossible to say that "he is the pupil of Neuhaus, Oborin, Flier and Zak." I hold to the opinion that if you are lucky enough to become a student of a good pedagogue you shouldn't give him up; on the contrary, you should get from him everything he can give you. And I consider this to be the major drawback of the western system of rearing musicians.

MZ: The statement you've just pronounced is perhaps quite correct, but it is by no means unquestionable. There may be, for instance, a wonderful pedagogue, an artist, a vivid personality like your revered teacher Yakov Zak. But can he or any other pedagogue of his rank turn a mediocre student into a pianist of the highest class? Naturally not. However, having taken the Conservatory course from such a pedagogue, this student has every right to call himself Zak's pupil like you do. At the same time, if a young musician who knows what he is seeking (and it is the most precise indication of the significance of his talent), is truly gifted, what harm do you see in his adopting something from Horowitz and some other things from Arrau? Of course, I don't mean the one-time pedagogical "injections."

NP: You are absolutely right but with only one reservation: this young personality should be very forceful. On the other hand, if it is a truly powerful personality who achieved maturity early, it still remains a question as to whether we can, strictly speaking, call him

During his tour of Japan, Nikolai Petrov met many young pianists and established a great reputation for himself.

159

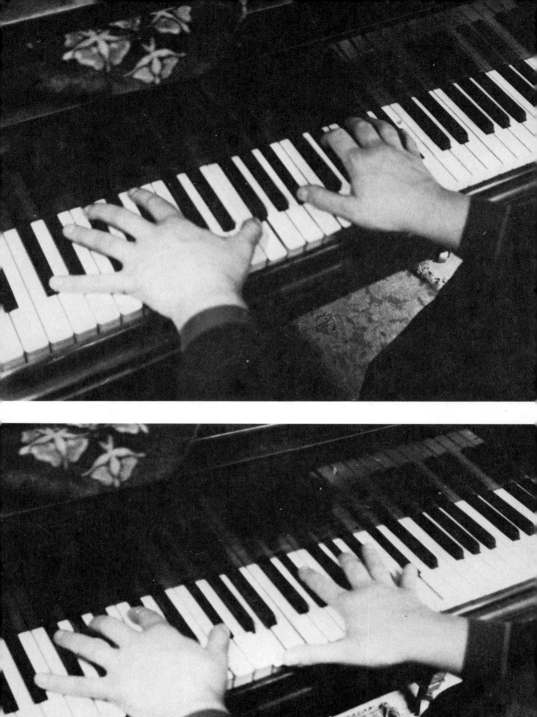

the pupil of that particular pedagogue who was his tutor. Have we the right to call Pletnyov the pupil of Flier with whom, in fact, he studied so little?

MZ: Right you are. But in my opinion, the talent of a student (I mean a grown-up student) is also manifested in his ability to take, to adopt from the pedagogue that which he needs most. As far as the pedagogue is concerned, his art consists of his skill to preserve the originality of a talented pupil, to choose for him a repertory that would reveal and develop his abilities to the utmost.

NP: I fully agree with you on this point.

MZ: As far as I know, making chamber music is very popular with young musicians in the West. Is it somehow connected with the characteristics of teaching chamber music in America and other western countries or are there any other reasons for that?

NP: It is common knowledge that human relations in this country are much simpler, are of a much more natural character than in the West. To drop in on someone is a natural thing with us and usually both the guests and the hosts are quite happy about it. But students of music getting together specially to perform chamber music is a much more frequent occasion in the West than it is here. And such contacts are so vital for a young musician! We can say without exaggeration that probably the major part of classical music is written within the frames of chamber music. I, for one, regard as some of the most significant of my achievements my participation in chamber music. To my mind, a pianist who declines the offers to make chamber music simply robs himself of something essential.

MZ: In what do you see the difference between the performer's condition and his "duties" in solo and chamber performance?

NP: Nowhere is the culture of a musician revealed better than in a chamber ensemble. In a chamber ensemble, it becomes obvious at once whether or not the musician comprehends the style, the correlation of sonority of the instruments, even how to behave at the instrument. Playing in a quintet, for instance, a musician can

Petrov has huge hands and uses them to great advantage playing all the virtuoso pieces many other artists shy away from.

neither feel, nor behave as a soloist. A pianist should not rock himself at the instrument or swing his head and hands, even if it is his habit when he plays solo, while the other performers in the ensemble sit modestly without displaying their emotions. A trifle? Yes, but a very important one.

MZ: Judging by the urgency with which you expounded your ideas on pedagogics, I felt that you were really concerned with these problems. But like most concertizing performers, evidently you prefer not to split your activities. Maybe this suits you but I can't help regretting the fact. The point is that you've accumulated considerable pianistic experience that could be so beneficial to young performers. Isn't it so? Didn't the example of your own teacher Yakov Zak inspire you?

NP: You've touched on a sore spot, because I do want very much to teach and I know I can do that. But I have not had the opportunity yet for teaching, though I'd like to very much! A lesson with a student, even if it is a poor student, to a certain extent is useful for the pedagogue himself. But if one feels truly responsible for whatever he is doing and leads such an intensive concert life as I do, for example, with a schedule of 70-80 concerts a year, systematic teaching is out of the question. Why should the students be blamed if they lose their tutor for different periods of time every now and then? As we've remembered Yakov Zak, I'd like to note that he had never "deserted" his pupils, even those who were careless, undeserving students. I would say he was the only pedagogue of the Conservatory who would not miss a lesson with a student even on the day of some crucial concert.

At that point we had to call it a day as Nikolai Petrov was hurrying to a rehearsal of the coming concert in Moscow.

Several days later we met again, but that time it was not in Moscow but in a picturesque spot in the suburbs which is called "Nikolina Mountain." At one time Sergei Prokofiev and Nikolai Miaskovsky used to spend the summer months there. And at present some of the inhabitants of this little spot are also famous musicians — Sviatoslav Richter, Gennady Rozhdestvensky. The permanent residence of Nikolai Petrov is here as well.

I found the host in a large workshop, the walls of which were lined with hammers, chisels, hand-saws, drills and all kinds of other implements carefully selected and kept in immaculate order.

"I am very fond of busying myself with making things," Petrov says, greeting me and telling me with pride how he has collected his tools. "It is the best imaginable way of rest for me," says the pianist.

It turned out that the whole workshop had been constructed by him, from the foundation to the roof. And in the house itself we can see many things Petrov made with his own hands. He tells me with animation how he reconstructed the simple wooden hut into a beautiful convenient and cozy house.

"Now I see," I remark half jokingly when we make ourselves comfortable in the sitting room to go on with our talk, "why some critics analyzing your style of performance point out as one of the major characteristics your brilliant 'engineer's' way of thinking. Do you agree with such a definition?"

NP: I am afraid of any labels at all. People writing about art, some music critics, mix up two essentially different things: defining the features of the performer's style with slapping labels on him. For instance, Vladimir Sofronitsky was somehow linked only with Scriabin; Clara Haskil, with Mozart, etc. By the way, Sofronitsky usually took offense when called a "Scriabinist." Indeed, he was a universal pianist.

MZ: Evidently you appreciate universality most of all in a pianist, don't you?

NP: I would say I do. So if I were to speak of those who in the days of my youth stirred my imagination most of all, I'd say it was undoubtedly Sviatoslav Richter who fascinated me, particularly with his universality. In my opinion he is the most universal pianist, though I cannot say he is my favorite pianist. I don't think I have one favorite composer or performer, or some favorite composition. I play what I admire and I admire what I play—that is my credo. The only thing I have noticed is that my repertory affections are "cyclic," lasting for a year or two.

MZ: And once again, as at the beginning of our talk, we touch upon the topic of repertory. How is it accumulated? Do you take the piece out onto the stage straight away or do you prefer to delay it until you feel more at home with it?

NP: I can't help remembering my teacher Yakov Zak in this connection. He used to say to me: "Learn new pieces. Learn the repertory in store. Learn while you are young, because after forty, it will be much more difficult. One's memory gets weaker. Learn! Let it be half-finished things, quarter-finished, but you'll nevertheless make use of them later and it won't be difficult to bring them to perfection then." I've followed my teacher's advice. During the fifteen years after my graduation from the Conservatory, I learned a great number of compositions, really made a storehouse from which I draw even now. Zak had one more saying: "You should never push the pie onto the table right out of the stove." To put it differently it is necessary that, after being learned, the composition should "rest" a bit and only then be produced for the judgment of the audience.

MZ: One of the most serious difficulties confronting a young musician is the way to approach a new piece, its selection, the direct work at it, perfecting its performance. In connection with this it would be interesting to know what are your major principles of approaching a new piece.

NP: First of all a piece should be learned in the rough and put aside for a while, for a month or even longer. As for the further stage, two viewpoints are known to exist concerning the work at a piece: from the particulars to the whole and from the whole to the particulars. My standpoint is to proceed from the whole to the particulars. In my opinion, you first have to have the general idea of the composition as a whole and only then to dwell on details.

MZ: What sound intensity and what tempo do you choose when commencing your work at a new piece?

NP: I completely reject "beating out" the sounds. I hold the opinion that one should learn a composition not in a quick tempo and as softly as possible, entirely preserving the conceptual background of the piece. Mechanical hammering out of the notes simply sickens me.

MZ: We've just touched upon maybe the most important aspect of the piano art—tone production. What would you point out as vital in this problem?

NP: I believe the culture of tone production is best acquired by a combination of practicing technique with working at sound quality simultaneously.

MZ: This advice must have been prompted by your own experience and is founded on your own unique makings of a virtuoso granted to you by Nature. But it is unlikely that this advice could be taken by a young player who lacks such innate technical resources. Unfortunately our craft often demands that we should practice, particularly the technique.

NP: You are welcome to do so! But for this purpose there exists a great number of exercises, scales, "Hanon"—a certain set of instructive études. On this material the musician who feels the need for it may very well polish and develop his technique, go in for "drill" if he finds it necessary. But not on the repertory!

MZ: Turning back to the problem of tone production, I'd emphasize that grasping the very essence of the piano tone, searching for one's own sound palette is a process which to my mind involves many points that are beyond verbal description. Don't you think so?

NP: At one time a certain musical authority arrived in Moscow to deliver a number of lectures on the nature of the piano tone. "What is the piano tone?" he questioned and then replied: "It is a certain vibration caused by the finger touching the key and the hammer striking the string accordingly. And consequently," he asserted, "no matter what we touch the key with, be it a finger or a fountain pen, the physical nature of the sound is the same. " It is absolutely clear that assertions of this kind are sheer nonsense. In the piano tone, in its nature, in the very "stemming" of the sound there is a mystery that can't be defined with words. I'll give one more example. We've been taught that one should play leaning "deeply into the piano," that a beautiful deep sound can be drawn forth "from the bottom" of the key. When I was lucky enough to listen to Vladimir Horowitz (he kindly received me at his place and played specially for me) I unexpectedly discovered that he produced the sound in quite a different manner: he strikes the keyboard as if plucking at the key, a kind of pizzicato, "rebounding" attack on the key, not "into" the piano but "out of it." I was sitting next to him and saw it with my own eyes. Thus, the question of tone production is strictly individual, depending on the physiology of a given person. I for one, play with a "wrong" hand position because I have unusual hands. It goes without saying that if I happen to advise some young pianists, I'm not going to call upon them to hold their hands as I do.

MZ: If you remember, Anton Rubinstein recommended learning how to "sing" on the piano from vocalists. Don't you think that some secrets of tone production could be perceived by watching string players?

NP: I did give it a thought when I was once watching the devices a guitarist employed while playing: after plucking the string he "roves" over the string with his hand as if conjuring, which must be regulating the resounding sound. We pianists can do something of the kind by means of correct employment of the right pedal, that is regulating the distance between dampers and strings. Generally speaking, I am convinced that a beautiful deep and rich sound as to its timbre can be extracted only from the "bottom" of the key.

MZ: You are absolutely right in saying that in the devices employed for good tone production as in many other devices of playing the piano (pedalling etc.) there are many points that are hard to explain. And your last remark is a brilliant illustration of that. Yes, in general the pianists finds the beautiful sound at the "bottom" of the key. But let's recollect the finale of the Chopin *B Flat minor Sonata*. The effect of ominousness, mysteriousness of this "Perpetuum Mobile" is created only by playing on some "superficial" layer. This music simply can't be played "at the bottom" of the key.

NP: Yes, of course all our pianistic recipes are quite relative.

MZ: What is the major flaw that you can point out in the performance of young pianists whom you happened to advise?

NP: I have said it to myself over and over again, and repeated the same thing to those young musicians who turned to me for an audition that the essential thing was the "horizontal"! What do I mean by that? Most young pianists dissect everything they play into quarter-bars and half-bars. There are no lines, no ability to see on the broad scale. Music can't be spelled out. It seems to be quite a comprehensible idea. However, it is particularly that kind of interpretation, just "spelling out" which can be often heard. I am all against thinking in "vertical," that cuts the music into pits, breaks the music to pieces.

MZ: In your opinion how thoroughly should the pianist know the score of a piano concerto that he plays on the stage, in particular the orchestra part?

NP: Not long ago I was on tour in Odessa with the Liszt *First Concerto*. On the music stands of the members of the orchestra there were the scores of their parts all speckled with marking-out, the scores from which this composition had been played dozens of times . . . And suddenly at the rehearsal I clearly heard a false note in the orchestra. I stopped playing, looked into the score; looked at the "voices"; there was an obvious error. I pointed it out to the conductor and the players. They were of course embarrassed at first, but then admitted that they had always played like that. It means then not a single soloist had ever heard it. I am telling you this episode not for the sake of boasting but to express my explicit conviction that the overwhelming majority of young pianists (and perhaps not only the young ones) do not know the score. There was a similar incident with the Prokofiev *Third Concerto*. In general I daresay that I know the score of the concertos I play better than 90% of the conductors under whom I happen to play. One of the reasons, to my mind, is that some conductors regard the accompaniment as secondary music.

It was not accidental that Nikolai Petrov chose as an example the compositions of Liszt and Prokofiev. Nowadays Petrov is rightfully considered to be one of the best interpreters of Liszt's and Prokofiev's compositions. He is especially eminent in performing the works of Sergei Prokofiev. Petrov in general possesses astoundingly keen sensibilities in relation to contemporary Soviet music, being one of its most ardent popularizers. Some of his programs, for example, the performance of four concertos for piano with orchestra in one program, Aram Khatchaturian's, Rodion Shchedrin's Tikhon Khrennikov's and Andrei Eshpai's, are a memorable event in Soviet piano art. The recordings of these programs are in great demand with the music-lovers and professionals.

Recording became the topic of my next question addressed to the pianist.

MZ: The role that recording plays in contemporary performance has been broadly discussed of late. Its advantages are apparent and hardly need any elaboration. But what are the problems of recording that you perceive, as a musician whose artistry is "imprinted" on records and video records, and as a listener of other artists?

NP: Recording is a blessing to us performers. However, some pianists make use of the opportunities offered by all possible technical arrangements and innumerable doubles and allow themselves to be "dishonorable" in the professional sense, achieving a high quality performance by means of the technical advantages of recording. Of course it will be imperceptible to the listeners. But can a musician himself be content with such a "torn" performance recorded in several steps? Therefore, I consider "live" recording especially valuable. Of course the opportunity to immortalize a performance is a marvelous thing. For instance, how very interesting it is to listen to the three recordings of the Tchaikovsky *Concerto* made by Artur Rubinstein at different periods of his creative life! But having listened to many recordings made even by eminent musicians, I can't help quoting a witty aphorism of Leningrad pianist and pedagogue Professor Natan Perelman: "Recording is a document that eventually turns into evidence."

As I know that Nikolai Petrov's daughter has already started study of the piano, I ask him if he cherishes the hope of his daughter becoming a professional musician.

NP: I am quite skeptical when musicians begin to teach their children music, first of all because it entails great effort and at times dramatic disappointments. With the seemingly wonderful opportunities for the young musician's life to turn out quite successfully, at the same time he is exposed to danger at every step and possible failures lie in wait for him. While not long ago the title of a laureate (and we know how difficult it is to obtain it) was a sure guarantee of stable solo concertizing, today "crowds" of laureates wander about absolutely unsettled and sometimes curse the moment when in their childhood they were found to have a good ear for music. Many of them simply cannot understand why they are not offered the opportunity to perform. Besides, in our craft, when the musician is still a teen-ager his unsettled professional career entails great disappointments. Professional training takes up so much of one's strength that, as a rule, there is no "way back." And one has nothing left but to choose the profession of musician.

MZ: I don't share your pessimism. It is true that our profession of musician demands tremendous moral, physical and psychological strain, not to speak of the time expenditures. First of all, having chosen a path that is not easy, say, your daughter or mine, who is also studying at the Gnesin Music School, enters the world of music which is wonderful in itself. Secondly, if your daughter does not become a soloist and does not follow in your footsteps, repeating your brilliant career, she'll perhaps make a good accompanist, pedagogue, musicologist . . .

NP: Certainly; you are right. The parents should help their children in the field in which they have achieved something themselves. It is quite natural and only fair.

MZ: So would you or would you not like your daughter to become a musician?

NP: It is difficult to give some definite answer to this question. I can only say that my daughter Zhenya (she is six years old now) has a keen sense of rhythm and wonderful hands, just like mine were in my childhood. Now she attends classes in a specialized preparatory group where she studies solfeggio and the piano. Incidentally, her piano teacher is the laureate of the Van Cliburn Contest, Alexander Mndoyantz.

MZ: How is your usual working day scheduled?

NP: At present I do not practice more than three or four hours a day. You may judge for yourself; I'm not yet forty but my repertory includes over forty solo programs and approximately the same number of Concertos with the orchestra, so the amount of time I practice is evidently sufficient for me. Undoubtedly before the Van Cliburn Contest I practiced some seven to eight hours a day but I remember that time as a sheer nightmare. Once, after I had spent ten hours at the piano, I had a nervous breakdown, after which I slept for over 24 hours at a stretch. Thank God it was for the first and the last time in my life.

MZ: What is the "supertask" you set yourself in your creative work?

NP: The public is as a rule extremely conservative. That is why I consider one of the most vital tasks to somewhat extend the boundaries of their idea of a certain composer, his creative life. I am conscious of having chosen a more difficult and less gratifying path. I dream of introducing on the concert stage many overlooked or neglected compositions and consider it the duty of concertizing pianists to play the major part of the existing repertory.

Vladimir Krainev.

Vladimir Krainev

Vladimir Krainev was born April 1, 1944 into a family of doctors. His native town is the Siberian city of Krasnoyarsk, but half a year after his birth, the mother and the son moved to Kharkov where Vladimir lived until he was 15.

His natural musical aptitude was revealed in early childhood. At the age of five he became a pupil in the preparatory class at the specialized music school for gifted children.

His first piano teacher was Maria V. Itiguina, one of the leading teachers of music in Kharkov. In the senior grades, Vladimir Krainev studied in the Central Music School in Moscow, under Anaida Sumbatian who has trained many a famous pianist. At the Conservatory, Krainev's tutor was Heinrich Neuhaus, and later his son, Stanislav Neuhaus, under whose tutelage the young pianist graduated from the Conservatory and the post-graduate course.

While he was still a student, Vladimir Krainev brilliantly performed at International contests. In 1963 he became the winner of the Silver Medal in Leeds (England) and a year later the winner of the Vianna da Motta pianist International Competition in Lisbon. However, it was the victory in the Tchaikovsky Competition (1970) that brought him the greatest fame, when he shared the first prize with John Lill from England. "He possesses the same brilliant technique that is characteristic of Richter and Gilels and to a certain extent the same all-embracing musicality," wrote the *Daily News* after the Competition.

171

Vladimir Krainev's repertory is vast and there are no stylistic restrictions for him. He performs with equal success the compositions of Bach, Viennese classics, Chopin, Liszt, Tchaikovsky, Rachmaninoff, Debussy, Ravel, Prokofiev, Bartok, and other contemporary composers. Rich and versatile is his sound palette. But evidently, the strongest facet of his artistic individuality consists of his rare pianistic magnetism, his special gift of joviality, of establishing contact with the audience. "He captivates his listeners by his sincerity," noted the *Rochester Times* reckoning Vladimir Krainev "among the most brilliant performers and subtlest pianists in the world of music today."

★   ★   ★

Two features of Vladimir Krainev's character become apparent when one is in close contact with him: great inner warmth and a sense of humor which brightens up many of his stories about himself. With humor, Krainev speaks of his physical constitution, hinting at his relatively small height. With equal wit he relates how stubbornly he refused to play at the Tchaikovsky Competition of 1966 when he tried to prove jokingly during a talk with the leaders of the Soviet delegation (which was no joke) that he simply could not play, or which of the Soviet pianists was going to get the Gold Medal at the Tchaikovsky Competition of 1970 (in hindsight we'd say that it was just how it turned out). But through all these jests one can't help feeling that there is nothing more serious in his life than his art, outside of which he does not exist.

Our talk started traditionally with the pianist's story of his childhood.

VK: Not only was there no one in our family who would be a musician, but there wasn't even a single person who was known to have tried to play a musical instrument or simply to have hummed a melody ... True, my mother is a musical person, and what's more important, a great lover and connoisseur of music. I start with her because I am obliged to her for almost everything.

MZ: Did she make up her mind to teach you music professionally as soon as your musical capabilities were revealed?

VK: No, at first there was no question of that. When, at the age of five, I was brought to the preparatory group of the music school,

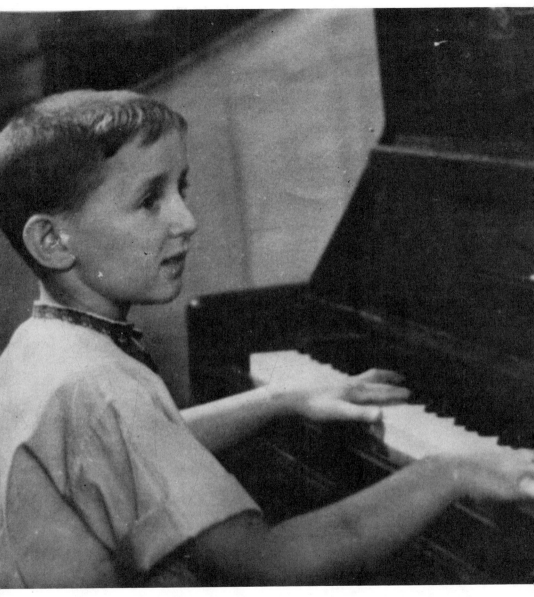

Vladimir Krainev. The picture was taken right after the young pianist's performance of the Haydn D *Major* Concerto *at a school concert.*

Vladimir Krainev with his first teacher, Maria Itiguina.

on examining my hands the pedagogues decided to assign me to the violin class, to which my mother protested vigorously, saying: "The boy is going to play for himself and on the violin it is hardly possible." That is how I became a pianist.

MZ: Who was your first teacher?

VK: At the school I entered there were two leading pedagogues—Regina Samoilovna Horowitz (Vladimir Horowitz's sister) and Maria Vladimirovna Itiguina. Quite by chance I got into the class of the latter. She enjoyed a special reputation. When a child begins to study music, probably the most important thing is not to divert him from his process, to instill the love of music in him. And she could do that brilliantly.

MZ: Since from the first years of studies you have been regarded as perhaps the most gifted of Itiguina's pupils, it would be interesting to know on what repertory, on what program she nurtured you—the traditional or a special one?

VK: Really, I soon appeared to be the "No. 1 star" not only in Itiguina's class but in Kharkov in general. But judging by the repertory, Itiguina reared me on quite a traditional program.

MZ: Can you remember which of the children's compositions especially contributed to the love of music?

VK: In the first grade, that is at seven, I attracted attention by a truly "outstanding" (Krainev smiles) execution of *The Dance of the Little Swans* from the Tchaikovsky Ballet *Swan Lake*. During my first performance, there suddenly awoke in me an incredible love for the stage. What had been apparently innate in a child was awakened at once and showed vividly. Playing that unpretentious piece I was literally dying of rapture! Three years later, I played the Haydn *D Major Concerto* with orchestra, first the school orchestra and then the Philharmonic, and at the age of ten I performed the Beethoven *First Concerto*—all three movements. I must say that I was playing almost standing up because my height hardly allowed me to reach the pedals.

MZ: To what extent did your mother help you in your home practice?

VK: In the first years, mother was present at all the lessons, accurately recording all the critical remarks and recommendations of the teacher. I began to practice on my own when I was ten or eleven years old.

***The young winners of the All-Ukrainian Contest of Young
Pianists: Yevgeny Mogilevsky and Vladimir Krainev.***

Heinrich Neuhaus, his assistant (now Professor) Lev Naumov and Vladimir Krainev after the victory in the Competition in Leeds (England).

MZ: In your childhood how many hours a day did you spend at the instrument.

VK: Very many. At the age of nine or ten I used to play for six hours a day. I practiced eagerly. And I've preserved that faculty to this day: I sometimes practice for five to seven hours a day. But at times I wouldn't play at all for several days.

MZ: Some words about your technical development in Itiguina's class, please.

VK: I think I've played all that was possible to play: Czerny-Germer, Czerny *op. 299* and *op. 740*, Clementi, Moshkovsky. And beginning with the seventh grade, that is since the age of fourteen, I have been working at the Chopin *Etudes.*

MZ: Did you play a great deal of scales in your childhood?

VK: I did not play them at all. Moreover, I hated them.

MZ: And what about exercises?

Vladimir Krainev. Facing page: The presentation of the prize to the Laureate of the Competition Vladimir Krainev (Lisbon, 1964).

VK: Never, I hold exercises to be necessary only to those who cannot manage something in a certain type of technique. But this type of technique is sure to exist in some specific works. So, why not study these works instead?

MZ: That means you are an advocate of mastering technique in the repertory rather than instructive exercises?

VK: Assuredly. And it is not an innovation of mine. Heinrich Neuhaus spoke about it. "Trills do not come out well," he used to advise his pupils. "Take the Beethoven's *Thirty-Second Sonata* or any Sonata of Mozart and learn the trill fragments from them until you feel that playing the trills is as natural for you as everything else." And it is absolutely right! A better exercise simply cannot be found, first of all because these are not abstract trills but a piece of music having some meaning. One should not deal with "naked" technique, that is technique out of context.

MZ: What place was assigned to chamber music at school?

VK: At school, I am sorry to say, we did not study chamber music at all. But by mere chance there studied together with me a girl of genius, Tanya Grindenko, and we performed together quite a lot. For example, I remember very well when in the first part of our concert we played the *Mozart Sonata* and some other pieces and in the second part I performed Beethoven's *Pathetique Sonata* and Schumann's *Intermezzo*. I was 12 and she was about nine.

MZ: Apart from study of music what were you drawn to in your school years?

VK: Sports, of course. I was not bad at playing tennis. And I must admit I made good progress at it. At 14 I took part in the Championship of the Soviet Union and in general I was so absorbed in sports that at times I forgot to play the piano.

MZ: Have you retained your fondness for sports to this day?

VK: Yes, in a very specific form—in my fondness for my wife who is directly connected with sport! She is the figure skating coach, Tatiana Tarasova, whose name might be much more familiar to the American public than mine—at least to sports fans.

MZ: Was your pianistic development gradual or was there a moment when a sharp spurt occurred?

VK: A noticeable sharp spurt occurred at 14. There was announced an All-Ukrainian Contest of schools, colleges and Conservatories without any age restrictions. The first prize was awarded

Tatiana Grindenko, a great violinist who at one time was married to the violinist Gidon Kremer. She and Krainev became great musical friends.

Vladimir Krainev's hands.

Vladimir Krainev.

to me and Yevgeny Mogilevsky, the future winner of the Queen Elisabeth Brussels Competition (he was 13 then). And soon afterwards another Competition of all the Ukrainian 10-year music schools and colleges was held in Kiev. What happened was that Mogilevsky won the first prize and I, whom I considered to be the leading pianist of Kharkov, holding a rather high opinion of myself by that time, did not get anything, no prize whatsoever. It was a shock to me. It turned out that though I played quite well, musically, my program was not complicated enough for those days. Then, on my own initiative, without my teacher, I took up the *Seventh* and *Fourteenth Sonatas* of Beethoven, the *Second Scherzo* of Chopin, the *First Concerto* and *Liebestraum* by Liszt, Chopin's *Etudes,* Mozart's *Sonata,* Schubert's *Impromptus.* Of course, my teacher was in the know but actually I worked at these compositions independently. In fact, I learned them in several months. The first victory was the Liszt *Concerto* with an exorbitant number of octaves, that I had not played earlier, but coped with nevertheless. It was really a spurt because I was finishing the eighth grade with the Liszt *Concerto* that I performed with the orchestra. And on the conductor's stand was our marvelous conductor, Israel Gusman.

MZ: In spite of the failure in Kiev you were making progress in your studies. What was the impetus to your moving to Moscow?

VK: My first teacher, Itiguina (we should give her credit for that) did not confine herself to our Kharkov circle—that is to a certain extent to a provincial circle. She used to go to Moscow, frequented the Central Music School and was aware of the highest level of musical skills, which the best students of that school had always served. During one of her visits, she auditioned Anaida Sumbatian's pupils, and on her return to Kharkov she said to me: "That's the teacher under whom you ought to study." And we decided to move to Moscow.

MZ: How were you received in the Central Music School and what impression did your achievements make on the teachers who auditioned you?

Vladimir Krainev.

Vladimir Krainev, Gina Lollobrigida and Imelda Marcos.

Vladimir Krainev and Stanislav Neuhaus.

Vladimir Krainev during his performance for the workers of the "Ilyich plant."

Vladimir Krainev with his wife Tatiana Tarasova, the eminent figure-skating coach.

VK: I must admit that my first encounter with the pedagogues of the Central Music School caused nothing but disappointment on the part of both. The matter was that as a result of strenuous work at difficult repertory before leaving Kharkov I turned from a very musical boy into a "pure" virtuoso—"ringing" virtuoso roaring with octave and other passages. The reaction of the Moscow pedagogues proved quite a surprise to me. Many of them said: "Why admit to our School such an "unmusical" student?" But Anaida Sumbatian, whom I had visited a year earlier, had her say and I was admitted.

MZ: How did the lessons with Sumbatian qualitatively differ from those with your first teacher?

VK: It was apparent in the repertory itself, even in the amount of the repertory. I got Beethoven's 32 Variations and the *Seventh Sonata,* Chopin's Third Scherzo and six *Etudes* straight away. But it was not merely the matter of the repertory. The character of our studies as such, the requirements, everything was different. For instance, it was regarded as unacceptable to bring to the first lesson a piece not learned by heart. This was new to me. Further, there was an absolutely different approach to the text. Previously the text as I imagined it was nothing but notational signs. The rest was showed to me by my teacher: she counted for me, pointed to certain shades of coloring and so forth. Sumbatian began to teach me an "adult"

The rehearsal of the Beethoven **Triple Concerto for Piano, Violin and Cello:** *Vladimir Krainev, Oleg Kagan, Natalia Gutman and conductor Dmitri Kitayenko.*

reading of the text from the start. All dynamics, fingering, even differentiation of the composer's and editor's instructions—all that was revealed to me in all its significance. More profound was the work at the tone, at the phrase.

MZ: How much was that change to your liking; how did you enjoy tackling new tasks?

VK: Very soon I developed a taste for the work at the tone, at the phrase, to the quest of the image-bearing interpretation of a piece. I appreciated Sumbatian's method of analogies to illustrate the idea, the image-bearing contents of the composer's text. I became fond of drawing out of the text what someone else must have missed (not contrary to the text, but proceeding from it). The work was so tedious, so minute that when working at the Beethoven's *Variations* we stopped on almost every bar and never reached the end. I remember that my shoulders and loins ached because of the strain. Moreover, after classes I often wondered what else was wanted from me as I had painstakingly carried out everything to the letter. I must say I studied selflessly.

MZ: Which of the pedagogical methods of your teacher Anaida Sumbatian would you point out as the most effective for you?

VK: Anaida Stepanovna Sumbatian had never gratified her pupils as far as repertory was concerned. She would give some piece to humor me, something that corresponded to what I could do at the moment, while all the rest were 'to run me up the wrong way.' For instance, I was almost never offered the chance to play Prokofiev. She used to say: 'You'll always have time to do it yourself. For example, as soon as I learned several *Fleeting Moments,* the *March* from *The Love for Three Oranges, Prelude,* and the *Third Sonata* of Prokofiev all by myself, I brought this all to her lessons. She listened and said: "As to that, when you grow up you'll play it on your own."

MZ: As far as I know, your living conditions left much to be desired. Did it somehow affect the quality of your studies?

VK: The conditions were truly nasty. My mother and I rented a room. I did not have any instrument at all. Therefore, very early in the morning I used to come to school and play before classes began. And also in the evening. But on the whole I practiced a lot.

MZ: What was the first piece of the school repertory to be performed at an open concert?

Vladimir Krainev.

VK: During my time, there existed the tradition that the open concerts of the Central Music School were held in the minor Hall of the Conservatory and it was all very solemn. It was at such a concert that I performed for the first time the Chopin *Third Scherzo*. It was my little Moscow debut. Beginning with that performance I started to catch up with the leaders of the Central Music School, and it was not easy. The pupils at that school were very strong. My classmate was Alla Postnikova. One year my seniors were Nikolai

Vladimir Krainev and Dmitri Kitayenko. Krainev is linked with Kitayenko not only by creative bonds but also by bonds of friendship. As Krainev admits himself, there is no other conductor with whom it would be so pleasant and convenient for him to make music as with Kitayenko.

Petrov, Alexei Nasedkin, Tigran Alikhanov, Valery Kamishov—now all of them are laureates of many competitions.

On entering the Conservatory, Vladimir Krainev became the pupil of professor Heinrich Neuhaus who estimated the talent of one of his last pupils at its true worth. "It is a real, great gift", he said about Krainev. And though Krainev's studies under Heinrich Neuhaus lasted only for two years, he may be rightfully called a pianist of the Neuhaus school.

I asked Vladimir Krainev to share his impression of Neuhaus, Senior and to tell of studying under him.

VK: Heinrich Neuhaus is a truly great phenomenon both in performance and pedagogics. And apparently each young student who studied in his class experienced a serious shock at the beginning, as he came in touch with the vast new world of Heinrich Neuhaus. Probably, for me it was to a certain extent easier than for others since my former pedagogue, Anaida Sumbatian, who worshipped Neuhaus, in a measure adhered to his method of bright comparisons, unexpected and very vivid associations. It is well-known that that method was one of the principal devices of Neuhaus the pedagogue.

MZ: How did an ordinary lesson with Neuhaus proceed?

VK: One of the major peculiarities of his lessons consisted of their being held in the very special atmosphere of a concert, when there were present some 15-20 students from other classes or simply musicians. So, whatever he said was addressed not only to the pupil with whom he was working at the moment, but to all those present. And the pupil himself played not just for his pedagogue, but as if he were on the stage.

MZ: How regularly did you attend the lessons?

VK: In general all of us Neuhaus pupils used to come to the lesson twice a week, but only those who wanted to do so played. For instance, I recollect the episode when I first played *Aurora*. I arrived at the classroom which was already crowded from a previous lecture. Hardly had he seen me (I was his favorite already) when he asked: "Vovochka, what are you going to play today?" *Aurora*, I answered. A peal of laughter in the classroom. It turned out that just before me two students had already played *Aurora*.

MZ: It was particularly in the years when you began studying at the Conservatory that you first participated in competitions.

Vladimir Krainev among his friends, former co-students at the Conservatory, at a friendly party celebrating the thirtieth birthday of each of them.

Vladimir Krainev and Aram Khatchaturian.

Please, tell of your competition biography.

VK: In 1963 (I was 19 then) I won the second prize in Leeds. A year later I was awarded the Gold Medal in Lisbon, after which I decided that my competition battles were over. However, I was mistaken. Six years later I played at the Tchaikovsky Competition where I shared the first prize with John Lill.

MZ: What was the reason for your reluctance to participate in the Tchaikovsky Competition? Were you confused by the program or were there other considerations?

VK: In 1966 I did not find myself prepared well enough in order to win a contest in which, in addition to excellent foreign pianists, there took part such musicians as Nikolai Petrov, Georgy Sirota, Alexander Slobodianik (16-year-old Grisha Sokolov who finally became the winner of that Competition was not taken seriously by anyone at that time). And in 1970 I simply was afraid to run the risk; by that time my name was famous enough. I had tours all over the world, a very good press and if I were to lose at the competition (even if it were the second place), it would amount to a failure.

MZ: In the Tchaikovsky Competition, you came out not from a teacher, but, so to say, by yourself. But not long before that you had graduated from a post-graduate course in Stanislav Neuhaus' class, your last teacher. Will you say something about your studies under him?

VK: If by studying with Heinrich Neuhaus I had learned some general musical things like the approach to a piece, perceiving the essence of music, etc., from Stanislav Neuhaus I learned all the sound technology. All told, I studied under him for about five years. In all fairness I must admit that on account of different temperaments, different views on compositions (and by the time I became his student I had already been twice a laureate coupled with the arrogance of a youngster) it was difficult for me to study under him. We argued a great deal and usually the golden mean was found between what he advised me and how I imagined it. Stanislav Neuhaus himself always said: "I'm not a pedagogue."

Vladimir Krainev.

And to a certain extent it was true. If his father had never thrust his interpretation upon his students, Stanislav was much more imperative.

MZ: Having been the pupil of such wonderful teachers have you never been urged to teach?

VK: Studying with Stanislav Neuhaus at the Conservatory and in the post-graduate course, I used to assist him in working with his pupils. But at present I am not teaching. The reason is quite common for us concertizing pianists: unwillingness or the difficulty of being torn apart by two pursuits. Tours, many hours of practicing at home, constant renewal of the repertory, and with every year it grows more and more difficult—all this does not allow devoting to teaching with all the earnestness it deserves, if it is tackled honestly and professionally. Teaching is a great expenditure of emotional strength. But at the same time, unofficially I am always teaching because there are young people whom I have been fostering for a long time; there are some who, when preparing for competitions, plead to consult with me, at times quite frequently and regularly. Sometimes these are schoolchildren whom I begin preparing for the Conservatory a year or two in advance.

MZ: In the process of teaching what brings you the greatest satisfaction?

VK: Of course, it is pleasant to work with students who have either entirely solved all the purely technical problems or such problems do not present any difficulty for them. I am most delighted to deal with the questions of interpretation and the integral solution of a performance piece.

MZ: What edition do you prefer to work at with students studying the Bach *Well-Tempered Clavier?*

VK: As a rule it is the edition of Mudgilini.

MZ: And what about the Beethoven *Sonatas?*

VK: I don't attach much importance to whose edition it is.

MZ: Are you sometimes tempted to compare the Urtext with the edition you are working at?

Vladimir Krainev.

VK: I wouldn't say so. Those "archivistics" do not interest me.

MZ: Do you think that in working with a young pianist (especially of the conservatory age) there is one problem which is underestimated by some pedagogues? Mastering certain technical devices, dealing with particular tasks, the student often fails to see their direct connection with what comprises the core of a profound interpretation.

VK: You are absolutely right. It is a most serious problem. I am sure that until the age of 28-30 a pianist can "hide" behind a beautiful tone, virtuosity and other attributes of pianism. But the older you become, the more your human nature, your true "interior" (be it spiritually rich or poor) comes to light, so that there is no concealing the lack of steadfastness behind a pseudo-harsh sound, or stupidity and narrow-mindedness behind pseudo-wisdom. Therefore, I hold that how richly your nature was developed in your formative years inevitably tells upon our art.

Turning to the discussion of the pianist's repertory, I was tempted to question him on different composers. As a matter of fact his repertory envelops all stylistic layers. It was no accident that the English *Daily Telegraph* wrote after Krainev's tour: "He is endowed with the gift of employing all colors, all peculiarities of such different musical individuals as Scriabin, Shostakovich, Prokofiev." In that quotation there is only a small part of the list of composers whose works Krainev performs. Taking into account the limited opportunities of this article I decided to dwell at greater length on the composer to whom he feels a close affinity—Chopin.

Being the pupil of Heinrich and Stanislav Neuhaus, outstanding Chopinists, Vladimir Krainev appeared to be their worthy successor. "His fine technique, his might and absolute sincerity amazingly match the Chopin music he performs," pointed out the French *Diapason*. "Chopin found a new great poet to perform his compositions," wrote another critic in connection with Krainev's record of Chopin.

"Teaching *and* performing are difficult since both are full time occupations. How do you know which should suffer the most? How can you refuse to help one of your students?"

Chopin

The last words refer directly to the Chopin *B Flat minor Sonata*. I asked Vladimir to speak of the work on that composition.

VK: It was one of the pieces on which I learned to play Chopin under Neuhaus. Forever is engraved on my memory the short program he offered me: *The Death of a Hero*. At greater length it was as follows: the first chords—the curtain is raised, then the two first movements—the life of a hero; the third movement—burial of a hero, and at last the finale—the wind blowing over the tomb of a hero; the last two chords—the curtain drops. Of course, he did not go into detail; it all depended on the pupil's imagination.

MZ: There exist two opinions on the repetition of the exposition of the first movement. Which of them do you adhere to?

VK: I do not repeat the exposition by any means. There passes the theme of the part of the exposition containing the first subject and the second theme, further on—the final one. But then there occurs a kind of development of the relations between "Fate" and a certain personality—a hero. For me a repetition is the same thing as watching a thrilling film and, after seeing some first important events, pressing the button, and reeling back the film to see the same thing all over again. It should be remembered that the second and third sonatas (I am not talking of the first one) and concertos are written in a strictly classical form. Therefore, I think the repeat signs in sonatas to be a formal tribute to the classical traditions.

MZ: In some of Chopin's miniatures—waltzes, mazurkas, nocturnes, there arises the problem of the diversity of repeated episodes—articulational, dynamic, etc. How do you tackle this problem?

VK: I hold to the opinion that they should not be diversified anyway at all. It is marvelous to play the repeated episodes identically.

MZ: But there is surely a certain evolution of the image. Just as it is impossible to enter the same waters twice, it is impossible to play a repeated episode in absolutely the same way.

VK: Apparently, both points of view have the right to existence. It does not matter how one plays, if only it sounds convincing, vivid. For instance, I've just finished work on all the *Chopin*

Krainev maintains that Chopin's miniatures should not be diversified in any way at all and that the repeated episodes should be played identically.

Ballads and allowed myself to listen to the recordings of great artists. It was Cortot, and Richter, and Stanislav Neuhaus, and Pollini, and Argerich. And though, as it seems to me, my interpretation is unlike any of those mentioned, many executions of outstanding masters are convincing to me and I appreciate them greatly. They have their own logic, wholeness of conception and its realization, and I have my own.

MZ: You've told me that your teachers Anaida Sumbatian and Heinrich Neuhaus aroused the pupils' imagination by resorting to different images, literary and other associations, and that it was very understandable to you, that you reacted keenly to it, thus finding the way to the interpretation sought for, your own "clue" to the composition. Years passed. And now, as a mature pianist, you take, say, Chopin's *Ballads*—pieces that are known to be rich in inner image-bearing contents and to have allusions to literary analogies (I mean Mitzkevich's *Ballads*). In what measure do you now employ in your work that image-associative system of devices?

VK: I understand your question. In particular, in that case turning to the Ballads, I did not reread "Sviatizianka" but fed exclusively on the figurativeness latent in that music of genius which, as you've already noted, is exceptionally rich in this respect. It should be kept in mind that I've played a great deal of Chopin. With the exception of *Preludes,* I have played compositions of all other genres. So the perception of Chopin's style permits, when commencing a new Chopin's work, not taking it as something absolutely new for oneself.

MZ: Which of the four Chopin *Ballads* proved most complicated for you?

VK: It was not easy to play the *Third Ballad* with, as I conceive it, its feminine images. But undoubtedly the most difficult is the *Fourth Ballad.* Take, for instance, the first page—it is by no means easy to communicate to the audience the integrity, the unity of this theme, so that it does not fall into separate fragments, "scraps," to play the enormous fragment, up to the octaves, at one breath.

> *Krainev works alone as he practices.*
> *If someone is in the room he "plays"*
> *rather than "practices."*

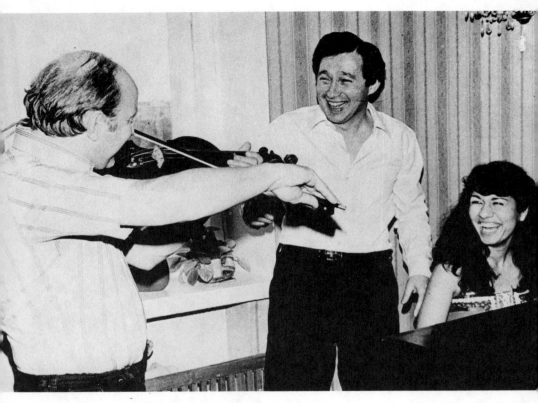

As a rule, Soviet musicians have a more rounded musical education than most Western artists. They learn more than one instrument, besides minor courses in composition, conducting, etc. Krainev proves this by taking Mihaela Martin's violin. Mihaela sits at the piano and Dr. Zilberquit can hardly believe what's happening!

MZ: As long as we are on the subject of the first theme of the *Fourth Ballad*, do you interpret it as more of a vocal or of a recitative type?

VK: Indubitably, it is more of a recitative type. Generally when I approach a Chopin work I never commence tackling any other problems until I make out its form in detail, until its structure is absolutely clear to me. I do not mean, if we were to speak of the *Fourth Ballad*, the general design, but the smaller fragments making up large parts: exposition, thematic development, coda, etc. It is especially here that the pianist is exposed to danger—to articulate the music being performed into small phrases. It is of utmost difficulty, yet it is essential that the general message of each fragment be defined and comprehended and the logic of the interconnection between them be revealed.

MZ: Certainly in this respect both the *First* and the *Second Ballads* are no easier.

VK: It is in general most complicated to play Chopin and I seem to have sized up the greatest difficulty: at the moment of performance, one's condition should be correlated to the music being performed, one's mood, feelings should match the spirit of that music. Otherwise, you enter into a contradiction with the mood of the

Krainev, Mrs. Evelyn Axelrod and Nikolai Petrov. The Moscow musical community is a small one, and most of the artists are friendly with each other.

*Vladimir
Krainev and
Mark Zilberquit.*

music you are performing. True, this can be compensated for by one's experience in playing these particular compositions; one attunes himself to a necessary frame of mind.

MZ: How many concertos with the orchestra are there in your repertory?

VK: Over thirty.

MZ: Under what prominent conductors did you perform?

VK: I have played under a lot of brilliant conductors. These were, for instance, Pierre Boulez, Gennady Rozhdestvensky, Erich Leinsdorf, Antal Dorati, Carlo Maria Giulini. I'd like to speak separately of Dmitri Kitayenko. This conductor, apart from his wonderful musical qualities, is my friend and it is most convenient for me to play under him like under no one else. There is a rare human and musical mutual understanding between us.

MZ: Have you ever been at variance with the orchestra, with your partner-conductors?

VK: That has happened. For example, I play the *Third Concerto* of Beethoven much slower than we are used to hearing it. It is very complicated for the orchestra. In that case everything must be played more expressively; even playing all the notes is not that simple for the members of the orchestras (I mean the *Finale*). I recollect that when quite young I performed Prokofiev's *Third Concerto* with a conductor now deceased who in his time was highly respected by everyone and was reputed to be a superb accompanist. No matter how hard I tried to explain to him my conception, he adamantly insisted on playing his way. He thrust upon me his tempos, the tempos that were convenient to him, to the orchestra. And I was compelled to say to him: "Now I understand why you are considered an outstanding accompanist. It is because you are being accompanied by performers."

MZ: You have been leading the busy life of a solo pianist for many years already. It has its roses and its thorns. So, what is most delightful to you in that way of life and what does not quite appeal to you?

VK: The thorns are that the strenuous concert life engulfs you, at times interferes with the quiet creative character of practicing. But, thank God, my teachers taught me to "scour," that is, after the concert routine to shed the thin coating of "road dust" and give the compositions their original freshness. And what appeals to me in that life primarily is that I am continually associating with people, with listeners. It means that I can always express myself, speak in terms of my art with the public. And it often occurs on the first-class stages of the world, where I play for most exacting audiences for whom the outstanding artists of older generations have performed. Undoubtedly, it brings great delight and deep creative satisfaction.

Dr. Mark Zilberquit and Mihaela Martin, winner of the prestigious Indianapolis Competition, with Krainev. Martin made a huge impression during her New York debut, which was hailed as . . . "the debut of the year!"

ЭМИЛЬ ГИЛЕЛЬС

Emil Gilels

Emil Gilels was born October 19, 1916, in Odessa. Very serious, professional study of the piano began at a very early age, in his pre-school years. That was promoted by his unique ear for music and the hands that, according to the words of his first teacher Yakov Tkatch, were as if specially created for playing the piano.

Swiftly developing as a child-prodigy, Emil Gilels made his debut when he was 13. The concert, consisting of two parts and including such compositions as the *Pathetique Sonata* of Beethoven, Chopin's and Liszt's *Etudes*, compositions of Scarlatti, Schumann and Mendelssohn, proved to be a sensation for Odessa which was in the heyday of musical art at the time.

The greatest contribution to his education, according to Emil Gilels himself, was made by his Conservatory teacher Bertha Reingbald, a profound musician, a pedagogue by calling. Under her tutelage he studied there until 1935. But two years earlier, Emil Gilels scored a triumphant victory at the First All-Union Contest of musicians and performers (1933).

After his studies in Odessa, Emil Gilels perfected his skill at the School of Artistic Mastership (at present the post-graduate course), under the guidance of the celebrated Soviet pianist, pedagogue and musical writer-professor Heinrich Neuhaus. These years coincide with Gilels' victories at Internationals—the second prize in Vienna (1936), and a triumph in Brussels (1938).

But no matter how brilliant the artistic success of Gilels of the 1930's, his talent was revealed with much greater force in the postwar years when the pianist reached the acme of true maturity. He concertized a great deal, as a soloist was a great success in a chamber ensemble (one of his permanent partners was the famous Soviet violinist Leonid Kogan, the husband of Elizabeth Gilels, the pianist's sister and herself a marvelous violinist with whom Emil Gilels used to perform in his youth).

Emil Gilels.

Particularly at that time, in the mid 1950's, Gilels was discovered by America. "He is one of the greatest pianists of our times," wrote Harold Schonberg after Gilels' debut in New York. The newspaper, *The New York World Telegram and Sun* called Gilels "the Giant of the piano" after his concert in Carnegie Hall. The pianist met with equal success in many other countries of the world.

But it would be a mistake to think that his whole life and creative path was strewn with roses. He had to overcome stagnation of a certain circle of the critics; therefore the unique evolution of Gilels as an artist is primarily connected with the amazingly high standards he set for himself. He makes equally high demands of his daughter Elena, who has followed in his footsteps and performs successfully both in the USSR and abroad.

Today Emil Gilels is rightfully considered to be one of the contemporary giants of piano performers. His distinctive features are his powerful virtuosity, stylistic purity in reading the composers of different epochs, and the subtle poetry of his art.

However, it is characteristic that no matter how distinctive the performing style of Emil Gilels, critics of different national cultures recognize in his art the features of the typically Russian-Soviet piano school. The Montreal *La Patrie du Dimanche* wrote: "Gilels confirms the fact that his motherland is the motherland of pianism. The country that gave the world Rachmaninoff, Brailowsky, Lhévinne, Barer and Horowitz still remains an inexhaustible source of talents. Gilels is the incarnation of the best features of the Russian School."

A more modest role in his career in comparison with his performing activities is played by pedagogical work which he has been carrying on since 1938 (among his pupils are Igor Zhukov and others).

Great is Gilels' authority in the musical world. It was no accident that he was chosen to head the jury of the first four Tchaikovsky Competitions. Emil Gilels is an honorary member of the Queen's Academy of Music in London; bearer of the gold medal of Paris; Belgan Order of Leopold I; and many others, including the highest Soviet awards.

Emil Gilels at the age of 10.

. . . It was in 1933. The Great Hall of the Moscow Conservatory was overcrowded. All the cream of musical Moscow were gathered there. It was the audition of the pianists of the First All-Union Contest of Musicians and Performers. On the jury were Alexander Goldenweiser, Heinrich Neuhaus, Konstantin Igumnov, Samuel Feinberg and other greats of Soviet pianism. Young musicians stepped out onto the stage in succession. And then a stocky red-haired youth appeared at the instrument. One piece sounded after another. The tension in the house swelled and reached its peak when, like the eruption of a volcano, the *Fantasy on a Theme* of *Figaro's Wedding* of Mozart-Liszt was being performed. The audience was shaken and greeted the pianist with tempestuous applause. The members of the jury looked at the young musician with obvious approval, stating with satisfaction that they had just witnessed the discovery of a foremost talent . . .

That's how Moscow first got to know Emil Gilels.

At that time of course, neither he himself nor any of those present knew that exactly a quarter of a century later he would find himself presiding in that very house in the role of the Supreme Justice, as the head of the I. Tchaikovsky Competition Jury.

But let's get back to Gilels' Moscow debut. Awarding Gilels the first prize set off an outburst of popularity and interest in the young pianist. The reason such close attention was paid to him, both on the part of the public and the music critics, lay not only in the fact that he had gained the first place, leaving behind many other performers (the competition was highly representative and strong as to its participants). In Gilels' performance the leading critics saw the embodiment of the very best features of native talent.

And it was in connection with Emil Gilels that there began the talk of a new Soviet style of performance.

"When one gets to think of the forming style of our musical performance," wrote one of the authoritative musical reviewers, "the first thing to occur to one's mind is Emil Gilels. Gilels is characterized by amazing wholeheartedness that knows no comparison, by simplicity and lucidity of thinking, the ability to fulfill the tasks the performer sets himself, no matter how difficult and complex they may be. Hence, that striking force of rhythm and sense of form in his playing, his unbending willpower, exuberant

Emil and Elizaveta Gilels. Being three years younger, Liza developed as impetuously as her brother. At the age of 18 (1938) she was awarded the third prize at the Ysaye Competition in Brussels. In their childhood and youth the brother and sister played together a great deal.

energy, emotional freshness and spontaneity ... There are no pianistically insuperable difficulties for him, and with exclusive freedom, outwardly with lightness and simplicity, he overcomes any hurdles whatsoever ... Look how precise, economical in his movements the pianist is, but at the same time how great his sweep, audacity ... what iron self-control."

In that description giving a rather accurate portrait of young Gilels, the estimate of both his pianistic and intellectual qualities is interesting, but what is perhaps no less significant is the first definition: "amazing wholeheartedness," because at the time when these words were pronounced Emil Gilels was only sixteen years old.

That event, the victory at the Competition—brilliant and triumphant—became the starting-point of Gilels' independent artistic life. He has become one of the most significant figures in piano performance of the middle of the 20th century—no less a role, compared to his purely musical pianistic qualities, was played particularly by his wholeheartedness and the strong willpower that had been formed early in his green years—the more so, as his life in art was far from ordinary and easy.

Following the victory at the Competition the young musician, still a student of the Odessa Conservatory at the time, was besieged with numerous offers of concerts. It was too big a temptation. And Gilels, an unknown student, became a celebrity overnight, a fashionable concert star, ardently greeted by the public. One tour followed another; cities and concert halls flashed by. And there was almost no time left for practicing, learning new compositions.

We must do justice to the willpower and mature self-criticism of the young pianist: having sensed in time that the development of his artistic skill had actually stopped, he resolutely cancelled all the contracts and returned to Odessa with a firm decision to give up concertizing until he had graduated from the Conservatory.

Under the guidance of his Conservatory tutor, wonderful pedagogue Berta Reingbald, Gilels plunged into work again. He learned many new compositions: Bach's *Preludes and Fugues,* Beethoven's *Sonatas,* songs of Schubert-Liszt and other pieces;

Emil Gilels.

From left to right: Y. Flier, E. Gilels, P. Serebriakov, I. Mikhnovsky and the member of the Jury of the International Brussels Competition, S. Feinberg, in Brussels before the beginning of the Competition while no one yet suspects Emil Gilels is to become its winner.

preparing for his graduation a complicated program that he had thoroughly thought out together with his pedagogue. It consisted of Beethoven's *Eighteenth Sonata*, Schumann's *Arabesques* and *Toccata*, the Chopin *First Ballad* and Liszt's *Spanish Rhapsody*.

The November night of 1935 was retained in the memory of those present for a long time, for that was when in the Concert Hall of the Odessa Conservatory the final examination of Emil Gilels took place.

In the autumn of the same year Emil Gilels, a laureate and Conservatory graduate, became the pupil of the famous pianist and pedagogue Heinrich Neuhaus at the School of Higher Artistic Mastery in Moscow.

To study with Neuhaus was extremely interesting and at the same time very difficult. Pianist-thinker, pianist-poet, Heinrich

224

Neuhaus taught his pupils Art in the broadest sense of the word. He roused their imagination and in whatever he was doing, he proceeded from music, from the sound image. A man of rare erudition, Neuhaus nurtured thinking artists rather than narrow-minded professionals. After the academic methods of Reingbald, and after the rigid lessons with his first teacher Tkatch who had paid primary attention to the development of the technical apparatus, Neuhaus' lessons were unusual for Gilels. "You've become used to taking the shortest way to reach the aim," Neuhaus used to repeat to Gilels at the beginning. "Now learn to solve a problem by the synthesis of opposed devices."

Neuhaus worked a great deal with his pupils on the tone, nuances, and pedalling. Technique as such did not exist for him at

H. Neuhaus, B. Reingbald and E. Gilels.

all. There was concrete musical material, and image-bearing concept that was possible to reveal by means of certain technical devices. "I often remind my pupils," Neuhaus wrote in his book *On the Art of Playing the Piano*, that the word "technique" comes from the Greek word "téxvy," and that "téchné" meant Art."

For Gilels who had been accustomed to many hours of practicing scales and exercises since childhood, for whom quite recently the attainment of fluency, evenness, accuracy had been one of the most important separate purposes, all that was quite a novelty.

"I was literally 'choking' on Neuhaus," Gilels remembered later, "and for a long time in these fireworks of aphorisms, comparisons and brilliant examples I couldn't digest what was the essential, the thing to catch at in order to stand upon sure ground."

But Gilels hadn't "choked." He very quickly realized what had been beyond his understanding in interpreting a composition before, what had constituted a certain one-sidedness of his pianism, and he absolutely reformed his studies. The "difficult" Neuhaus lessons and zealous work gradually began to show the first results. His pianism became much better, richer as to the coloring, his comprehension of the image-bearing contents of the compositions more profound. Gilels' repertory as such changed. There appeared in it the last Beethoven *Sonatas*, compositions of Brahms, Ravel, and Rachmaninoff.

The first year in Moscow Gilels seldom appeared on the concert stage. It was a time of thorough, painstaking work, the results of which revealed themselves quite soon. When in one of his rare concerts Gilels played *Isolda's Death* of Wagner-Liszt, one of the critics who had before reproached the pianist with exceeding fondness of virtuoso music wrote: "It was a striking performance. Indeed, how could the young pianist know and understand the languor and torments of Wagner's heroine, how could he perceive all the profound essence of that music?"

These lines were written soon after Gilels had been awarded the second prize at the International Competition of Pianists in Vienna (1936), a year before his performance at the Brussels Competition.

Emil Gilels performing
for the sailors of the ship
The Paris Commune.

226

Emil Gilels with the great Polish violinist Henryk Szeryng.

Heinrich Neuhaus. *"I was literally 'choking' on Neuhaus, and for a long time in these fireworks of aphorisms, comparisons and brilliant examples I couldn't digest what was the essential, the thing to catch at in order to stand upon sure ground."*

"In my childhood I slept little. At night when everything in the house calmed down I used to take father's ruler from under my pillow and start conducting. The small dark bedroom turned into a dazzling concert hall. Standing on the stage I felt behind me the breathing of a large crowd and in front of me the orchestra was stockstill with expectation. I raise the baton and the air fills up with marvelous sounds . . . My child's thoughts were entirely devoured by music . . ."

Even today, when the number of Internationals can be counted by the dozen, we may safely say that the Brussels Competition of 1938 was one of the most representative (95 pianists from 23 countries) and serious in the entire history of competitions. It is enough to say that on the jury were R. Casadesus, Artur Rubinstein, L. Stokowski, W. Gieseking, E. Zauer, C. Zecchi, S. Feinberg and other authoritative musicians. The final round of the Competition proved difficult as the pianists were to perform a complicated, inexpressive Concerto of Jan Absile which they had to learn in one week (a manuscript of forty pages!).

Gilels' performance at the Competition turned into a real triumph that became a part of the triumph of the whole Soviet School of performance. (The third prize was awarded to Yakov Flier who had been the first in Vienna.)

However, neither the public who ardently greeted Gilels in Brussels and then in Paris, nor even the members of the Jury could guess that at that Competition Gilels had in fact scored a double victory. For him as an artist not only the victory as such was important but particularly due to the compositions with which that victory was won. Preparing for the Competition, Gilels selected each composition with special care and thoroughness. Several variants of the program were compiled and in the discussion not only did Neuhaus participate, but also the Odessa tutor of Gilels, B. Reingbald. There were some doubts concerning polyphony—(it was decided for sure to play two compositions—Bach-Ziloti *Prelude* and Franck's *Prelude, Chorale and Fugue*; but the third, Bach-Godovsky *Fugue G-minor* or Leily-Godovsky *Gigue*, was discussed—and the final virtuoso piece (Balakirev's *Islamey* or Liszt's *Spanish Rhapsody*). But the main point of discussion was Chopin's *B Flat minor Sonata*. Many musicians close to the young pianist categorically recommended he not include it into his program. It was then that the pianist's willpower, creative audacity and perseverance became evident. He did not want to give up the Chopin *Sonata* by any means, [no matter how hard the process of working on it was for him, of overcoming the difficulties of Chopin at this point in his career, and yet . . .] he played in Moscow with amazing subtlety and rare understanding of Chopin's style. "The brilliant performance of this Sonata," wrote the newspaper *Soviet Art* not long before the Brussels Competition, "showed that the young pianist was right, and the skeptics limiting his capabilities by the frames of a certain style were wrong . . . Gilels has always been notable for great musical and artistic flair. But what had been intuitive earlier gradually turned into a more and more conscious and deliberate skill of the artist who had mastered the craft of his art."

With the Brussels victory, the pianist's world fame began.

If the All-Union Contest revealed Gilels as a great, spontaneous, courageous and profoundly original talent, the Brussels Competition revealed Gilels as an artist, a mature and independent musician.

Emil Gilels.

The history of performance knows more than one case where a musician with a vivid and original gift, having appeared like a bright star, vanishes from the musical firmament. So, in order to climb to the musical Olympus it is not enough to be gifted by nature, to be a success with the public and even to possess the highest competition rewards. It takes something greater.

That "something" which we'll now try to define is what Gilels decidedly possesses.

Let's note one remarkable peculiarity of Gilels' creative life of the 1930's: each "final chord" of a certain period (the victory at the All-Union Contest marked the end of the Odessa period) was at the same time the starting point of some new stage, the tasks of which (the essence of that important "something"!) Gilels could most exactly and clearly define for himself. He defined them for himself, but as these tasks were undertaken with the intuition of the truly thinking and great artist Emil Gilels is and were solved on the highest artistic level, they proved to be not only the achievements of the pianist himself but also to a certain extent of the world art of performance in general.

Gilels' triumph in Brussels was a kind of summing-up of the pianist's studies in Odessa and Moscow. Yet, the victory could by no means make easier the hardships of the creative quest of the years to follow. His contacts and studies with Neuhaus changed Gilels' approach to the process of working on a composition, the aims of this process and even finally the repertory itself. Therefore during all these years Gilels, with his rare memory and his ability to master an unfamiliar piece extremely fast, learned a comparatively small number of new compositions. Main among them were: *The Symphonic Variations* of Franck, *The B minor Sonata* of Liszt, the Schumann *Concerto*, Chopin's *Fantasy-Impromptu*, De Falla's *Dance of Fire*, and *the Preludes* and *Etudes* of Debussy. Besides these compositions, such pieces as *Variations on a Theme of Paganini, Intermezzos and Rhapsodies* of Brahms and the Chopin *B Flat minor Sonata* learned by the pianist in recent years, are repeatedly interpreted and re-interpreted by him.

By casting a passing glance at this repertory two things draw our attention: the first is the propensity for complicated many-sided compositions—sonatas, concertos, big variation cycles—that later became one of the characteristics of his performing style. It

Emil Gilels, his wife Fariset Gilels and the French journalist Dominique Desantie, during a tour in Paris.

naturally arose from the peculiarities of Gilels' artistic make-up which is far from the "chamber" style, so typical of many pianists, the necessity to "pour one's heart out" in a close circle. On the contrary, Gilels' bright palette, his very special talent of a musician-tribune (noted by many critics in different periods of his creative life) revealed itself best of all, especially at the time of acquiring the creative maturity we are now speaking about, in large "canvases."

The second point is that in the repertory of that period there is an obvious accent on the romantic composers. Why does Gilels place emphasis on the music which demands softness and warmth of tone, phrasing, and particular frankness?

In order to understand that, evidently, we must go back to an earlier period, the pianist's childhood and youth.

Gilels grew up in the large family of a poor Odessa white-collar worker. Financial hardships of the family, the tense atmosphere of the first years after the Revolution in Odessa, left its mark on the forming character of the future pianist. The boy grew too taciturn and sullen for his age. Almost the only delight of his young years was music. "In my childhood," Gilels remember, "I slept little. At night when everything in the house calmed down I used to take father's ruler from under my pillow and start conducting. The small dark bedroom turned into a dazzling concert hall. Standing on the stage I felt behind me the breathing of a large crowd and in front of me the orchestra was stock-still with expectation. I raise the baton and the air fills up with marvelous sounds. The sounds are streaming stronger and stronger. Forte, fortissimo . . . But at this moment my worried mother would open the door and interrupt the concert at the most interesting point . . . My childish thoughts were entirely devoured by music . . ."

As a boy of five Gilels entered the class of the pedagogue Yakov Tkatch, famous in Odessa, and for eight years he plunged into the atmosphere of beautiful but somewhat narrow professionalism. With persistence and talent, Tkatch was making Gilels a little virtuoso. However, work on the tone, phrasing, penetration into the image-bearing contents of the compositions performed always remained in the background, if there was any such work at all. And the lessons themselves, which were turning into a many-hour drill, made the boy even more reticent both in everyday life and in music.

Overcoming the difficulties connected with the discrepancy between phenomenal technical development (at thirteen Gilels easily played Chopin's *Etudes,* the Beethoven *Pathetique Sonata,* Liszt's *E Flat Major Concerto*), and those aspects of pianism that demanded warmth of tone, the ability to spontaneously, humanely "interlace thought and feeling," express oneself on the instrument, was particularly what Gilels worked at both in Reingbald's class and mainly in that of Neuhaus.

The first significant landmarks in the complicated process for the pianist became *Isolda's Death* of Wagner-Liszt and the *B Flat minor Sonata* of Chopin. However, the period we are speaking about was the crowning stage of "overcoming oneself," because now it was no longer the initiative of his tutors but the personal artistic demand of the pianist himself.

We may safely say that in those years the balance between all the elements of Gilels' performing arsenal was established once and for all. And in connection with this the main distinction of Gilels' pianism, the feature that was most impressive of all, was seen in a new light—his virtuosity.

Yes, the virtuosity of Gilels was "the talk of the town" among many music critics. However, surprising as it may seem, more often its discussion narrowed—Gilels' virtuosity was regarded apart from other facets of his pianism. For a long time many of those who wrote about Gilels (at the end of the 1930's to the 1940's and later) would not deviate from the appraisal, labels and epithets that appeared when Gilels came to prominence on the performing horizon. The pianist was often "lectured" which at times ran into absurdity: someone quite "competently" advised . . . that he almost entirely give up performing virtuoso music!

Is it possible to imagine Liszt, the performer, knowing how emotionally he performed the Beethoven *Sonata—Quasi Una Fantazia—op. 27, No. 2,*how poetic and inspired his piano sounded in slow cantilena pieces, without his legendary virtuosity? Would he have gone down in the history of piano performance had he not been a matchless virtuoso? Evidently not.

Emil Gilels.

The same is true of Gilels, whose virtuosity is the heart and soul of his inimitable individuality, that very virtuosity due to which his art has become one of the standards of technical prowess of the 20th century, a remarkable phenomenon in the history of the piano as an instrument of powerful varied orchestral resources. One of the highest peaks in the development of a performer is meeting the demands that Beethoven made of the piano when the limited dynamics of the harpsichord were found to make the instrument inadequate for the purpose. That is why it is so difficult to imagine Gilels of the 1930's to 1950's at the harpsichord.

In the mid-1950's, one of the most prominent Soviet historians and experts on piano art, G.M. Kogan, wrote of the exceptional force of the influence of Gilels' virtuosity, its steadfast, tough origin: "Few of the piano virtuosos in the world are capable of 'electrifying' the audience by the technical brilliance, chiselled rhythm, dynamic vigor of their performance . . . The pianistic gift of Gilels excels almost all contemporary pianists. His virtuosity . . . is not to be 'liked'; it overwhelms, it is spontaneous . . . The masonry of the broad and steady constructions he erects affect the audience irresistibly and joyfully. His rhythm rules over the people, the waves of his ascents nearly 'wash the listeners away from their seats.' "

Thus Gilels' virtuosity became one of the principal means of broadening the spectrum of impressions of piano playing. Such broad understanding of virtuosity is in a large measure identical to the notion of "mastery." It is especially mastery that should be spoken of in the broadest, universal sense of the word when Emil Gilels' art of performance of the period of his creative maturity is meant.

"Mastery in the art of performance begins when technical brilliance disappears, when we are listening only to the music, admiring the inspired performance, forgetting how and by means of what technical devices the musician has achieved one or another

Emil Gilels with the students of the Budapest School of Music Art.

expressive effect . . . All the richest technique of such musicians, a truly infinite complex of expressive means they possess, is always subordinated to the task of a possibly most vivid and convincing realization of the composer's idea, of driving it home to the listeners." These words belong to one of the most outstanding composers of our times, Dmitri Shostakovich. It is very significant that, to confirm his thought, Shostakovich gives as an example several noted performers (D. Oistrakh, Sviatoslav Richter and others), naming Emil Gilels the first.

What are the essentials in the creative life of Emil Gilels that have lasted for several decades?

To find a simple answer to that question when speaking of such an eminent artist as Gilels seems very difficult if not impossible. However, in the case of Gilels and his complicated and versatile individuality, it is possible (with certain reservations) to point out one such feature: it is the permanent evolution of the pianist; not the evolution of his mastery in the narrow sense of the word (it would be absurd to speak of it), but the general evolution of Gilels the artist, Gilels the musician.

Without the understanding of that evolution, it is impossible to truly appreciate the art of Gilels (especially of the latest period), as it is equally impossible to comprehend the role that the amazing feature of the pianist plays in the art of performance of our times.

Heinrich Neuhaus, who was a man of rare insight, pointed to that quality of the pianist unaware of the cardinal changes that Gilels' art would undergo in the 70's: "Gilels' biography" he wrote in 1962, "is remarkable for its steady and consistent line of development and growth. Many, even very talented pianists get stuck at some point beyond which no more progress is observed. With Gilels it is quite the contrary. From year to year, from one concert to another his performance is blossoming, getting richer, more perfect. When he was beginning his pianistic activities as a young boy, it was clear to everybody that the brilliant basic material was obvious, but he still lacked high artistry, spirituality. Gradually the spirit —the spirit of music—penetrated into all the pores of that magnificent flesh, brightened it up, allowed the performer more and more to achieve the major aim—his personal interpretation of the author's idea without diminishing, depreciating it, but creatively illuminating it with his own light."

"And again Gilels confirms the fact that his motherland is the motherland of pianism. The country that gave the world Rachmaninoff, Brailowsky, Lhevinne, Barer and Horowitz still remains an inexhaustible source of talent. Gilels is the incarnation of the best features of the Russian School."

Emil Gilels in the Juilliard Music School (1955).

It is in that direction of continuously acquiring higher artistry, imparting even greater spirituality to the performance, that Gilels' evolution developed.

The easiest way to trace this evolution is through the example of concrete compositions, but also, in a sense, to rise to the level of the most prominent interpreters of Liszt. For instance, the performance of *Figaro's Wedding* of Mozart-Liszt by 16-year-old Gilels exceeded the limits of his performance at the competitive audition, and became a significant event in the art of performance of the 1930's. However, at that time it was still too early to speak of the young pianist mastering the entire profundity and depth of Liszt's style.

Emil Gilels after a rehearsal.

An appreciable qualitative advance became obvious after the Brussels Competition, when in the art of his favorite composer Gilels became more concerned with the subtle lyrics, bright poetry, inner dramatism of Liszt's compositions. All that, together with Gilels' perfect technique which conformed completely to Liszt's pianism, permitted him to create a marvelous interpretation of the *B minor Sonata*—the central composition of Liszt's piano repertory. In the integrity of that monumental canvas, in the steadiness of its separate fragments, the "Faust" images created by the pianist stand out vividly and boldly. Lyrical episodes are also permeated with true profoundness and meaning. In their almost vocal speech-melody, Gilels always manages to find that important measure, the lack of which, even in the case of some talented performers, turns Liszt's elation, pathos, dramatism into pompous theatricality.

The years were passing. Gilels' passion for Liszt's music was far from a youth's "crush"; it was earnest for the rest of his life. Trying to grasp the meaning of Liszt's compositions, penetrating deeper and deeper into the inner world of his music, Gilels comprehended better its versatility, and above all, its poetic and philosophical contents.

It is also interesting to trace the evolution of the pianist's attitude to the music of Brahms.

In Odessa Gilels actually did not know Brahms' piano music. The young pianist got his first "taste" of it when he entered the class of Heinrich Neuhaus, who was an ardent propagandist and a subtle, refined interpreter of Brahms. But to become fond of something is one thing, and to find a convincing, interesting interpretation is another. For Gilels, who had immediately felt a strong attraction to the music of Brahms, the way to grasp the complicated style of the composer constituted a quest of many years—not only for "the golden mean" between the "academism" and "romanticism" of Brahms, (in the opinion of many performers and especially musicologists that is "problem Number One") but

Friendly caricature of Emil Gilels.

primarily of bringing to light with no extraneous features the frankness, charm and profound concentration of Brahms' music. "To speak his own language" in Brahms proved far from easy for Gilels. But today Gilels, who includes the *Second Concerto, Variations on a Theme of Paganini* and numerous miniatures of Brahms

Emil Gilels.

The Head of the Tchaikovsky Competition Jury, Emil Gilels, congratulating its winner, American pianist Van Cliburn.

in his repertory, can be called one of the most inspired (among, un-fortunately, very few!) interpreters of Johannes Brahms.

Gilels' performance of the Beethoven *Sonatas* and *Concertos* is the most telltale confirmation of continuous evolution of the artist.

The fortitude and severity, "iron" rhythm and inclination to compositions presenting broad canvases, the vivid "concertism" of Gilels' technique noted by almost all the critics early in his youth—all that comprises the important component required to play Beethoven successfully. And Gilels did play Beethoven; at 13, as we already know, he played the *Pathetique Sonata*, then other compositions. But the more he familiarized himself with the crea-tions of the great Master, the clearer he saw that mere pianistic capabilities, temperament, and a sense of rhythm for a truly beautiful interpretation of this music was not enough. Each newly learned Beethoven composition made him observe from different angles the pieces he had played before. Thus, in constantly plung-ing into Beethoven's world there was born not only a more com-plete interpretation of every piece, but also the whole concept of performing Beethoven's music. (Goethe had asserted that concep-tion in art was everything.)

The best idea of that conception may be given by Gilels' inter-pretation of the Beethoven Concertos. It would be hardly an exag-geration to say that the performance of Beethoven's Concertos by Emil Gilels was not merely the top achievement of the pianist in his own Beethoveniana, but also a great phenomenon in the world art of performance. And those who managed during two evenings to hear Gilels perform all the *Five Concertos* of Beethoven consider themselves lucky, not without reason.

"Gilels plays Beethoven with ardent fervor, in full measure revealing the dramatism of his speech, agitated and sharp, tender and elated," the famous Canadian critic Pierre Socier wrote. "His performance is sweeping, which is indispensable for these pages permeated with passion. The power of the performance reminded one of an orchestra. Is there another pianist in the world capable of arousing equal enthusiasm?"

We have mentioned Liszt, Brahms and Beethoven. However, similar illustrations in the same measure may be presented by the compositions of Bach, Scarlatti, Ravel and Prokofiev, which also occupy an important place in Gilels' repertory. Sensitive and

ПРОГРАММА
ПОСВЯЩЕННАЯ 50–летию
ПЕРВОГО КОНЦЕРТА

Бетховен – Соната до минор № 8 соч. 13
Шуманн – Романс фа диез № 2 соч. 28
Шуманн – Карнавал соч. 9

Скрябин – Этюд фа диез № 2 соч. 8
Скрябин – Этюд до диез соч. 2
Скрябин – 5 прелюдий соч. 74

Рахманинов – 4 прелюдии

си бемоль № 2 соч. 23
соль бемоль № 10 соч. 23
си мажор № 11 соч. 32
соль минор № 5 соч. 23

The program devoted to the 50th anniversary of the first concert by Emil Gilels.

serious listeners who follow the pianist's performing activities must have felt his evolution in any part of his repertory.

But even those who knew of the talents of the artist and became accustomed to hearing in almost every season, almost every performance another, a different, Gilels could not fail to note that the Gilels of the 1970's is absolutely a new phenomenon.

"The symptoms of novelty in today's art of Gilels are seen, so to say, with the naked eye," one of the music critics wrote quite recently. "Slow tempos, emphasized unhurriedness of musical narration. Muffled tone, muted colors, employing nothing too bright, striking the eye, playing sotto voce when every word is pronounced softly, yet forcibly, significantly, with great dignity. The emphasized declamatory style of the speech-melody, expressiveness of each intonation, melodic idiom intensified to a head. Listening to Gilels one feels at times as if his phrasing were oozing, bleeding with inner expression . . ."

How can such a change be overlooked? If, for example, even the Schumann *Toccata* that Gilels had always performed with bravura, with "steel" non legato, in one of the concerts quite suddenly sounded gentle, lyrical, almost like a melodious piece – unexpected but cogent. Similar transformation occurred in Gilels' performance of Schumann's *Arabesque* and *Concerto;* the cantilena parts of the Beethoven *Sonatas* became even more profound and concentrated.

Some other signs of novelty: could it have been imagined some twenty or thirty years ago that Gilels would include into a concert program Mozart's *D minor Fantasy* or 'Lyric Pieces' of Grieg? Today we hear them performed by Gilels and wonder at the ingenuousness, charm, sincerity of the execution.

What caused such changes in Gilels' playing? It is not a simple question. One thing that can be said is that Gilels has achieved the contemporary interpretation of some compositions, his new manner of playing quite organically, indicating a constantly searching artist who never marks time.

Gilels' art has always been distinguished for its great lucidity and simplicity of expression. Today we can speak of the classic clarity of his art and the simplicity that permeates Gilels' performance.

No matter how the art of Gilels is transforming, one thing, perhaps the essential quality in his art ever remains unchanged. It is the feature that had been noticed even by Heinrich Neuhaus:

". . . Gilels is admired most of all for his indefatigable vitality, because he so loudly and imperiously proclaims "Yes!" to life. His voice is clear to anyone, answers the innermost desires and expectations of the people. In short, the art of Gilels helps to live."

Andrei Gavrilov.

Andrei Gavrilov

Andrei Gavrilov was born September 21, 1955, in Moscow. The pianist's parents are people of art: his father was a painter, his mother, Assanetta Yegicerian, a former pianist. It was she who became his first teacher.

The study of the instrument began at an early age—at three—when the rare musical capabilities of the boy and his keen perception of music were displayed.

At the age of six Andrei Gavrilov entered the Central Music School (CMS), the forge of many a talented Soviet musician. There he became the pupil of Tatiana Kestner who had nurtured many famous pianists. However, during all his schooling his mother continued to watch over his pianistic development along with Kestner.

Intensive professional work in his school years under the guidance of persistent and competent tutors produced wonderful results: at the age of fifteen, still a schoolboy, Andrei Gavrilov was quite a success at the All-Union Contest of performers winning the title of a laureate. And two years later he became the winner of the Gold Medal at the V Tchaikovsky Competition.

"Andrei Gavrilov," wrote the Soviet Press at the time, "is a real volcano. Obviously, his performance cannot leave anyone indifferent. The versatility of his talent, the unique makings of a virtuoso of the young pianist are such that he is due to occupy one of the foremost places in the pianistic world."

At the time when he scored the victory in the Moscow Competition, Andrei Gavrilov was already the student of the noted Soviet pedagogue, Professor Lev Naumov. Under his tutelage he took the entire Conservatory course.

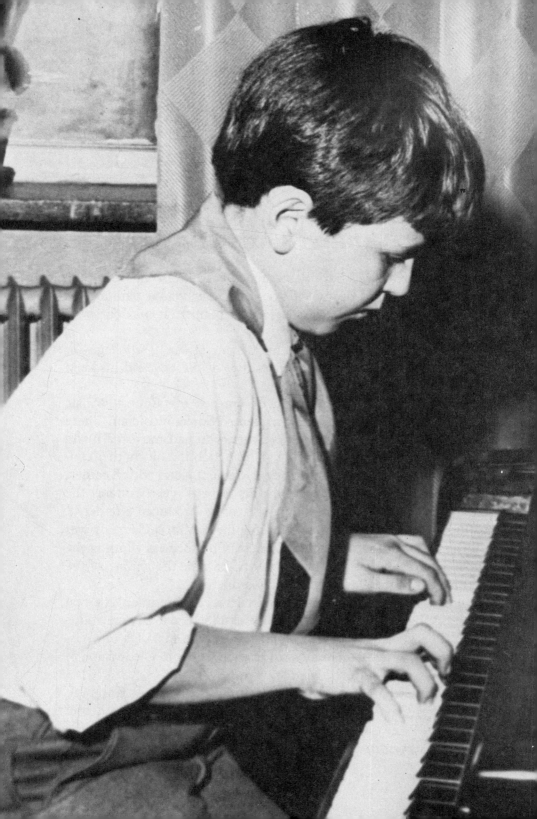

Today in the unanimous opinion of many musicians and critics, Andrei Gavrilov is one of the most interesting and original Soviet pianists of the young generation. Some of his programs of recent years in all confidence can be called unique as to grandeur of the design and the quality of execution; as, for example, the interpretation of all the clavier concertos with orchestra of J. S. Bach, as well as the cycle of concerts in which Andrei Gavrilov, together with Sviatoslav Richter, each performed eight *Handel's Suites.*

Now the circle of creative aspirations of Gavrilov is broad enough and covers different stylistic layers—including Ravel, Britten and even the most contemporary, experimental music.

*   *   *

In Andrei Gavrilov's study-drawing room, the center of which is occupied by two grand pianos, all the walls from floor to ceiling are hung with pictures. And this surrounding of musical instruments with pictorial canvases is very symbolic: two arts have been living side by side in Gavrilov's family for a long time—music and painting.

"These are the pictures painted by my deceased father," says Andrei Gavrilov. "Some of his works are exhibited in the Tretiakov Gallery and other museums. He was a very serious and original painter. I was fond of watching him work and of course I also dreamt of becoming a painter. I was supposed to be taught painting and my mother planned for my elder brother (he is three years my senior) to study music. She was a pianist who had had a Conservatory education. She had been tutoring him quite zealously for three years and he was to enter the Central Music School with a rather complicated program for his age, when out of the blue I came up to the piano and . . . played his entire program by ear. Since that moment there was a reorientation in our family. As a result my brother has become a painter and I, as you know, a musician . . ."

Andrei Gavrilov speaks of the years of his childhood with humor. His voice becomes soft and even. While he is speaking it is

Andrusha Gavrilov at the age of 10.

difficult to imagine him at the piano – one moment in a frenzy, as if at the point of smashing the instrument with his large athletic hands, another moment dreamily delicate . . .

I asked the pianist to recollect the most vivid musical impression of his early childhood.

AG: I was about three or four years old when I saw the Italian film *Prelude of Fame* with little Roberto Bentzi. When I heard Bach's *Dorian Toccata* and *Fugue D minor* for organ the impression was so great that I burst into tears.

MZ: Your first teacher was your mother, wasn't she?

AG: Yes, she applied herself to the work with me with the same earnestness, persistence and patience as she had been first working with my brother.

MZ: And what happened to your passion for painting?

AG: It was strictly pursued. My mother must have feared that painting would win out. And that apprehension of hers was not devoid of grounds. A child is much more inclined to mess about with colors and brushes rather than tackle something at the piano. And still I carried on with my studies of painting more or less until a certain age. By the way, Father liked some of my works and considered that I had more talent for painting than for music.

MZ: It is no surprise that it is awfully difficult to study with one's own children. Therefore it would be interesting to know how your lessons with your mother went. Were they more of a game for you, or was it a "stern" everyday working life?

AG: I cannot say if it was a kind of simplification on her part, but it was certain that the elements of a game were lacking. It did not come easy to me; at times I was bored to death. Moreover, in the secondary grades at school there were moments when I simply wanted to give up music for good. But now when I realize that without the technical "apparatus" formed by serious and persistent studies since early childhood, I wouldn't have achieved anything in music, I think of my mother with deep gratitude.

MZ: So what were your first achievements?

AG: By the time I entered the Central Music School (I was six) I was playing the Handel *F-Major Concerto* which, incidentally, I am going to perform next season.

MZ: Who was your school teacher?

AG: On entering the Central Music School I became the pupil of

Andrei Gavrilov not long before the Tchaikovsky Competition, rehearsing with his mother.

Andrei Gavrilov with his teacher Tatiana Kestner.

the wonderful pedagogue Tatiana Kestner for ten years. She was the former pupil of Alexander Goldenweiser and a practitioner of his school, the principles of which are different from those of Heinrich Neuhaus, to which Mother belonged and to which, I reckon, I myself belong to a great extent. It is well-known that Goldenweiser's school is characterized by a somewhat speculative, rational attitude towards music. And it did me a lot of good. Mother was an advocate of emotional richness in music. So I was developing in two directions, as my mother kept watching over me almost until the Tchaikovsky Competition, that is throughout all my school years.

MZ: In other words, during your school years you were studying almost all the time with two pedagogues simultaneously. Did not the differences of their views bring about conflicts?

AG: Such conflicts were continual, especially in the first years of studies. But eventually my mother and my teacher became kind of collaborators because both methods seemed to "bear fruit."

MZ: At the age of fifteen you were already a success at the All-Union Contest where you were the fourth. And already by that time your phenomenal technique became "the talk of the town." Please, tell me how your technical development was proceeding in your school years.

AG: I was made to practice a great deal indeed. It is enough to say that for at least an hour and a half I used to play scales, exercises, Hanon including. As a result, by the time I left school, technical hurdles of any kind practically ceased to exist for me. For instance, I developed such deftness of fingers that now it makes absolutely no difference to me with what fingers to play the trills: 1-3, 2-3 or 3-4 and 4-5.

MZ: Did you do this work willingly?

AG: Of course not. I especially disliked the Czerny etudes. But what could I, poor thing, do about it? I was gripped in an "iron vise."

MZ: There is a saying: "Winners are not to be judged." Paraphrasing it a bit, we may say that "parents of the winners of competitions are not to be judged . . ." Nevertheless, the question arises as to whether such intensive and forced pianistic development was truly necessary.

AG: It is difficult for me to answer this question. For instance,

Sviatoslav Richter began studying music later than is customary. But never in his studies had there been any forcing. As a result he had certain technical hurdles that he had to deal with later. But on the other hand, he studied playfully, and hence his attitude towards practicing. That important quality has been preserved by him up to the present. But times have changed. It is difficult to judge what attitude is the correct one.

More than once in our talk Gavrilov mentioned Sviatoslav Richter. The last several years of their close friendship have, so to say, lit up the life of the young artist. Perhaps, it may be accounted for by Richter's finding a "kindred soul" in the younger colleague. In the opinion of some musicians, Andrei Gavrilov at the instrument is somewhat reminiscent of the young Richter. Whether it is so or not, it is obvious that Gavrilov possesses a rare feeling for the stage anyway. I asked the pianist to answer the question about his first performances on the stage.

AG: In this respect I am very much obliged to Kestner. Apart from all the other things, she marvelously performs with small children (I am no expert in it myself), she amazingly and naturally introduces them to the stage. In her pupils she nurtures an attitude of modest efficiency, which completely conquers the feeling of stage fright. I remember that everything down to the smallest detail had been trained for and practiced: how to step onto the stage, how to make one's bows, how to put the footstool under one's feet, and many other "trifles" that will later make up the behavior of an artist on the stage, which is molded in early childhood. And besides all that she was very careful not to let her pupils boast because of their performances on stage, which is often the case with young children.

MZ: No matter how hard you studied music, you must have had some non-musical interests in your childhood.

AG: Naturally. It was sports. I went in for tennis and even made good progress in it. But in general, what on earth did I not go in for? In the period when I lost interest in music, I became in-

Ilya Grubert and Andrei Gavrilov (the last on the left)—the would be "Gold" laureates of the Tchaikovsky Competition at the graduation evening party at school.

fatuated with history and architecture. Then I began to dream of becoming an archeologist together with my friend who eventually became a rather famous one. So I undertook excavations, looked for ancient coins, made stylized pots of the time of Neolithic and Paleolithic periods. But all my passions didn't prove to be serious. Piano was the main thing indeed.

MZ: With all our intensive practice, when the rough work takes up so much time and effort, certain periods of cooling off to music and even disappointments are in all probability natural, as natural as the moment when in an adolescent a conscious attitude towards studies, towards art is suddenly awakened.

AG: You are absolutely right. I experienced such a moment, such a turning point when I was playing the Saint-Saëns *Second Concerto*. I was 14 at the time and I suddenly felt that I could greatly enjoy the very process of the work itself.

MZ: Was it at about that time that you became Lev Naumov's student?

AG: Yes. I became Lev Naumov's pupil when I was still at school, a year and a half before I won the Tchaikovsky Competition. But when I came to his lessons for the first several times, everything was a novelty for me. New understanding of the essence of music, new attitude to the form, to the psychology of performance. There was no technical training; we were concerned exclusively with the creative quest.

MZ: It must have been difficult to accustom yourself to work of another character as you were, to a certain extent, a fully developed musician; it was no accident that your performance at the All-Union Contest was noted by a laureate title . . .

AG: True, it was not easy for me at first. On the one hand there was my ungovernable temperament—I was simply raging at the instrument and was already playing super-difficult compositions, but on the other hand there was no profound understanding of music yet.

MZ: Lev Naumov is a pedagogue blessed with God's gift. But he almost never plays as a performer himself. What's the reason for that in your opinion?

AG: Naumov is a striking personality—very complicated, gifted in many ways. He could perform wonderfully, but he is bursting with numerous ideas. It is most interesting to associate with him; one can work with him at a piece forever and discover something new.

Andrei Gavrilov and Lev Naumov at the time of the preparation for the Competition.

The head of the jury of the pianists, composer Otar Takta-kischvili, present-ing the award to the winner of the V Tchaikovsky Com-petition, Andrei Gavrilov.

MZ: To conclude discussion of your early student years. I'd like to ask who was your idol at that period of your life?

AG: All my life, literally, since the age of three, my idol has been Sviatoslav Richter. In my childhood I even had a game with my mother: when I played well, in order to encourage me, she would say that I played just like Sviatoslav Richter. And then I was in seventh heaven. At that time, of course, I could not even suspect that Fate would grant me such happiness as to have close contact with that outstanding musician.

MZ: Sviatoslav Richter is one of the great "mysteries" of contemporary performance. He has never taught and only rarely was he in such close creative association with any pianist other than yourself. That's why I ask you this question: in what way did you perceive the influence of that extraordinary personality?

AG: It is impossible to describe it in few words. You are asking about the influence . . . We often interpret the notion of influence in the negative sense of the word, that is, meaning overwhelming an individual or such influence that encourages imitation. But this is not the case with me. Richter's influence has never showed itself as an overwhelming force. It has been rather a guiding and directing force. Richter is not even a "school." It is a kind of biofield in which you start feeling and thinking differently.

MZ: How did you make music together?

AG: The most significant and interesting form of our musical association was our joint reading of Handel's 16 Suites. It is difficult for one person to play such a cycle and we decided to play eight suites each.

MZ: In the process of working at these pieces was there discussion of any kind between you?

AG: No. And there is more to it. Having chosen the eight suites neither of us had ever heard the other eight before. We played them to each other for the first time in France. It occurred under unusually romantic circumstances. We met in an ancient castle, on a balmy evening. We had had a supper of French cheeses with red Burgundy and we then moved to the adjoining hall and began playing to each other. It was Sviatoslav Theophilovich who played first and I was hanging on each of his notes. Then I played. When the last sounds died away we didn't say anything to each other—we were absorbing the music we had never heard before. It was just

The congratulations of the winner of the competition, Andrei Gavrilov, from the head of the Composer's Union of the USSR, composer Tikhon Khrennikov.

three days before our joint concert.

MZ: Didn't you discuss each other's performance in those three days either?

AG: No, we didn't, except for getting acquainted with the text of the other eight suites in order to be able to coordinate the turning of the pages. Each of us took into consideration the wishes of the other. Sviatoslav Theophilovich is very thorough in this respect. He had marked everything in advance, where and how to turn the pages and it was much easier for me. He is a man who thinks everything out; nothing escapes him—even such a thing as the turning of the pages. But then I understood that this was not a mere trifle. Much depends on how accurately the page is turned.

MZ: What was the reason for your playing the Handel *Suites* from music?

AG: Actually, we played from memory. There is one principal consideration in this. Richter believes that the classics up to the 19th century ought to be played from music, as it creates a different atmosphere. And in general he may be right. I've just performed a cycle of the Bach *Concertos* from music and I've arrived at the conclusion that it does create a different atmosphere indeed and different penetration into music and musical emotions. When the top of the piano is down, the score is on the music-stand, the light is subdued, the perception of music is different; making music as such is of a different character.

MZ: We often dwell on the Bach *Concertos* in our talk; this is only natural, as you've been working at them a great deal and are still "living" in that music. Your turning to this music must have been prepared by your entire evolution as a performer. Isn't it so?

AG: Absolutely. Since my childhood I've dreamed of performing all the Bach *Concertos*. I wanted to do it when I was 15 and when I was 20. But I set myself an age limit—to play them not sooner than when I reached the age of 25. That's precisely the way it came about. When I was 25 I played the first four Concertos and recently I've played the other three. Incidentally, when I say:"I dreamt to play," I also mean that involuntarily in my thoughts I turned to that music time and again. Sometimes I heard it in my sleep, under circumstances quite alien to playing the instrument. So when I began working at these compositions, some problems proved to have been already solved.

Andrei Gavrilov.

MZ: Have you ever wanted to perform the entire *Well-Tempered Clavier* of Bach?

AG: You've hit the nail on the head. Just recently I've commenced working on it and I hope to perform it in the not-too-distant future. I think I'll play it from music.

MZ: Your reasons?

AG: What's the point of playing 48 preludes and fugues from memory? I don't think it was envisaged by the composer to play *the whole* cycle. And why do that gigantic absolutely unnecessary work anyway? It is necessary neither for the pianist, who will simply traumatize his memory, nor for the audience.

MZ: Of all the recordings familiar to you, for instance, those of Samuel Feinberg, Sviatoslav Richter, Edwin Fisher, which is the most compatible to you?

AG: Each of the pianists mentioned by you has something with which I agree. But I would never undertake to work at a composition which has been performed so perfectly that its interpretation could be regarded as ideal, if I didn't think I could say something of my own, something new in it.

MZ: Have you happened to discuss with Sviatoslav Richter why he never plays arrangements?

AG: No, I haven't, but I agree with him. I don't like arrangements either, though I make an exception for the songs of Schubert-Liszt. I enjoy listening to them and maybe I'll play them some day. But in general, why turn to arrangements when there is a lot of original music that is performed precisely as the composer envisaged it? I believe the arrangements to be the natural self-expression of the musicians who made them. That's the way I accept them, but not as independent pieces of the piano repertory.

MZ: What editions of the Bach compositions do you find the best? Which of them coincide with your own idea of the contemporary style of interpreting the eighteenth century music?

AG: I hate any kind of editions and always try to work with the Urtext. I hold it to be the only correct way. It does not mean that I never acquaint myself with the commentaries of authoritative musicians of a certain composition. In particular, playing Bach's *D minor Concerto* I studied the remarks of Edwin Fisher with great interest. I took into account certain things and I rejected others. That is acceptable. But when the editor's hand pushes through into

per andrei Gavrilov

con grande stima, du

Renato Guttuso

The sketch of Andrei Gavrilov's hand by Italian painter Renato Guttuzo.

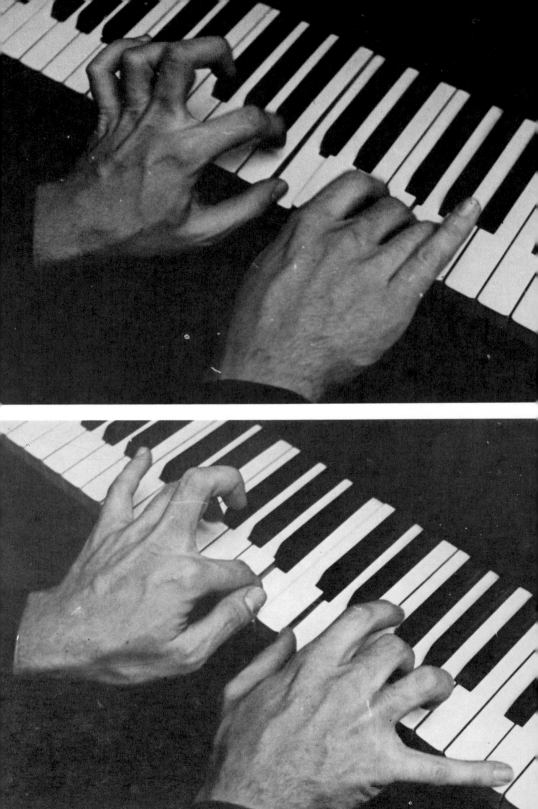

the staff, it drives me crazy.

MZ: While working at the Urtext, do you keep in mind or make notes in the score of your dynamic and articulation commentaries?

AG: In romantic music, I do not mark anything at all in the score as a rule. But in the compositions of Bach I immediately mark in the score everything that occurs to me, as Bach's Urtext is exceptionally ascetic. As a rule, there are only note signs without any kind of articulation or dynamic recommendations.

MZ: What are your views concerning articulation in Bach's compositions?

AG: I am not sure; perhaps my comprehension of music in a great measure is conditioned by my being the son of a painter, but the finales of Bach's *Concertos*, for example, are imagined by me as mosaic multi-colored panels. Therefore I try to employ most varied articulation devices from staccato to legatissimo, that is, to resort to all the possible colors the piano permits.

MZ: Recently you've been fond of Bach's polyphony. We know one of the sacraments of Bach's music lies in the fact that this is Art for all times, it is eternally contemporary . . . And each generation offers its own reading of Bach in the person of its most talented performers. In what do you feel Bach's contemporary essence?

AG: First of all, today's music without polyphony does not fascinate me at all. In polyphony there appears the strongest friction of the elements of music tissue, the highest tension in music that excites me to the utmost. To go deep into all the details of the intricate interlacing of the parts and try to bring it to a certain perfection is a great delight to me. Secondly, it seems to me that polyphony has reverted to its original "position" but on a new level. It is now comprehended more profoundly, loftily, correctly. In our complicated times when we have already had romanticism and impressionism and other "isms," Bach's biblical polyphony brings us up to some new level of perception. There have been horrible wars, Man has stepped into Space, new categories have appeared. And today Bach is acute as ever in a new way. He does not simply fascinate, but grants us, performers, the opportunity to have our say, to express ourselves.

Andrei Gavrilov's hands.

MZ: When preparing to perform the Handel *Suites* or the cycle of Bach's *Concertos* you completely plunge into the style of that music. But your repertory is very versatile. Do you experience any difficulties when switching from compositions of one style to another?

AG: It is known that compositions of one style are characterized by certain technical formulas not typical of another. Therefore if one has not played romantic compositions for a long time, it will be difficult to turn to classical music because the classics are based on scale-like passages, which is closer to Czerny's technique. So, I believe that one should strive not to divert for long from any type of technique, to put it in more general terms, not to withdraw into one style for a long time. If, for example, one plays romantic music for two years, it will take some period of time to feel at ease in another style.

MZ: Young musicians who are already working at the instrument conscientiously but have not yet worked out any rigid practicing habits are keenly interested in rational ways to arrange their working day.

AG: The most essential thing in practicing is regularity. If one practices for seven or 14 hours two days running and then does nothing another two days, everything will go to rack and ruin. You may practice for four hours without forcing yourself and that will give much better results. That's my principle. And I'll formulate my other opposite principle: if for some reason I miss a day or two of practicing, I do my best to make up for the lost time and work off my "debt" afterwards. For instance, at the moment I owe myself some 150 hours that I've got to work off . . .

MZ: Do you count your summer holiday among your "debts"?

AG: I haven't had any summer holiday for two or three years now. In general I try not to make any intervals in my practicing. Because if I don't play these 20 days I'll have to make up for it anyway. And that allows me to think that I did practice. Psychologically it's very comforting and gives one the feeling of steadiness.

MZ: You place great emphasis on regularity and the amount of working hours a day. Isn't the arrangement of the material of some importance?

Andrei Gavrilov with his mother.

For many years there has existed a creative bond between Andrei Gavrilov and Soviet pianist of genius Sviatoslav Richter. In the 1980/81 season they performed all the Handel Suites. They played from the score. The photo shows Andrei Gavrilov performing the Handel Suites while Richter is turning pages for him. Even in that, remembers Andrei Gavrilov, Richter showed himself as an unusually punctilious person, having marked in the score in advance the point at which one or another page should be turned.

AG: As a rule, I try to envelop everything I am dealing with at the moment, but it is awfully difficult to manage more than two programs at a time. As for these two programs, solo and symphony, I do my utmost to play all the notes of these programs while practicing and to drill some difficult passages so that I can specially concentrate on something, though to my mind it does not play a decisive role. It is the amount of time that counts.

MZ: You say you prefer to work at not more than two programs at a time. How many new programs do you usually prepare during one year?

AG: I've made it a rule for myself to prepare four new programs a season: one classical program with the orchestra, the second—not standard, untraditional. For instance, last season it was an opera for children with a boys' choir. The third program is traditional orchestra. I've recently played Franck's *"Djinns"* and Ravel's *Concerto for the Left Hand.* And finally, the fourth is the traditional solo program. For example, soon I'm going to play the Schumann *Sonata* and four Chopin Ballads.

MZ: Your "repertory policy" is quite curious and may set an example of versatility for young performers. When you were talking of your repertory plans I paid attention to the fact that an important place in your creative activities is occupied by performing with the orchestra. It means that you've got to work with conductors a great deal. In your opinion as a soloist what are the rights and duties of a conductor when a concerto with orchestra is being performed?

AG: I think to assert that the conductor accompanies the soloist is erroneous in principle. There is no accompaniment as such; there is making music together. It should always be the synthesis that is, however, so difficult to achieve. The soloist and the conductor leading the orchestra are two partners enjoying equal rights.

MZ: Under what prominent conductors did you play and which of them was most compatible to you and most "convenient" as a partner?

AG: I was lucky to play under marvelous conductors. I'll start with Yuri Nikolayevsky. I believe the recordings made with him still to be the best I have recorded with a chamber orchestra. Nikolayevsky is a brilliant, erudite musician, an honest servant of Art. Sviatoslav Richter thinks that no one would have coped with

Andrei Gavrilov at a solo concert in the Great Hall of the Moscow Conservatory.

Andrei Gavrilov during his tour of the USA.

At the Kogans' (from right to left): Mark Zilberquit, Pavel Kogan, Andrei Gavrilov, Mrs. Helena Zilberquit and Mrs. Lubov Kogan.

the Berg *Concerto for Piano and 13 Wind Instruments* better than Nikolayevsky. I recorded the Tchaikovsky *Concerto* with Riccardo Muti—a wonderful master. It is appropriate to mention here that not long ago I was scheduled to make a recording of Rachmaninoff's second Concerto under Karajan on his initiative. Our collaboration hasn't taken place yet. I'd like to specially note the German conductor Hörst Stein with whom I managed to obtain the greatest synthesis of the piano and the orchestra.

MZ: Has there been any crisis in your creative biography?

AG: Speaking of crisis, in principle, it is always present. The matter is probably in my being a highly emotional, impulsive person, so that one day is not like another with me. I can give way to despair, ten times a day, to emotional crisis. But maybe it's the fate of all artistic people to be constantly tormented?

MZ: You've studied with wonderful pedagogues. Haven't you ever taken the role of a teacher yourself?

AG: No, I am absolutely convinced that it is impossible to serve two gods. One should choose either performing or pedagogics.

MZ: What excites you most of all in Art?

AG: I love literature, theatre, cinema very much, not to speak of painting. I love whatever is nice, whatever is beautiful, whatever is

Mark Zilberquit, Andrei Gavrilov and Pavel Kogan at the Kogans' home.

talented. All the rest does not exist for me. No matter what serious faults a person has, if he is truly talented the shortcomings move to the background and in the foreground there remains only the Talent.

MZ: What are your views concerning recording?

AG: Perhaps recording is too recent for generalizations and conclusions. Of course, recording is our final product, but it is getting unrestrainedly out-of-date with time. Such is the sad peculiarity of our art.

MZ: You speak quite pessimistically about it.

AG: Yes, in this respect our profession is really unfortunate. We are eternally pouring water into a sieve. That is why I am envious of painters. All their accomplishments are materialized in canvases that go on living their own lives after their creation and, what is of utmost importance, if their author is truly talented never do they grow out-of-date.

MZ: Andrew, I don't share your pessimism. It is enough to watch the public listening to you during a performance to assert that, by your art, you affect the audience no less, and in a sense, even more than does a painter.

AG: You may be right. Our art of performance wields a special power. It is the most communicable means of intercourse, however ephemeral. The concert is over and only memories remain. But that is not insignificant either.

MZ: Assuredly, the words pronounced by Claudio Monteverdi almost four centuries ago are by no means out-of-date nowadays and may become the motto of any musician-performer: "The purpose of true music is to stir one." And to my mind, it is marvelous that your life is devoted to such a lofty goal.

Richter and Gavrilov during their performance in the Pushkin Art Museum in Moscow.

Eliso Virsaladze.

Eliso Virsaladze

Eliso Virsaladze was born in Tbilisi, on September 14, 1942, on the day when fascists bombed the city for the first and the only time. The first and the principal teacher of Eliso was her grandmother, famoust pianist-pedagogue Anastasia Virsaladze. Under her tutelage, Eliso Virsaladze studied in the Tbilisi School for Gifted Children and graduated from the Conservatory. Later she perfected her artistry in Moscow with Heinrich Neuhaus and Yakov Zak.

The pianist's debut took place in Tbilisi when she was 16. That concert was a kind of prologue to her successful performances in competitions in later years. She scored her first victory in 1959 at the World Youth Festival in Vienna, where she was awarded the Silver Medal. Her name acquired wider fame after she became the laureate of the Tchaikovsky Competition of 1962, the youngest of its very strong winners.

"The rare gift of 20-year old E. Virsaladze (. . .) has drawn the attention of musicians in recent years," wrote the *Soviet Music* magazine after her performance. "Her participation in the Tchaikovsky competition in all three rounds adorned the contest. Virsaladze demonstrated wholeness and fascinating poetic spirituality of interpretation. The richness of her insight and the exceptional will power of the pianist are captivating."

The competition period of Eliso Virsaladze ended with her winning the Gold Medal in 1966 at the Schumann Competition in Zwickau.

Eliso Virsaladze at the time of her performance at the Tchaikovsky Competition in Moscow, 1966.

Having gone through a brilliant schooling of marvelous pedagogues, Eliso Virsaladze very early revealed her own vividly individual style. As a performer she can be characterized by an organic combination of classical rigid style with romantic freedom, bold colorings and subtle poetry. Her naturalness and willpower are also impressive. Among her favorite composers are Mozart and Beethoven, Schumann, Scriabin and Prokofiev.

Interesting facets of the performing manner of Eliso Virsaladze are revealed in chamber ensemble. Her frequent partner is the prominent Soviet cellist Natalia Gutman.

Since the late 1960's Eliso Virsaladze has been teaching in the Moscow Conservatory. Because of the pianist's intensive solo activities her class is not large. But she treats her pedagogical work as well as the main pursuit of her life—performance—with equal earnestness, passion and selflessness.

The artist tours a great deal in the Soviet Union and abroad. The serious critics of Germany, Spain, Italy and the countries of South America invariably write about her as a "profound and original" musician. *Augetburger Allgemeine,* for one, ran an article entitled "Fascinating Pianist": "Eliso Virsaladze (. . .) is a star from the inexhaustible reservoir of the young generation of Russian pianists . . . E. Virsaladze's performance is more than a demonstration of flawless technique and surprising musical originality. It is the synthesis of an extraordinary gift and spiritual command of musical "matter" in a single picturesque sounding . . ."

The great Russian poet Boris Pasternak (incidentally, he is one of the most "musical" poets belonging to the same intellectual circle as Heinrich Neuhaus, Sviatoslav Richter) pronounced the following words:

"The purpose of creation is in selflessness,
Not in sensation, nor in the success . . ."

These words occurred to me when we met and talked with Eliso Virsaladze. Being quite a down-to-earth person, she lives the typical life of a concertizing musician: hard but one rich in events. But neither fame, nor success, nor publicity—none of these outward attributes of a brilliant artistic career—seem to matter to her at all. It is apparent from whatever we touched upon in our talk—her first success in her school years, her competition victories, her reputation today as an artiste, press reviews of her performances, even her students—that nothing not pertaining directly to her art exists for her.

Her manner is very gentle, delicate, feminine (which cannot be said of her performance, which is energetic, powerful, temperamental and impulsive in the best sense of the word). Her unassuming manner of speaking with people, her sincerity and unpretentiousness immediately kindle deep liking for her.

Anastasia Davidovna Virsaladze, Eliso's grandmother, who nurtured Bashkirov and Vlasenko besides Eliso.

For example, Eliso Virsaladze speaks quite simply, without a hint of sensationalism, of her first steps in music, the initial period of her study of music.

EV: In the house of my grandmother,—Anastasia Virsaladze, where I was brought up, music sounded from morning till night. So from early childhood I have been "stewing in musical juice." But my granny was a very wise woman and pedagogue—she wouldn't "drill" me at the instrument beginning at the age of three or four; quite the contrary—she began rather late (I was eight years old then), after she made sure that I really ought to study.

MZ: In what way were your musical capabilities revealed that convinced your grandmother of the necessity to teach you?

EV: First, the ear for music and memory. I used to welcome Grandmother's pupils, playing their pieces by ear. I was in general fond of playing by ear. Then, by the time I was eight it was apparent that my hands were very good for the piano—large, elastic with innate fluency.

MZ: It is common knowledge how difficult it is for relatives to teach their children or grandchildren. What were your relations with your grandmother-pedagogue?

EV: Indeed, under such circumstances the pedagogue sometimes turns into just a coach. But it didn't happen in my case. My granny worked with me once or twice a week and I played on my own the rest of the time. Of course, it was very difficult for her to work with me. Like all children I was sometimes lazy, did not want to do what was required of me. I remember one image my granny invented in order to convince me how essential it was that I should study. Once she said to me, "Just imagine that you are walking down a bridge throwing pieces of gold into the water—if you don't study music, it amounts to the same thing."

MZ: In other words, one way or the other, your grandmother succeeded in finding the "key" to you and making your studies fruitful.

EV: Yes, but it was not only the matter of her gift of persuasion. Now, when I am bringing up a daughter myself, I become more and more sure that if a child does not see a live example, no words have the power to be convincing. My granny used to practice daily from 9 A.M. to 1 P.M., setting me the example of industry and a serious attitude towards music. Even in her old age, when she could not leave the house, she continued regularly practicing on the piano. And all of that, her love for music, the way she served it, was so effective that it was worth a dozen of the most perfect pedagogical devices.

MZ: How much did you practice daily in your school years?

EV: In my childhood I practiced very little, and the same is true of today. Now if I practice for some three hours, it is the limit. In my childhood I spent an hour or an hour and a half at the instrument. And there were days when I did not practice at all.

MZ: We know very well that a child of eight or ten, even if he loves music, would gladly play the tunes of his favorite songs, improvise sitting at the instrument, but to work at what the teacher demands of him is boring to him. Therefore practicing, as a rule, doesn't prove very productive. Perhaps, such was not the case with you?

EV: When at eight years old I began to study the piano, I already had a certain innate technique that later also allowed me not to spend much time at scales and exercises. Besides, my granny always worked with me at the repertory which was invariably interesting to me. It is enough to say that probably from the very beginning of my studies I did not have a single composition that I wouldn't be able to include in the program of my concert today. In fact, I did not play children's compositions as such at all.

MZ: But haven't you ever played the Clementi *Sonatinas,* the traditional children's études, scales?

EV: I've never played Clementi's *Sonatinas.* Of études I remember only one—that of Cramer. I played the scales only in that short period when I had to take my credit-test in scales at school as I absolutely hated them. But then by the time I was leaving school I played ten Mozart's *Sonatas.* I have been studying Mozart's *Sonatas* since the third grade, that is, since I was ten years old.

Eliso Virsaladze after she won the Gold Medal in 1966 at the Schumann Competition in Zwickau.

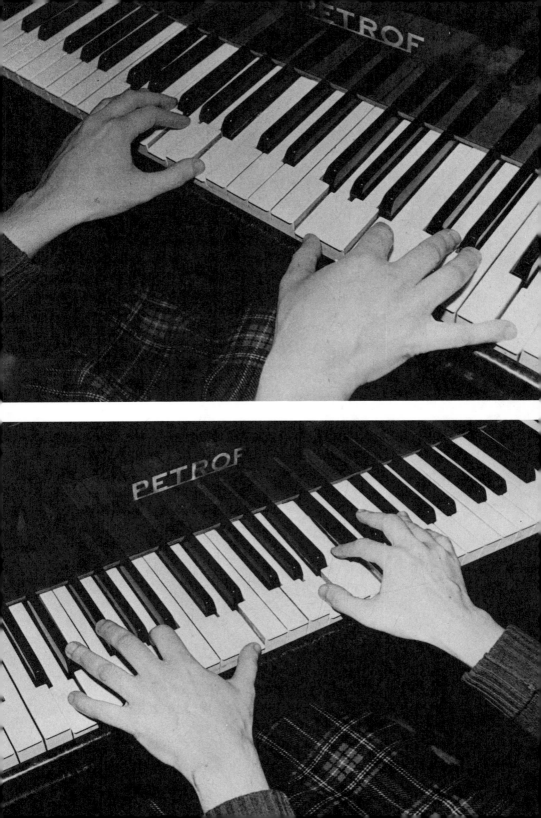

The love for Mozart which Eliso Virsaladze had even when a small child, multiplied by the skill acquired over the years, has resulted in her being rightfully considered one of the best interpreters of the compositions of the Salzburg genius. "When the pianist executed the Mozart *B flat major Sonata*," wrote one of the reviewers, "the outstanding interpreter of Mozart of the first postwar period, Rumanian Clara Haskil, immediately came to mind . . . In Eliso Virsaladze's performance there was everything that distinguished her from all the rest: the pure poetic essence, sparkling gaiety. It is an example of the natural, unpretentious approach to Mozart . . ."

MZ: Was it the general method of your grandmother or was it the way she worked only with you?

EV: Of course, it was my individual path and I am not going to assert by any means that it is suitable for anyone. At the same time I am not of the opinion that overcoming technical difficulties that are inevitable in one's childhood should be turned into an end in itself. And when the child is confronted only by that problem, it is particularly what the reluctance to study stems from. I had not experienced anything of the kind. In my first year of studying at school (though I was considered to be in the third grade), I played the *G Major Sonata* of Mozart, and the next year already the Beethoven *Third Concerto*. In the fifth grade I played with the orchestra for the first time the *Third Concerto* of Beethoven.

MZ: You present one of the rare examples of acquiring the piano technique omitting quite a large amount of obligatory etudes, such as those of Loeschhorn, Czerny, Cramer, Clementi, Moszkowski, etc.

EV: And nevertheless, it is quite so. I've never played any exercises, because I have never been offered any isolated technical tasks. And since the age of 11-12 the work at the Chopin *Etudes* began. There was simply no need for special technical training. The point is that in the Mozart *Sonatas* the technique is so complicated that, with all the difficulties contained in them being overcome, there is no more need for études.

MZ: With what compositions did you make your debut?

Eliso Virsaladze's hands.

EV: My first solo concert occurred when I was finishing school. In the first part I played the *Overture* of Bach-Saint-Saëns, and two Mozart *Sonatas;* in the second part, the Brahms pieces *op. 119,* the *Eighth Novelette* and *Prophetic Bird* of Schumann, *Dedication* of Schumann-Liszt and two pieces of Rachmaninoff, *Polka* and *Etude-Tableaux.*

MZ: By that time your grandmother must have been content with the results of her pedagogical work as well as your own achievements.

EV: Of course, she was. However, she could not attend that concert, as in all my performances in the senior grades, because of an injury she had had. So never in her life had she heard me in a solo recital.

MZ: From your grandmother, you turned to Heinrich Neuhaus, a prominent pedagogue and inspired poet of the piano. How did you take that transition from one pedagogue, especially since she was your close relation, to Neuhaus?

EV: There was no abrupt change for me, because almost throughout all my student years he kept an eye on my development. I played for him for the first time when I was nine. And whenever he came to Tbilisi, which was quite frequently, he always auditioned me.

MZ: When did you begin studying with Neuhaus regularly?

EV: Unfortunately, it did not last long. Beginning with 1961 for almost a year he was considered to be my official advisor in my preparation for the Tchaikovsky Competition of 1962.

MZ: Heinrich Neuhaus is acknowledged to be a great pedagogue of music, of Art in the broadest sense of the word. And it is undeniable. However, I am convinced that those pupils who brought him the greatest fame as a pedagogue, and you are one of them, will remain in the annals of piano performance particularly because they themselves knew how to take from their brilliant teacher exactly what they needed.

EV: It is a very correct idea. When I began to study with Neuhaus I was very well aware of how little I knew and could do.

Eliso Virsaladze.

"Heinrich Neuhaus was a man of rare artistry . . . he made music live from the first note to the last note."

But if I had attended his lessons oftener than I did and followed all his requirements, I would have hardly been able to participate in the Competition. One of the major points in performing is absolute confidence in whatever you are doing. When it vanishes you are not capable of saying anything. When I achieved something all by myself, I was eager to consult him. So I intuitively chose a ratio between his advice, most valuable, useful to me, and my own very personal perception of the composition due to which I felt confident on the stage. During my preparations for the competition, I preferred to perform more in concerts rather than to attend classes. I emphasize that my "strange" attitude to the lessons with Neuhaus was accounted for by the coming participation in the competition. When in 1964 I moved to Moscow and Heinrich Neuhaus passed away, I grieved because I was no longer able to carry on with my studies under his tutelage. What he had given me while I was preparing for the competition and those few lessons I got from him afterwards were invaluable experience for the rest of my life — not only in respect of the work at the compositions we had studied together, but in general in understanding piano art as a whole.

MZ: We know there are no universal pedagogues. But since Neuhaus had produced such different piano personalities from his class as Emil Gilels, Sviatoslav Richter, Yakov Zak, Stanislav Neuhaus, and you at last, it means that each found something in him, some important response. In what did you feel he was spiritually close to you as a musician? What "key" did he find to you in particular?

EV: Heinrich Neuhaus was a man of rare artistry. For me it was of utmost importance that, on the one hand, he made music live from the first to the last note, and on the other hand, he demanded an exceptionally strict approach to the text, to the comprehension of the composer's concept. That combination was most precious. He insisted that any emotion should be based on precise knowledge of the musical "tissue." I did appreciate that combination, but it was most difficult to realize it.

MZ: Did you have any other teachers besides your grandmother and Heinrich Neuhaus?

EV: In the post-graduate course my tutor was Yakov Zak. I consider myself lucky for the years of my studies under him. I used to show him all my new works.

MZ: It was the Tchaikovsky Competition that brought you the greatest fame. Will you please tell how you were prepared for it?

EV: I'd start with the fact that I was very much against taking part in it. I was appointed to play in the competition from the Tbilisi Conservatory. When I raised my protest in the rector's office, I was warned that if I flatly refused to play in the competition I would be made to attend all the lectures. I chose the lesser of two evils and began to prepare for the competition.

MZ: You mentioned that you were burdened by the attendance of the lectures in general subjects. What was it caused by? Did you feel aversion for certain subjects or was it your reluctance to fritter away your time on anything but music?

EV: Undoubtedly, the latter was the reason. I prepared with great conscientiousness every subject, but I really begrudged all the precious time for anything beyond music, beyond the piano. It was wearing for me and I preferred to take my exams without attending lectures.

MZ: I understand that some musicians, though today it is not typical, because of certain individual qualities do not want to participate in competitions. But what was the reason for your reluctance?

EV: I did not want to learn *The Thought* (*Dumka,*) of Tchaikovsky that I do not quite like . . . Now, I certainly think it was a great stroke of luck that I did play.

MZ: Please, remind us, Eliso, of your rivals in the competition of 1962.

EV: The first prize was awarded to Vladimir Ashkenazy and John Ogdon. American pianist Susan Star won the Silver Medal. I won the third prize.

MZ: You know, Eliso, I've noticed one curious peculiarity about the Tchaikovsky Competition. The stature of this Competition is valid with just one important reservation. Practically all the Soviet musicians honored with the prizes of the Tchaikovsky Competition remain up to the level of the prizes they have been awarded, if not grow higher than it while at the same time many of the winners who come from the West, with years, vanish from the stage or simply cannot stand the test of the time. For instance, Susan Star rose a step higher than you at the Competition. But her first tour in 1963 disappointed Muscovites, and nowadays she does not perform at all.

"*The first prize (Tchaikovsky Competition, 1962) was awarded to Ashkenazy and John Ogdon. American pianist Susan Star won second prize, while I took third prize.*"

"... in 1966 I performed at the Schumann Competition and was awarded the Gold Medal there. And I eagerly drew an end to my 'tournaments.'"

EV: I guess Susan Star's success in the Moscow Competition was to a great extent accounted for by the fact that she was seized with a kind of "sporting fever." And, at a competition, at times that has a magic effect on the public and on the jury. In her performance there was temperament, "high voltage" . . .

MZ: And your last competition was the Schumann Competition, wasn't it?

EV: Yes, in 1966 I performed at the Schumann Competition in Zwickau and was awarded the Gold Medal there. And I eagerly drew an end to my "tournaments." Incidentally, when I began teaching, in the performance of my official duty I had to sit on committees selecting students for competition. More than once it occurred to me that if I had known that "other side" of the medal, I would probably have lost any hope for success long before stepping out onto the stage. Now I know that there exists a whole "industry" of producing laureates. As the students say, some pedagogues are 100 per cent secure, while others are, in their opinion, "not reliable" in this respect.

MZ: You've already disclosed the secret of how you were "forced" to play in the first competition. But why did the second happen to be particularly the Schumann Competition?

EV: Schumann is one of the composers most congenial to me. I have always delighted in playing his compositions since I was a schoolgirl. Going to Zwickau was not so much a matter of playing in a competition as it was just playing Schumann. For me the three rounds were like three separate concerts. I must also say that I took part in the Schumann Competition several months after my mother had died. So it was not easy for me at all. She had known I was to play at the competition and I wanted to do so as if in her memory.

Eliso Virsaladze's confession of her passion for Schumann brings to mind the enthusiastic comments of the press on her interpretation of the compositions of the great German composer. One of the major authorities, Dr. Karl Gantzer, wrote after her tour in Germany in April, 1980: "Musical lucidness, profoundness of performance found reflection in the exceptionally expressive execution of both pieces of Schumann at the beginning of the concert. It should be specially noted how subtly were performed the often underestimated *Arabesques C major op. 18* and, first of all, how vividly was interpreted the *Sonata F sharp minor op. II,* so delicately telling of the inner struggle of the composer. In the musical declaration of love for 16-year-old Klara Wieck, Eliso Virsaladze expressed all the stages of pensive dreaminess and passionate appeal succeeding in it through subtlest tone and deliberation, making the keys sing. We haven't heard such Schumann in concert halls for a long time."

I reminded Eliso of that review to which she modestly remarked shrugging her shoulders: "Critics are apt to exaggerate everything."

As we dwelt on the competitions I asked the pianist to express her opinion on this point.

EV: Of course, there are many contradictions concerning competitions, and some of them are simply insoluble. For instance, many musicians don't want to play in competitions as they are simply not inclined to partake in sporting contests at the piano, but from the force of contemporary conditions for young performers to establish themselves on the concert stage, they are obliged to go through that "crucible." But there are also surprising things in competitions. You are quite right in saying that many western pianists, having shone at the Tchaikovsky Competition, did not stand the test of the time, but their performance at the competition sometimes proves to be an unforgettable occasion in itself.

MZ: Do you mean anyone in particular?

EV: I know that Van Cliburn does not perform almost at all at present. Yet, for me his performance in Moscow in 1958 is the brightest, the most unforgettable musical event of my life. I remember from beginning to end each of his appearances on the stage in all the three rounds, every phrase he played. I emphasize I mean the competition, but not his later visits.

MZ: Were you also disappointed in him later as were most of the Moscow musicians?

EV: Yes, very much indeed. Especially during his two last visits. It was not simply a disappointment. It is like you loved someone passionately, with all your heart, and then were disappointed in him. It is like the death of your idol.

MZ: How can you account for such a rare phenomenon, such a great talent, such marvelous, organic "blending" with the instrument, such harmonious, fascinatingly completed interpretation of all the composers he has played, and then that colorless impression

Eliso Virsaladze with her frequent ensemble partner, Natalia Gutman.

of his performance? Is that because the time advanced and Van Cliburn remained behind, on his youthful level?

EV: Might be, but I believe the main reason is insufficient love for music.

MZ: All your performances at competitions refer to the years of your youth. Which of the pianists inspired you, was probably your idol at the time?

EV: Like the majority of the pianists of my generation in my student years, I was under the magic charm of Emil Gilels and Sviatoslav Richter. I very well remember many of their performances, especially those of Richter, as if in the very name itself there was something legendary. I greatly appreciate Alexander Ioheles

Eliso Virsaladze with the author of this book, Dr. Mark Zilberquit.

who, incidentally, encouraged me a great deal at a certain period. I for one have never heard such an amazing performance of the *Thirteenth Sonata* of Beethoven as his. I also felt kindred with Maria Grinberg.

MZ: How would you define the moment, as applied to your own evolution, when you felt you'd crossed the boundary between a student's approach to a composition and the interpretation of a mature artist?

EV: Naturally, it is possible to answer this question only relatively as this "boundary" is relative in itself. Yet, I have such a criterion. It is connected with the classics. To attain in the classics the same freedom, naturalness of expression as in the romantics was the aim that became feasible only when I felt certain maturity.

Here is one of the latest examples. Recently in Milan there was held a cycle of concerts in which all the Beethoven *Sonatas* were executed by different pianists. I was to open that cycle, to perform the first four sonatas. I had played the *First* and the *Third* before, but I had to learn the *Second* and the *Fourth* specially for that concert. How much I gained as a musician while working at the Beethoven *Sonatas*!

MZ: Do you adhere to a certain edition when you work at the Beethoven *Sonatas*?

EV: I like to look at the edition of Artur Schnabel, because I highly appreciate him as a personality, as the most prominent in-

Eliso Virsaladze with her daughter Dariyadzhan.

Eliso Virsaladze with her daughter Dariyadzhan.

terpreter of Beethoven of his time, though it certainly does not mean that I strictly follow all his remarks, especially concerning the changes in tempos.

MZ: One of the debatable points in interpreting Beethoven is pedalling. It is especially demonstrative in comparing several editions of his sonatas. What's your opinion on the subject?

EV: I hold that pedalling shouldn't be marked in the score at all, the exception being the composer's pedal. Say, in the second movement of the *Third Concerto* Beethoven wrote infinite pedalling with all possible harmonic features. It is important for the performer to be able to grasp the composer's message and try to produce the desired tone.

MZ: What, apart from the composer's text as such, helps you to create your own conception of a new composition? Do you go into reading the composer's letters, or is musicological literature of any help at all?

EV: Sure, the more you know of the composition and its author the better. However, I never resort to the help of any accessory sources. The composer's text itself offers such an ample opportunity to meditate, to work.

MZ: What are your criteria in estimating a performance?

EV: I possess a happy peculiarity: I can listen to and be delighted

Eliso Virsaladze with her daughter Dariyadzhan.

with good music even if its performance is not quite up to the mark. As far as the estimation of the performance is concerned, I can say the following: when I am listening, for example, to one of the most outstanding performers of our time, Pollini, I involuntarily recall Heinrich Neuhaus. Both of them are characterized by a most careful attitude to the composer's text. But Neuhaus, remaining faithful to the letter, still made his performance exalted, inspired, creating the illusion of instantaneousness, while whenever I listen to Pollini I'm awfully bored. He plays "solely the text." This is just a case of my unprofessional judgment, because as a professional I should highly appreciate him for his craftsmanship. I was especially disappointed when after knowing him through his records I heard him on the stage in Moscow. There was absolutely no difference! But it shouldn't be so. A live performance is marvelous, it is valuable particularly for its spontaneity, for its being "live," but not recorded once and for all.

MZ: Were there any types of technique that were more difficult for you to master than others, and how did you overcome these hardships?

EV: Perhaps, because of the characteristics of my musical upbringing, and above all, psychologically, I have never experienced any particular technical difficulties. For instance, I had never played octaves until I was 18, that is, actually until I took up the Tchaikovsky *First Concerto*. I cannot boast of an absolutely flawless performance of octaves, but I coped with them quite well. In other words, as soon as I confronted some artistic tasks, the necessary technical problems were solved along with them simultaneously.

MZ: You perform rather little contemporary music. How do you account for that?

EV: It is really so. I must admit that I often play contemporary music because I have to do so, and I perform the music of the 18th and 19th centuries because I like to do so very much indeed. So usually when facing the alternative of whether to play some con-

". . . whenever I listen to Pollini I'm awfully bored. He plays solely the text."

310

temporary piece or to "touch" those numerous compositions of the past that I had not played before (and we pianists have an enormous repertory), as a rule, I opt for the latter. I begrudge the time.

MZ: Could you mention some repertory tendencies that you somehow do not approve of?

EV: Have you paid attention to the fact that Liszt's music has been heard rather rarely in recent years? It is considered to be almost bad taste to play some of his pieces. But I hold his music to be full of rare nobleness and I'll play it in the near future by all means.

MZ: By what other considerations are you guided in the choice of your repertory?

EV: As with other pianists, one of the most important principles for me is monographism. It is of utmost interest to play a monographic program because a performer searches not for some sole image of the composer but tries to reveal his versatility, the evolution of his style, though a mixed program is much easier to perceive.

MZ: I know your repertory to be vast enough, from Bach to contemporary Georgian composers. But still, couldn't you point out several composers whose compositions you perform most of all?

EV: Beginning with my school years and up to now in most of all my programs there may be found compositions of Mozart and Schumann. Certainly, it does not mean that I perform not enough of other composers. I play a great deal of Beethoven, Brahms, Chopin.

MZ: Listening to your concerts where the Mozart and the Beethoven *Sonatas* were played, I paid attention to the fact that in Mozart you did not follow the signs of repetition, while in Beethoven you repeated expositions whenever it was marked in the score (for instance, in the *First* and *Third Sonatas*). How do you explain it?

EV: I don't approach this matter from a strictly scientific, or to put it more accurately, formal point of view. I think that if there is a will, an assurance that in repetition you've got something new to say, something you did not manage when playing for the first time, it should be repeated. In this case formalism is irrelevant to my mind. For example, I used to repeat the Schumann *Symphoniques Etudes* just formally. But eventually I arrived at the conclusion that one could repeat only what he truly liked to.

"Have you paid attention to the fact that Liszt's music has been heard rather rarely in recent years? It is considered to be almost bad taste to play some of his pieces."

MZ: And what about the romantic sonatas, for instance, those of Chopin, Schumann?

EV: In the Chopin Sonatas, either in *B Flat minor* or in *B minor* I never make repetitions. In *F Sharp minor* and in *G minor Sonatas* of Schumann, I repeat the exposition.

MZ: As far as I know you have been performing a great deal of chamber music recently and most successfully at that. Did this fondness of chamber repertory begin in your school years or did it come about later?

EV: In chamber music I am attracted by the versatile opportunities to try oneself in a duet, a trio, a quartet, a quintet. I am ready to play chamber music interminably. And only because of my very intensive solo activities I can play chamber music only episodically, devote less time to it than is desirable. Unfortunately at school I played very little chamber music. I remember my first chamber piece was the Mozart *Quartet* which I played at about 12 or 13 years of age and a little later the Schumann *Quintet*. In fact, that is to what my performance of chamber music was limited in my school years.

MZ: With what musicians have you been playing in a chamber ensemble of late, and with whom do you find that ensemble most felicitous, or maybe even consider it to be a significant achievement of yours?

EV: I'll start with Natalia Gutman. The concert with her opened up for me the period of mature chamber music performance. My performances with Vladimir Spivakov are also memorable. In Leningrad a Sonata recital with the wonderful hornist Vitali Buyanovsky was also a success.

MZ: What about the nervousness you experience when on the stage? Perhaps you'll share your other feelings and sensations that arise at the piano when before the audience?

EV: I am very nervous at the concerts. I never know beforehand what I'll feel on the stage. Sometimes I feel absolutely free, emancipated. But it does not mean that this freedom, this ease has been

Eliso Virsaladze played with Vladimir Spivakov, Natalia Gutman and Vitali Buyanovsky, among others.

acquired for good. Already at the next concert I may be strained and not have the slightest idea of how to get rid of that constraint.

MZ: What hardships of a creative and personal character did you happen to encounter on your creative path?

EV: There have been hardships indeed. Probably it is even possible to speak of a certain crisis that occurred right after the Tchaikovsky Competition. I had the title of laureate, good press reviews, vast repertory. But when I began to perform after the competition a disappointment overtook both me and those who had a liking for me.

MZ: What was the matter?

EV: Obviously, psychologically I was not prepared to start an independent concert life. But there as well I found the way out of the crisis myself.

MZ: Can you remember any comic episodes from your concert life?

EV: There must have been a great many. Now, for instance, I remember the following one. Once I went on tour to Riga and suddenly it turned out that on the posters that were all round the city quite a different program from what I was going to play was printed. One Riga manager, a picturesque personality, was to blame for all that mess. And this is what he said to me: "Do you want to come to Riga on tour once again?" "Of course, I do. Why?" I answered. "Then you've got to play the Schumann *Kreisleriana* which is announced in the program." And I arrived at Riga right before the concert. So, hardly had I finished the first part of the concert when I rushed to the artists' room to "refresh" *Kreisleriana*. I realized I was doing something absolutely inconceivable (though this composition had been in my repertory).

MZ: And how long had you not played it before that?

EV: For about a year, probably a little bit less. However, there are pieces learned so thoroughly, so firmly stuck in your memory, in your fingers, that it does not take you long to bring them back to life.

MZ: How long have you been teaching?

EV: When a post-graduate student I was the assistant of Professor Lev Oborin, later Yakov Zak's assistant.

MZ: Do you carry on with your pedagogical activities?

EV: Yes, I am assistant professor of the Moscow Conservatory.

316

"Right after the Tchaikovsky Competition . . . psychologically I was not prepared to start an independent concert life."

However, my class is not large—one student and two post-graduate students. I cannot cope with many students as I perform a great deal (and consequently, go on tours) and certainly I am not spared innumerable family duties. Once when one of my students, a man of rare gift, died tragically, I made up my mind to give up teaching at all. But every time I tried I found I was "obliged" to do something for somebody, or I had promised, or I simply had to bring a student to the graduation from the Conservatory or even the post-graduate course.

MZ: Apart from solving some temporary problem, in what do you see the difficulties of teaching?

EV: The main thing is the constant feeling of great responsibility to the students. Therefore it is beyond my understanding how some pedagogues can have in their classes some 17 (!) pupils. I just don't consider them truly serious and honest pedagogues, no matter how many assistants they have. Each student requires special attention, just as every patient requires that the doctor be especially delicate with him.

MZ: What are your principles of selecting pedagogical repertory? Let's say, how independent are your students in choosing compositions?

EV: You've touched upon the question I gave much thought to, especially at the beginning of my pedagogical work. I still prefer to take a more difficult, at first, perhaps, a thankless way, that in the end leads to the main object. For example, I had a student who studied under my tutelage in the Conservatory and in the post-graduate course and became a very serious and interesting musician. I used to select a program for her so that she mostly played the pieces which, as it happened, did not come out well. She had a really hard time. Furthermore, in the first years she did not get excellent marks and only in the third year was she at last spoken of as an original musician.

"It is beyond my understanding how some pedagogues can have in their classes some 17(!) pupils."

MZ: It is a very interesting repertory principle—and apparently, at certain stages of development of every student it produces good results. But don't you think that irrespective of how much the teacher takes into consideration the individual peculiarities of his pupil (offering him compositions to "gratify him" or "rubbing him the wrong way" as in your example) there should be necessarily a clear repertory basis on which to build the pianistic development of each pupil?

"Nurturing a young musician is a very special field . . . perhaps more complicated than teaching . . . in a Conservatory. I know only two outstanding pedagogues of the kind." Shown below is Marina Young-Marshak, one of the special pedagogues, with Virsaladze's young student K. Dudnikov who, unfortunately, died at the age of 20.

EV: You are quite right. I believe there is a certain repertory foundation indispensable for every musician, whether he becomes a performer or a pedagogue. First of all it is the classics, that is, a certain number of Preludes and Fugues of Bach, Sonatas of Mozart and Beethoven (Haydn stands further because he is easier to execute). And the sooner the student starts mastering that "basis," the better for him. I don't mean to say that Schumann is easier to play. But it is quite a different matter. Classics are the basis.

MZ: How much importance do you attach to whether the pedagogue who is in charge of a student in the final stage of his development is a performing pianist or not?

EV: I don't exclude the possibility of being a brilliant tutor without being a concertizing performer. We do know such examples, though they are singular. Still, when a future performer is coached by a performer, even if the latter gives him fewer lessons than a pedagogue dealing only with teaching, it is of utmost importance for the student, the more so, as in this case I don't believe in quantity turning into quality. And maybe it is generally wrong to take exorbitant care of quite grown-up people.

MZ: Is the length of time of your lessons with your students restricted?

EV: Oh, no! Just the contrary! When I work with a student, especially after being absent, the lesson lasts for two and three hours—to the point of exhaustion.

MZ: If we ignore the natural professional inexperience of the student, what features in your pupil are important for you as a pedagogue?

EV: I attach great importance to the psychological compatibility of the pedagogue and the student. And one more consideration. I am always frightened and feel alienated from a student who enters my classroom with the sole intention of becoming a laureate of some International competition. When I am aware of this burden, it is very difficult for me to work with him.

MZ: Have you ever thought of teaching a pupil from the very beginning, or at least from the teen age period?

EV: Nurturing a young musician is a very special field of musical pedagogics, perhaps more complicated than teaching in a piano master class of the Conservatory. And it takes a very special talent. I don't know whether I possess it. It is enough to say that I know only two outstanding pedagogues of the kind. Marina Young-Marshak from the Gnesin ten-year school and the teacher of Central Music School Tamara Koloss.

MZ: How do you manage to combine the roles of an intensively concertizing pianist and a mother?

EV: Of course, it is not that simple. And as you may well understand I did not begin practicing more regularly before my daughter was born. A month and a half after she was born I played two solo concerts, one after another, in the Great Hall of the Moscow Conservatory.

MZ: Are you going to teach music to your daughter?

EV: By all means! Dariyadzhan, that's her name, already at the age of four shows certain musicality. She has wonderful hands.

MZ: Would you like to teach her yourself?

EV: That I have not decided yet. What I know for sure is that I'll do my best not to make music a burden to her. For me, practicing on the piano has never been work. That's my blessing. And I never cease being surprised that for such a pleasant way of spending my time I am being paid!

MZ: What is the main "spring" in the work of a performer?

EV: It often happens that you work at a piece, overcome certain hardships, perform it at last, and feel content, satisfied by your performance. Then after a year or two elapse, you get back to that composition and suddenly realize that earlier you played it badly. And so on. In that quest, in your eternal discontent with yourself and with the final result of your work is the driving force of your craft. We performers live from concert to concert. Stepping out onto the stage and fighting ourselves, our nervousness, we often live through many uneasy moments. But those instances, and at times whole concerts, when one manages to dispose of everything else but the process of truly creating at the piano, make up for everything. I remember these surprising sensations of content with one's own performance when one tells oneself: it is all worth it, even if it takes ever so much nerve and strength—it is worth it!

Gregory Sokolov

Gregory Sokolov was born April 18, 1950, in Leningrad. His life is connected with that city where he is now the leading pianist. His parents did not have any professional ties to music. However, his father, Lipman Girshevich Sokolov, from whom the future pianist must have inherited his musicality, learned to play the violin.

Regular study of music began when Gregory Sokolov was five years old, and at seven years of age he entered the School for Gifted Children, part of the Leningrad Conservatory. There, during all his 11 years of studies, his tutor was Leah Zelikhman. After leaving school, Sokolov continued with his studies in the Leningrad Conservatory under the tutelage of professor Moisey Khalfin. But Gregory Sokolov entered the Conservatory having already won world fame. In his ninth grade at school he became the "Gold" laureate of the Tchaikovsky Competition (1966).

Awarding the highest prize of such a prestigious competition to a 16-year-old pianist was at first considered by some critics and musicians perplexing. However, the years following the Competition showed that the jury headed by Emil Gilels had made no mistake in their judgment. All who heard Sokolov at that time were startled by the profoundness of his interpretation. "He possesses brilliant finger and chord technique, he easily wields the piano, so easily that he performs prestissimo of the last movement (of the Saint-Saëns *Concerto No. 2*) with truly refined lightness," wrote Harold Schonberg in the *New York Times*. "It was a startling performance. Doubtless we are going to hear much more about this young talented pianist. . ."

Gregory Sokolov

The words of the leading American critic proved prophetic. Today Gregory Sokolov is one of the foremost Soviet musicians. The profundity of his approach to a musical composition, the vastness of his repertory including compositions from Bach to Schoenberg, the earnestness and originality of his performing intentions, and the precision of their realization permit one to conclude that in the near future he is due to take his place among the most prominent performers of our time.

The pianist combines concertizing with pedagogics, being assistant professor of the Leningrad Conservatory; though, as he himself admits, teaching is burdensome at times. It may be because of his reluctance to be distracted by anything from performance which comprises the essence of his life.

Gregory Sokolov's life as a touring soloist is quite overcrowded. He tours a great deal in both his motherland and abroad. Four times he toured the USA (1969, 1971, 1975, 1979). Sokolov's art is held in the highest esteem in European countries.

★ ★ ★

I met Gregory Sokolov when he was on tour in the capital. We talked in a Hotel Moscow suite in the intervals between his performances and rehearsals.

The pianist's concerts in Moscow are always an important event in the musical life of the city. In Moscow, as in his native Leningrad, he has his own audience, constantly increasing but mainly consisting of those listeners who have been watching his creative development for 15 years; that is, since as 16-year-old Grisha Sokolov, an unknown in Moscow, he outstripped many an eminent favorite, and became the number one sensation, the "gold" at the Tchaikovsky Competition.

Talking with Gregory Sokolov, I often thought that I felt a kind of strain unusual for interviews of this sort. Later I realized the reason for it: Sokolov, as probably no other of his colleagues with whom I have spoken, is so concentrated in his speech, striving for utmost accuracy in the account of his thoughts and ideas. During all the hours of our discussions I did not hear him utter a single remark just by chance, a single word concerning the subject of our talk—piano performance, pedagogics, problems of music. In

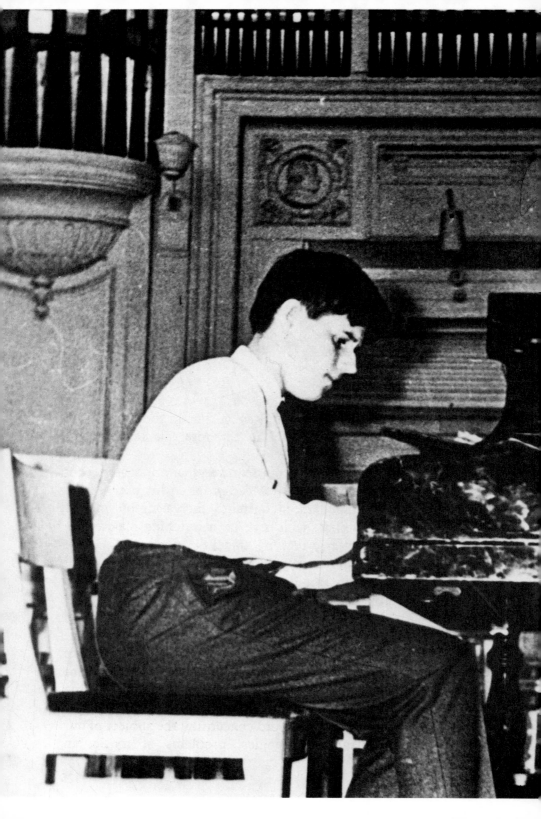

everything his extraordinary exactness and seriousness in respect to his pursuit, to Art on the whole is obvious.

Beginning our discussion, I asked Gregory Sokolov to tell of his evolution, from his point of view, after the victory in the Tchaikovsky Competition.

GS: Of course, in the years that have elapsed since my success in the Tchaikovsky Competition, almost half of my life, a great deal has changed for me as a performer, and I myself must have also changed greatly. However, I'm not going to renounce what has been done before. I find it absurd when people say that at 16 one was *one* musician and then that he "grows" into something different.

MZ: In other words, you consider the victory at the competition to be not so much the achievement of a student, as the commencement of your artistic career, don't you?

GS: The concerts I gave right after the competition already included such compositions as the Beethoven *28th Sonata,* Schubert's *A-major Sonata, The Wanderer, the B minor Sonata* of Chopin.

MZ: As far as I know, both the Soviet and foreign press highly appreciated your performances of the post-competition period. But perhaps your tender age and boyish looks really "hypnotized" some of the critics and affected their estimation.

GS: Critics are apt to stick to certain clichés and labels, for instance, "age" clichés, i.e., in their estimation that is their pseudobiographical approach. If the musician is young, it means that his performance is fresh and spontaneous; if the musician is no longer so young his interpretation is marked with wisdom and maturity. It is absolutely wrong. A true musician can and must be mature at a very early age.

MZ: The problem of the estimation of creative performance by critics is quite involved. And we'll certainly turn to it. But now I'd like to touch upon another question. Your study of music began when you were five, and at 16 you embarked upon the career of a performer. It would be most interesting to know of the main landmarks of that considerably short route, that is of the years when you were developing as a pianist.

Grisha Sokolov
performing at a
school concert.

GS: The beginning was quite ordinary: my parents bought a piano, and from that moment I could not think of anything else but becoming a pianist. My teacher, Leah Ilyinichna Zelikhman, a marvelous pedagogue, managed to arrange our studies in such a way that everything went smoothly and very naturally for me.

MZ: Your first teacher Leah Zelikhman, as well as your Conservatory professor Moisey Khalfin, were both former pupils of professor S. Savshinsky, a famous methodologist. To what extent can you describe a certain originality of your school teacher's method?

GS: I guess Leah Zelikhman did not have any particular "method" in the narrow sense of the word. It would be more correct to speak of something much more elaborate than a schematic method. She simply knew how to find a correct approach to a pupil in every individual case. She had no dogmas. For example, she wouldn't force her pupils to play scales; neither would she forbid them to do so. She used to give the example that some of the great pianists did play scales, but others did not. She held that it was possible to solve the same technical problems not necessarily on scales, but on actual works. Since the very first years there was a most earnest attitude to studies.

MZ: It must have also showed in your zealous studies?

GS: Certainly. Approximately in the fifth grade, that is by the age of 12, I was practicing for some five or six hours a day.

MZ: On what repertory was your pianistic development built? Was it given to you gradually or did Zelikhman resort to "leaps", that is, offered you compositions much more difficult than your level allowed for?

GS: I was taught a versatile repertory. I played a great deal of Bach whom I've appreciated since childhood, compositions of Viennese classics, Chopin and others.

MZ: It is common knowledge that artistic maturity is not reduced merely to a brilliant command of the instrument. This definition involves broad-mindedness, the ability to see and perceive what is going on beyond the immediate boundaries of one's profession, doesn't it? Evidently, such things were also taken care of in the process of your development.

GS: Surely there shouldn't be any such thing as limiting the development of a pianist exclusively to the acquisition of pianistic skills. It should be a person with an understanding of art in the

Grisha Sokolov not long before his performance in the Tchaikovsky Competition.

broad sense of the word, an understanding of the correlation between the intertwining arts. I for one have been fond of literature and painting since my school years.

MZ: Which of the great pianists inspired you in your years of studies?

GS: I began to frequent the Philharmonic Society very early. Later I also acquainted myself with the art of the great masters through records. As a result I acquired my own favorites. Of those whom I heard on the stage I'd like to name first of all Emil Gilels. Judging by the records, it was Rachmaninoff, Sofronitsky, Gould, Solomon, Lipatti. As to esthetics, I feel most close to Anton Rubinstein.

Gregory Sokolov with his teacher Leah Zelikhman.

MZ: Do you mean his enlightenment conceptions?

GS: Both as to enlightenment and performance, as we can envision them on the grounds of different reminiscences.

MZ: When did your first performance take place, in particular, your philharmonic debut?

GS: I participated in concerts, including those in the Philharmonic Society, beginning with the first year of my studies. And when I was 12, my first solo concert was held at our school. The program .there included compositions of Bach, Beethoven, Schumann, Chopin, Mendelssohn, Rachmaninoff, Scriabin, Liszt, Debussy, Shostakovich. At 14 years of age, I took part in the audition for the Bach Competition and a year later played at the All-Russia and All-Union Contests. After I scored the victory there, I began to appear in my own concerts in the Philharmonic Society.

MZ: We know laureates of two, three and even five Internationals. As for you, having scored victory at such an early age you never participated in competitions again. What's the reason for that?

GS: To my mind, competitions today have acquired a different meaning from what they were meant to. What's the main purpose of a performance competition? Today when there are so many young performers, a competition presents the only opportunity for them to gain the right to step onto the professional stage. But performances in competitions do not directly pertain to the profession of a pianist. All kinds of fuss do nothing but harm to art. Therefore I cannot understand the people who, having acquired the opportunity to take up the cause they wanted to devote their life to, suddenly go to some place again to compete with someone. It turns into something sporting. To win, to compete, to emulate – either it is not quite art, or some special sporting kind of art. I believe a musician ought to go through a competition to gain the opportunity to perform. But as soon as he has made his mark with the public, and the victory is won, what else has he to do with competitions? The competition has done its part and it is high time he got down to "business."

MZ: What you've just said about competitions seems to me one of the most correct and sensible considerations to this effect. The point is that for the performer participating in a competition, if he is a truly mature creative personality, it is far from easy to squeeze himself into the "bed of Procrustes" of certain limited terms of a

competition program. You yourself, after your victory, rid yourself of the necessity to play in a competition again, and thus could choose the programs that were more suited to your interests and creative aspirations, couldn't you?

GS: Quite right.

MZ: By the way, what are your considerations in choosing a program?

GS: It is very difficult to make up a program. It becomes different every time, sometimes even unexpected.

MZ: What compositions do you think unsuitable to combine in one program?

GS: I'll confine myself to one example. I would hardly play in one concert the *Second* and *Third Concertos* of Rachmaninoff. But in general, I don't have any set scheme of a program make-up. Usually a program is compiled gradually. Parts of it can be altered.

MZ: Quite recently I've heard you perform the Beethoven *Seventeenth Sonata* (in a television recording). Your interpretation is very unusual; for instance, the second and the third movements sounded much slower, didn't they?

GS: I know from the reviews that I perform the *Seventeenth Sonata* somewhat untraditionally. But this "unusualness" does not result from my artificially inventing something; it is dictated by my inner need. As for the tempo, after all, it is only a means of expression.

Obviously, that very special "hearing" of many pieces of the piano literature by Gregory Sokolov is caused by his need for a more profound penetration into very familiar compositions, for a new understanding of them in compliance with his attitude. However, it would be erroneous to put it down to the pianist's desire for "originality." That's just what is absolutely alien to him! And of course the considerably slow execution of certain episodes by Sokolov is not connected with any virtuoso hurdles that have actually never existed for him. Some meticulous critic has counted

Gregory Sokolov playing at the Tchaikovsky Competition. This victory brought him world fame.

that Maurizio Pollini plays the Chopin *24 Preludes* within 36 minutes and Gregory Sokolov within 48. It is quite a convincing comparison. But at the same time, that very critic points out that: "when Gregory Sokolov was playing the Chopin *Etudes,* the virtuoso level of the performer seemed just breathtaking."

Our talk with the artist continued.

GS: I'd like to add how, unexpectedly at times, a composition enters one's repertory. Once I was very reluctant to play the Beethoven *Seventeenth Sonata,* probably because of its popularity. It so happened that I began to work at it with my student at the Conservatory (he chose it on his own initiative). And when I "got in touch" with that composition, I realized that it sounded different to me from the way it had previously, how I had used to hear it. And I felt an urgent need to learn it myself.

MZ: Can you describe your perception of the music of the *Seventeenth Sonata,* and the difference between your treatment of it and the generally accepted one?

GS: It seems to me more dramatic, even tragic. In general, I hold that if the pianist has aroused puzzlement and questions by his interpretation, all subsequent commentaries are of no avail. Do you think it possible to describe the process of performance or even the way you comprehend this or that composition? Is it possible to put into words the music or our intuitive sensations, without distorting their meaning?

MZ: I can't agree with you. How is the teaching of performance carried out? Is it that you explain to your students your requirements only by resorting to the instrument? In that case, not offering any verbal explanation, you risk rearing only your own kind, imitations of yourself, because, being capable young people, they'll imitate you unwittingly, whether they want to or not.

GS: Truly talented students will never imitate. But, undoubtedly, teaching is not only showing how; but talks with the pupils either deal with more general things, or are connected with the semantics of the piece. In offering the student a certain verbal characteristic of the musical image, we thrust our own interpretation upon him. It is important to arouse his fantasy, imagination and independence rather than to palm off your own solution.

MZ: We've just touched upon another very important problem of the art of musical interpretation — the plurality of musical images

Gregory Sokolov receives the highest award of the Tchaikovsky Competition from the hands of the Head of the Organization Committee, composer Tikhon Khrennikov.

Gregory Sokolov and Emil Gilels. When Sokolov speaks of the eminent pianist most congenial to him he names Emil Gilels first. In his turn Gilels holds Sokolov to be the most interesting and profound pianist of the young generation.

and the performer's attitude to the composer's text. Many authoritative musicians made it clear that they adhered to the composer's text absolutely. Well, it is an indubitable consideration, but many concrete examples suggest how relative it is. Let's regard, for instance, such point as the markings for repetition in compositions of Bach, Viennese classics composers , romanticists. Is it obligatory to follow them? Many more such examples can be found. In this connection there arises the question of the limits for keeping strictly to the composer's instructions.

The solemn welcome to the winner of the Competition in his native Leningrad. Gregory Sokolov with his teachers (from right to left): Leah Zelikhman and Professor Moisey Khalfin (her husband).

GS: It is an important problem indeed. I am against servile submission to the text. The greatness of the composer's personality and inspiration, the constant development and mobility of music should not be reduced to the instructions in the text. One should clearly realize the relativeness of the signs that cannot express all the many meanings. One should love what is created and do his utmost to grasp it, with the help of the markings of the text, and realize what is beyond expressing by mere signs; and still "run it through" himself, through his individuality and his own new interpretation.

And is the text itself unambiguous? Even when reading the manuscript, different opinions and different treatments of the text may be formed. And what about the changes brought into the text by composers themselves?

MZ: Of course, we can recall different variants in the pieces by Chopin who made changes in the galley proof, or Scriabin who, according to the evidence of witnesses, played his own compositions in concerts often deviating from the text that he himself adjusted . . .

GS: As to repetitions, I like them and see deep sense and ample dramatic opportunities in them. But formal repetitions are utterly unacceptable to me—either of whole parts or separate notes (incidentally, that is just what often happens with students).

MZ: I absolutely agree with you. In such cases I don't take it for a repetition of one and the same idea (and usually put it to my students that way) but as continuation of its development.

GS: Yes, of course. But as far as repetitions are concerned, I don't have any dogmas either. For instance, I repeat the expositions in the Chopin *Sonatas*. I play the Bach *Goldberg Variations* with all the repetitions, but in the Bach *Second Partita* (*C minor*) I don't repeat all of them, and it was recorded that way in 1975. True, it was rather long ago and I am not quite sure how I'd handle it now; maybe I'd do the same, maybe not.

In general, dogmas in art are most harmful.

It is absolutely wrong to suppose that having allegedly followed all the instructions of the text, you prove faithful to the composer's cóncept. By dogmatically and blindly following the markings in the text you may stray away from the composer and his concept, from the life of the piece, its eternal changeability and plurality of its meaning.

MZ: But where is the boundary between the performer's permitted freedom and illicit arbitrariness? What is the means to help a young performer to establish that boundary?

GS: As a rule, there are attempts to establish that boundary from outside as a system of outward restrictions. But I am of the opinion that only honesty, the honesty of an artist will prevent crossing that boundary beyond which charlatanism begins.

MZ: Perhaps you'll find it possible to point to more objective criteria in this respect. Say, the notation of compositions in Bach's time when the dynamics, articulation and other instructions were almost non-existent, offers the performer much more freedom than when interpreting Beethoven's *Sonatas* as, on many occasions, he scrupulously defined the desired character of performance.

GS: Yes, the widespread opinion is that Bach allegedly offers broader possibilities for dynamics, for example, variation in a performer's reading. But I wouldn't like to oppose one composer to the other, perhaps because I generally prefer not to interfere with the inexplicable, mainly intuitive process of the approach to a composition. In any case I am against the assumption that turning to Beethoven, for example, the performer knows beforehand that there are things that are beyond his power to alter even if the incentive is quite weighty. If one has "lived through" the piece, tested it many times and feels that it is essential that something be changed, I hold the performer is entitled to do so, right up to the orthography.

MZ: I guess the majority of pianists of the older generation wouldn't share your somewhat "nihilistic" viewpoint. There still exists the notion of "style" in music, and no matter how relative the definitions, such as "baroque," "classicism," "romanticism" might be, they do exist.

GS: I don't think that music should be divided into "romantic" and "classical." I hold all these subdivisions to have been invented for the convenience of systematizing our knowledge. And really, isn't Bach's music romantic? Isn't Chopin a classic? It is another matter that the composer's language is different. But even at one and the same time, there exist personalities with different creative views. It all depends on the inner world of the composer.

MZ: Will you give examples of your correcting the orthography of the composer's text at your own discretion?

Chicago Tribune *of January 20, 1975 in the article* **Music
Coming from the Soul** *wrote about that particularly concentrated state of Sokolov when onstage: ". . .There is in
his manner on the stage something arousing bewilderment
. . .It seems that Sokolov tries not to notice the presence of
the live audience. At times there is formed an impression
that playing in public is not so much a joyful opportunity as
a solemn duty, responsibility."*

GS: For instance, I somewhat alter the build-up in the *First Sonata* of Scriabin.

MZ: It is common knowledge that in the recapitulation, Beethoven often changes the subjects of the main and secondary parts only for the reason that the range of the pianos at that time did not allow making it in the given key exactly the same as in exposition. How do you think it should be played: as it is written by Beethoven or by employing the opportunities offered by contemporary pianos?

GS: I hold both variants equally right. If you play as it is written in the score, you create an atmosphere of sound limits more typical of the instrument of that time. On the other hand, changing the text and repeating the recapitulation exactly, you'd do precisely what Beethoven would have done, had he had the opportunity. He was the one to react most swiftly to the widening range of the instrument.

MZ: What editions do you prefer to work with when performing the compositions of Bach and Beethoven?

GS: I acknowledge only the Urtext. It is awfully annoying when it is difficult to make out where whose marks are. In general, the problem of Urtext is of utmost importance. But there is no such thing as the performance of the Urtext because any performance is a kind of edition. It is no use criticizing the so-called performers' "editions" in favor of the Urtext. These are two different, in fact incomparable things. Urtext is meant for the understanding of the composer's message, his intentions; it is meant for the performer to "live through it." The performers' edition is one of the means to try to fix the interpretation to a certain extent.

MZ: What's your attitude to the existing opinion even among eminent pianists that transcription lies beyond the boundaries of the piano repertory?

GS: I do not share it by any means. On the contrary, I play not only the Bach organ choral preludes in my own arrangement, but also transcriptions of vocal compositions—for instance, the Third five-part *Motet of Palestrina* from *The Song of Songs*. In general I think no artificial hurdles should be created in music. There should not be any rules invented that would later be in the way. The attitude to everything a pianist does in music ought to be natural.

Gregory Sokolov's hands.

Gregory Sokolov during his first American tour.

". . . to be natural." How important is the idea formulated by Gregory Sokolov for himself as a performer?

Different features have been noted in the performance of the pianist. For example, Sokolov's playing made a great impression by its virtuoso scope, orchestral character of the tone. "*Never Rur Zeitung* wrote in 1977: "The three parts from the Stravinsky ballet *Petruschka* are the pieces that make even experienced pianists pale at one glance at the score. Sokolov performed that composition most difficult in the technical sense in such a breathtaking tempo and so confidently that his hands seemed nothing but a sheer white shadow. And the tone was such that you asked yourself if an orchestra could reveal to the listeners more nuances and versatility of inner voices and accompaniment than did Sokolov."

Other features of Sokolov, the performer, were also pointed to. But evidently the listeners are most particularly delighted with the naturalness of his performing manner, which as we know now is part of his artistic credo. That naturalness finds reflection in the interpretation of most diverse composers. For instance, it helps Sokolov to find his own key to Chopin's creations.

"In Chopin he can communicate to the audience much more than others," wrote one of the Bonn critics, "because he does not embellish anything in his repressed, fervent execution, but expresses himself with startling naturalness."

It should be said that critics in general highly appreciate Sokolov's art. When I drew his attention to this fact, the pianist reverted to the problem of judging a performer by the critics.

GS: With due respect for the work and art of criticism I can't help noting that as a rule it suffers from some chronic diseases.

MZ: You have already mentioned one cliché of contemporary criticism at the beginning of our talk.

GS: Unfortunately, it is not the only one. I could name at least two more. It is the biographical approach to the creations of the composer, that is, the direct transfer of the events of the composer's life into the character of the music created at that time and, finally, one more cliché: if the pianist plays thoroughly, flawlessly it is described as a performer of the alleged "classical kind"; but if he smudges or plays slovenly, it is the work of an allegedly "romantic" pianist. What nonsense! A musician can play very neatly and be a poet. What really matters is if these flaws "stick out" or not.

MZ: You've pointed to the shortcomings of, as I would put it, primitive criticism, while to my mind there are more serious deficiencies in the reports of some of our critics. At one time Rachmaninoff said with irony that only music critics could understand a new musical composition on its first hearing and only for the reason that they simply had to write about it. It is one of the most widely spread diseases of criticism—the pronouncement of a judgment (which, when published, becomes a document of a kind, at times denunciatory at that), pronouncement of a sentence after the first hearing of the performance. True, sometimes the critic falls victim to the circumstances: the pianist arrives in the city, gives one concert and the critics are expected to respond. But to what extent are generalizations justified in this case? That's the question.

Gregory Sokolov

GS: That's a question and a serious one at that—the question of the right to judge. My point of view is as follows: if I feel the performer is dishonest in respect to art, if I fail to believe him, if in his interpretation there are many superficial effects intended for making a success, I am ready to estimate him judging by one performance only. But if I see that he is an honest musician, sincere in his intentions, who has lived through the music he performs, one should be most careful in his judgment and preferably not on the grounds of one program only.

MZ: Since we have gone into the matter of music criticism at such length, what else seems unsatisfactory to you in this respect?

GS: I find it unacceptable to evaluate a performer from the standpoint of the tastes of a certain critic or a certain individual.

MZ: Apparently it is inevitable. It is a person, an individual with his own scale of values, his own taste, who pronounces his judgment. So it is hardly possible to speak of objectivity.

GS: It is not a matter of objectivity—there should be broadmindedness in the approach. And if a critic or a pedagogue cannot say: "It is not exactly my cup of tea, but it is good," it means that such a pedagogue would nurture pupils in his own image, and such a critic would estimate all performers with one "yardstick" of his views. I believe the tasks of a critic and a pedagogue should coincide in some major points: a performer should be criticized in such a way that it would help him to get rid of whatever hampers the realization of his idea, assuming the idea is of significance.

MZ: You've quite rightfully pointed to the analogy of the estimation of a performance by a critic and a pedagogue. A teacher must be a really thoughtful critic of his pupil, a critic whose advice and remarks help the young musician to reveal his talent more vividly. Being a pedagogue, you are sure to know that the potentials of a student are a far cry from his achievements.

GS: That is why I am usually wary of speaking of a student's talent. There are so many musicians who have left behind them nothing but a lot of talk about their talent! For example, a student plays badly in his first year, but he is said to be "very talented." Good. Two years later, he plays no better, but his wonderful talent is still spoken of. So I wonder what will come of that "talented" student in the end. If he is good at playing, I am ready to speak of his talent; if not, apparently, it is possible to speak only of his innate

Gregory Sokolov at the rehearsal with conductor Dmitry Kitayenko.

capabilities. He may possess a phenomenal ear for music, a marvelous memory, many other brilliant abilities. But I wouldn't call it talent; it is a person with a facility for learning. And it is quite a different matter when a person plays the piano well and interestingly, a thinking person, an artist.

MZ: You are teaching at the Conservatory, so you deal with the pianistic development of a student in the highest stage. What in your opinion are the demands of pedagogics in the initial stage?

GS: I can't take the liberty of formulating it. I think children's musical development is of a different kind. There are children's medical specialists and there are children's music teachers, the specificity of whose activities does not arouse any doubts. It is most difficult to work with children. Right before the eyes of the pedagogue the pupil's hands are growing, his organism is being formed. We, the Conservatory teachers, face a student about whose hands it is practically impossible to do anything, or it is dangerous to attempt anyway. In fact, the technical upbringing occurs at school. At least that's the way it should be. And I feel deep respect for children's pedagogues, but I'm no expert in it myself. I think only that children ought not to be forced to study.

MZ: I can't agree with you. It is common knowledge that there are children with brilliant professional abilities, but lazy and undisciplined, which is not that unnatural for their age. And if they are not "gripped in a vise" they'll just lose the time and a professional career will become impossible for them. As a matter of fact, there are many examples to prove my point. No one knows how the fate of Lazar Berman and Igor Oistrakh as performers would have turned out had their parents not forced them to study music. Another thing should be taken into consideration: for a child who loves music it may be a treat to play some pieces on the instrument, but children are usually reluctant to work thoroughly at their performance to bring it to the extent of perfection, as it bores them quickly. Possibly you belonged to those rare exceptions for whom a serious artistic attitude to practicing has been typical since early childhood. That is why you express such a "liberal" point of view.

GS: But still, at a certain age there should be a serious, professional attitude towards studies; otherwise nothing will come of it.

MZ: How do you advise your students to study virtuoso pieces—in a slow tempo or in the tempo close to the required one?

GS: There is a school of thought which believes that if a virtuoso piece is studied in a slow tempo for a long time, it will come out well in the end. I doubt it. One can work at a virtuoso piece in the tempo close to the real one. But I put forward this idea not as the only possible and correct one. My six-year pedagogical experience does not permit me to make any all-embracing generalizations. I must admit I don't find it possible to give any universal recipes. It may be good for one but harmful for another. The student himself must feel how he can achieve something. If he fails to learn it in the five years of the Conservatory, he'll prove helpless in the future.

MZ: Do you recommend some compositions to your students, or are they in the position to choose their repertory themselves?

Gregory Sokolov during his talk with Dr. Mark A. Zilberquit.

GS: My students, as a rule, choose their programs to their liking. The things we ought to study in the Conservatory can be studied in fact just as well in any repertory.

MZ: What are your considerations concerning fingering?

GS: I won't sound original if I say that the choice of fingering should be first of all prompted by the message latent in the composition, even if it happens to be counter to the seeming simplicity and convenience. But it is not the point I'd like to emphasize. I am sure that a true musician should have all the components, and fingering in particular, interconnected. By the way, it is exactly this lack of interconnection in the command of different elements in playing the piano that is one of the greatest troubles with students.

MZ: On the whole I agree with you. When one hears a complete original performance, it is difficult to break it up into separate components. But for the sake of methods, it can be justified or even indispensable at times. For instance, we often say that a student lacks certain culture of tone; or listening to several students of one pedagogue, we realize that he pays much attention to the beauty and intelligence of tone production.

MZ: Of course, a gifted student needs only guidance in the correct direction, just prompting, drawing his attention to something, but not coaching. After all, not everything can be taught.

GS: Yes, I do believe that no matter how comprehensive the teacher's help to the student may be, the essential, which is what makes him an individual, he has to grasp for himself. Even in the sense of technique, no matter how meticulously he is shown the most rational devices, how thoroughly his technical development is dealt with, his truly virtuoso achievements are possible only because of his own discoveries, the sensations he finds for himself.

MZ: Have you a large class?

GS: I have four students. But if we speak of pedagogics, I rather prefer a type of teaching such as "Meisterklasse." I mean lesson-consultations with mature young musicians, an exchange of opinions, so to say. On the whole, my attitude to my pedagogical activities is rather contradictory. It takes too much strength and nerve. And what matters most is the time.

MZ: Does it mean that you are inclined to devote yourself solely to performance?

GS: In general, yes. It is no accident that most concertizing performers do not deal with teaching.

MZ: How is your ordinary working day scheduled?

GS: I don't follow any rigid regimen. Usually I practice for some six hours in the course of the day, but with intervals. I prefer to practice twice—in the morning and in the evening.

MZ: How early do you begin working?

GS: I can get up very early, but if you'd like to know whether I am an early riser or prefer working in the evening, I'd rather choose the latter.

MZ: Do you warm up before you start practicing?

GS: No.

MZ: How quickly do you learn a composition?

GS: It is difficult to give a simple answer. It all depends on the composition itself. And what do you mean by "learn"? The work at the piece may begin before it is learned with your hands. A piece should be learned as long as is necessary; it must grow naturally. In general I hate fussing. But it has happened that I've had to learn a composition in a very short time (that's the way it was before the competition).

MZ: Commencing your work on a piece, do you strive to memorize it as soon as possible, or do you prefer it to "sink" into your memory naturally, all by itself?

GS: As a rule, I don't learn a composition purposely. But a natural memorization does not mean being passive.

MZ: If you are going to have a concert, do you practice only the compositions you are supposed to perform?

GS: It depends. As a rule, I do my best to look through the entire program.

MZ: Do you remember any especially memorable concerts, any highlights of your career?

GS: Concerts are like children—they are all dear to you. The point is that every performance takes a piece of your life.

MZ: To what extent do you allow yourself to yield to some unexpected mood, to change the preconceived plan of the performance in the course of the concert?

GS: I think changes right on the stage are possible, but it is essential that they match the entire construction, the general concept of the performance.

MZ: In your opinion what are the difficulties of the profession of a pianist and what specific problems did you happen to encounter in your career?

GS: In art everything is difficult. It is a famous truth—in general it is easy to play the piano, but to play well is really difficult. I don't know if there are any easy professions at all. If one treats his profession in earnest, it cannot and should not be easy.

The last phrase of Gregory Sokolov that concluded our discussion involuntarily reminded me of the lines from two reviews of his

"I find it unacceptable to evaluate a performer from the standpoint of the tastes of a certain critic . . ."

performances. One of them is from an authoritative West German newspaper, *Never Rur Zeitung* which wrote: "Sokolov suffers and struggles literally for every note." The second review is from a modest bulletin published by old Leningrad actors who have given all their life to art and who are now living in the Home of the Veterans of the Stage. The short article was entitled, "For the Forthcoming Concert of Gregory Sokolov."

"He performed for us on the 29th of September, 1972. A memorable day! The artist shared his talent with us, lavished on us his strength and youth. And now he'll be here again. And again there is anticipation, excitement . . . We are looking forward to hearing the enchanting sounds of Chopin, and inimitable Scriabin will sound again. We are expecting you, dear magician."

And as such a magician of the piano, Gregory Sokolov remains in the memory of most listeners who have had the opportunity to become familiar with his art.

Sviatoslav Richter

Sviatoslav Richter's native town of Zhitomir is situated in the South of Russia. He was born there on March 20, 1915, in the family of the organist Theophile Richter. The future pianist spent his childhood and adolescence in Odessa where the family moved soon after his birth and where his father began teaching in the Odessa Conservatory.

Odessa was going through the period of its "Renaissance" at the time. Among the young people of Richter's age whose musical education began in Odessa were David Oistrakh, Emil Gilels and others famous today in the world of musical performance. However, the commencement of Sviatoslav Richter's path in music is absolutely unlike the mighty take-offs of these musicians. He had his first lessons from his father, but from the age of nine to ten he was actually deprived of any instruction and was left entirely to his own devices in his musical studies.

Without following every step of the traditional piano school, Richter nevertheless completely plunged into the world of music. He hungrily played at sight almost all the accessible compositions of opera and instrumental literature, and improvised and composed music himself. The circle of his artistic interests at that time was amazingly diversified. Simultaneously with music Richter tried his hand at literature and painting (incidentally, he has retained his passion for painting throughout his life). The musical atmosphere in Odessa of the 1920-30's was very "nourishing" and that must have had a certain influence on his development as a musician.

The growth of Richter as a pianist up to 1937 was quite peculiar. He practiced irregularly, combining his own intensive study of the instrument with work at the Philharmonic Society and the Opera Theatre.

Sviatoslav Richter.

Richter's debut took place in 1934 in the Odessa House of Engineers. The nineteen year-old musician performed a program of utmost difficulty and for the first time proclaimed himself a soloist (for many of those who knew him only as a brilliant accompanist it was a surprise).

In 1937 Richter moved to Moscow and entered the Conservatory into the class of Professor Heinrich Neuhaus. The teacher and the pupil proved to be strikingly kindred souls, and it was Professor Neuhaus who was the first to speak of Richter as a pianist of genius. He managed to find the correct approach to his unique pupil. Later Neuhaus liked to repeat that he had not taught Richter anything, but on the contrary had learned from him.

Even Sviatoslav Richter's student performances took place in overcrowded houses. He became the idol of the Moscow public. The programs were learned nearly instantaneously. In those years of his performance, along with his characteristic spontaneity and mighty temperament, there appeared more naturalness and ingenuousness of expression, making him a startlingly harmonious and wholehearted artist.

The formal recognition of Richter's phenomenal gift came with the triumphant victory in the all-Union Contest of Performers in 1945, when the Jury headed by Dmitry Shostakovich (Emil Gilels was also on the Jury) awarded Richter the highest prize.

"Sviatoslav Richter is an extraordinary phenomenon," Shostakovich wrote later. "He is the pride of the Soviet performing school. The enormity of his talent staggers and enraptures. All the phenomena of musical art are accessible to him, from most intimate lyricism to grandiose pathos . . . But Richter never stops at what has been achieved, never rests on his laurels. He is continuously moving ahead . . ."

Indeed, no matter how perfect Richter's interpretations of the 1940's might have been, they were even more stupendous in the 1950's. Richter's art reached the utmost perfection in the 1960-70's. Foreign listeners, in particular Americans, could make certain of it when they first got to know Richter at that period. And today many authoritative critics unreservedly call him "the greatest pianist of our times." "Rarely have the vaults of Carnegie Hall heard anything of the kind," wrote the eminent musician Professor Rosina Lhévinne of her impression of Sviatoslav Richter's art.

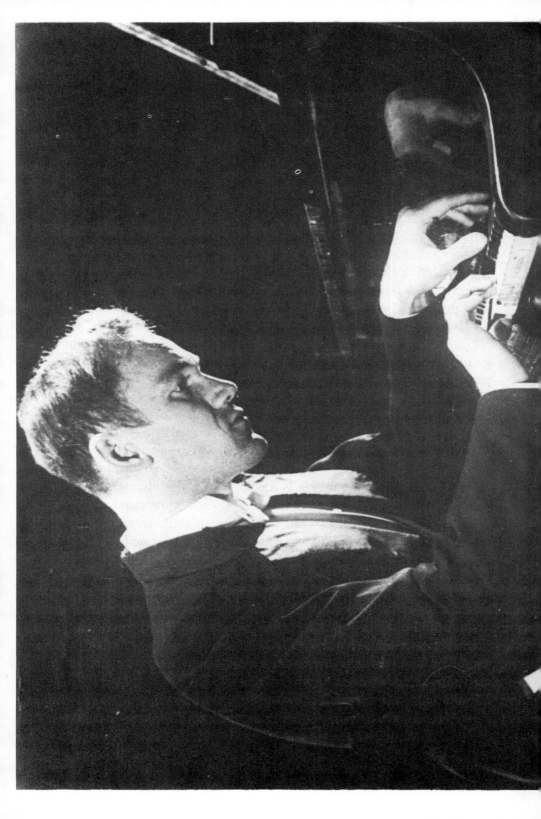

"Sviatoslav Richter is first of all a bright and inimitable individual ... Richter is an inspired poet of music and in that is his mesmerizing power ... Listening to Richter I caught myself all the time thinking that I was witnessing an exceptional phenomenon of the twentieth century."

★   ·   ★   ★

In the very center of Moscow at the intersection of Big and Small Bronnaya Streets there is a tall building—a tower. One of the uppermost floors in it is occupied by Sviatoslav Richter.

Undoubtedly, a contemporary "tower"-type block of flats bears little resemblance to the legendary "ivory tower"—in the opinion of aesthetes, the best haven for a man of art. Yet, to a certain extent it is symbolic: Sviatoslav Richter is not merely a creator of the beautiful—not a single step in his life is conceivable beyond the context of the high art to which he has devoted almost half a century.

The spacious apartment of Sviatoslav Richter, a passionate lover of painting and himself a naturally gifted painter, is decorated with the pictures of artists who are his friends. Remembering one of them, his friend Keato Magalazchvili, Richter wrote: ". . . she lived in her "tower" like an empress but at the same time it was plain living." These words in the best way describe Richter himself. He is quite unpretentious with those who are close to him, whose company is pleasant to him. For all the rest—numerous music-lovers, the majority of Soviet pianists—he is abolutely the "king of pianists," whom they have always worshipped and still idolize to this day. They speak of him as a demigod, adding to their judgment of his creative work and facts of his biography numerous "probably, obviously, perhaps"—because his life, even outwardly, is still full of "gaps."

It is difficult to penetrate into the inner world of this musician. Richter usually flatly refuses to give interviews, does not publish any articles, and never shares his ideas on specific authors or compositions. The sparse utterances dropped by him at times do not by any means reflect that unique phenomenon which is called "Sviatoslav Richter's Art."

Sviatoslav Richter performing the **Seventh Sonata** *of* **Prokofiev.**

Richter exists in his own world, aloof from the rest of the universe. The impression is formed that the cataclysms raging around him do not seem to concern him at all; he remains eternally in the sphere of his art. Even his own personal conflicts did not affect his powerful advance, did not leave their impact on his creative art that seems protected from everything external by selfless devotion to music, piano, by the fanaticism of an artist for whom there exists nothing else but art.

Richter cannot be described within the ordinary framework of an artist. A memorable example is the incident of Richter's participation on the jury of the first Tchaikovsky Competition. The quality of a performance was estimated by a ten point system. After hear-

Sviatoslav Richter and Heinrich Neuhaus. Praising Richter as no one else, Neuhaus wrote: "Richter is an outstanding phenomenon. The force of his penetration into the very essence of art, the fervor of his performer's temperament and the purity of feeling create a harmony in Richter, such precious fusion, that there is no resisting the power of its ascendancy."

Heinrich Neuhaus, Stanislav Neuhaus and Sviatoslav Richter in front of the building of the Moscow Conservatory.

ing Van Cliburn's performance in the first round, Richter gave him (and continued to do so in the following two rounds) one hundred points (!) and to all the rest . . . a zero. It was the first and the last time he was on the jury of a competition.

The attempts of critics to apply their usual yardstick to the most important facet – Richter's performing style, his enormous contribution to the treasury of piano performance – were similarly condemned to failure.

Nevertheless, let us try to look into the phenomenon of Richter guided by his own few utterances, by the precious testimony of those who happened to have had close contacts with him, and certainly, by his interpretations.

In one of the Soviet publications of the 1960's there was a friendly jest on Sviatoslav Richter. With several accurate touches, the painter depicted the characteristic features of his face, the body and the hands of the pianist melting into the piano. The inscription under the drawing was as follows:

Why be surprised at that unusual hybrid?
It is not Richter turned into the piano a bit.
Quite on the contrary,
It is the piano as such,
Turned into Music very much!

In that unassuming friendly sketch, the authors managed to observe the main features of the performing character of the pianist. Richter and the piano are always taken as a single whole, as something absolutely harmonious, indivisible. Whatever Richter is playing, however his performing style changed in the various stages of his evolution, or however differently he performs the music of different authors and styles, one has always been surprised at his absolute integrity with the instrument, the feeling that he was created for the piano, that he is pianistic by birth. It is not just an emotional reaction. There are objective data pointing to Richter's rare innate gift. It is difficult to imagine hands that would be better suited for the piano. Richter easily takes a twelfth (dodicesima) and his extraordinary stretch and elasticity of fingers allows him to take simultaneously the chords G-B Flat-E Flat-G-B Flat and on fortissimo F-A Flat-B-D-A Flat. But he is, above all, primarily a musician and only then a pianist. The piano for him is indeed merely an instrument, a means to penetrate into music in order to recreate it. That quality of his was noted by critics more than once. Julius Katchen wrote that in the article "The Greatest Pianist" in the London review *Records and Recordings*. "Richter is a complex of pianist-virtuoso with the brilliance of Rachmaninoff and Horowitz, with the rhythm characteristic only of him, with the depth penetrating into the very essence of music . . ." He is echoed by the Rumanian press: "Richter is music itself."

To that comprehensive sense of music, in which piano literature is only one of the parts, Sviatoslav Richter has been advancing since his youth. In Odessa, working as an accompanist, he played at sight and studied many opera pieces with singers. Later, as a Conservatory student Richter became the initiator (and the major performer) of the student circle where he used to play (often with

Sviatoslav Richter performing in a concert.

362

his Conservatory friend, pianist Anatoly Vedernikov) all the symphonies of Mahler and Miaskovsky, operas of Wagner, Richard Strauss and Debussy. And how diversified is Richter's work as a chamber musician!

His rare gift of reproducing on the piano large canvases belonging to orchestra and opera literature made musicians listening to him speak of the "conductor's" reading of the composition, of his striking talent to see any grand composition as if from the height of a "bird's eye view" that is so essential for a conductor. It must be said that this feeling was roused not only in the listeners. Encouraged by the warm welcome of his piano rendition of orchestra music soon after his graduation from the Conservatory, Richter began to dream of conducting.

There are few known, such bright examples of musicians brilliantly combining these two forms of performance. There were Franz Liszt and the brothers Anton and Nikolai Rubinstein; among contemporary musicians there are Carlo Zecchi and Daniel Barenboim. And Sviatoslav Richter also took his place on the conductor's stand. It happened in 1952. As might have been expected, the debut was a success, but never again has Richter performed as a conductor. What was he discontented with in his conducting? He has never revealed it even to his intimates. Nevertheless, there was every reason to suppose that, in conducting, his unique musicality would have also found its exceptional expression.

"Together with many others I was lucky to hear him at home perform the operas of Wagner, Tchaikovsky, R. Strauss, Debussy, Schreker, symphonies of Mahler, N. Miaskovsky, etc.," recalled Richter's spiritual and musical mentor Heinrich Neuhaus. That kind of "making music" made, perhaps, even a greater impression on me than his concerts. What a conductor has been lost, has not had his say!... He possesses in a great measure what is usually called the sense of form, the command of time and its rhythmic structure. Proportion, harmony, stemming from the very depths of classical disposition . . . —that's his main power, the major quality that makes us dream so much of him conducting!"

Sviatoslav Richter performing in a concert.

That dream was not destined to come true. However, in everything Richter does at the piano we see primarily a great musician for whom all the other facets of musical creation—opera, symphony, chamber music—have penetrated into him, live within him; he has lived through them like he has lived through his music.

The span of Richter's approach to music is revealed primarily in his repertory.

"I am an omnivorous creature and I want a lot of things. It is not because I am ambitious or try to do a great many things simultaneously. I simply love very many things and the desire to bring to the listeners all that I love never leaves me."

These words belong to Sviatoslav Richter himself. They were pronounced by him as early as in the late 1940's. Even at that time his repertory was surprisingly varied. Today we can speak without any reservations of the universality of the pianist. It goes without saying that, with the boundless range of piano art, it is impossible to speak, as applied to one performer, of enveloping all the composers who have left a considerable impact on piano literature. But Richter did not set himself any such task; neither did he set himself the task of playing "all" of Chopin, "all" of Beethoven. Speaking of Richter's universality we choose another criterion: no matter what composer Richter "touched" he did not need any kind of "overcoming"—either of the material or of himself—in order to create magnificent interpretations.

At one time the legendary Josef Hofmann was famous as a universal pianist. However, when his truly vast repertory was subjected to detailed analysis, it turned out that the major place in it was occupied by the Romantics. The musical genius Vladimir Sofronitsky, in spite of his undeniable versatility, remained, in the memory of those who had heard him, an inspired interpreter of Schumann and Scriabin. Obviously, the late Glenn Gould will also go down in history not as a universal pianist, but as one of the most outstanding and original interpreters of Bach's music. Sviatoslav Richter is a different matter: it seems absolutely impossible to point out one or several composers most congenial to him. All of those whose works he performs are without exception "his."

". . .Richter is the most significant of the living pianists," wrote Paul Moor in *Fono Forum* in 1960. "I heard the *"Big Sonata" B dur*

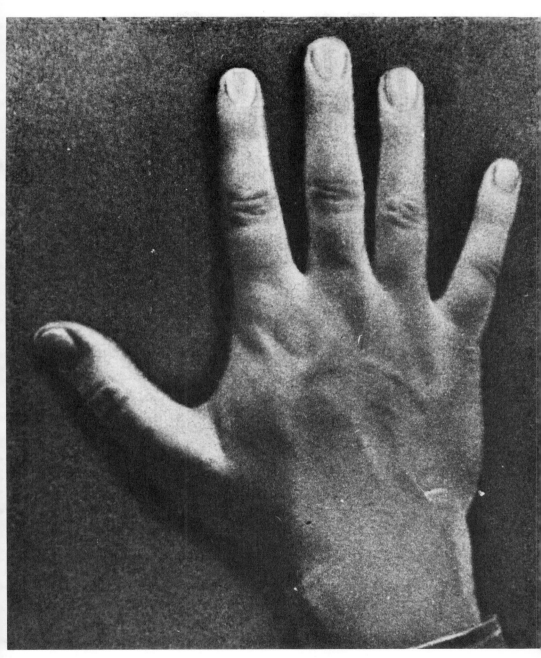

The pianist's hands are practically ideal for playing the piano. He easily takes twelfths.

Sviatoslav Richter (standing third from right) at the time of
his Conservatory studies under Heinrich Neuhaus. At the

piano is Heinrich Neuhaus. Fourth from left in the first row is Yakov Zak.

of Schubert performed by Gieseking, Schnabel and Kempff; but Richter made it even more expressive and poetic . . . Schumann's *"Toccata"* sounded as a newly discovered composition . . . Prokofiev's compositions . . . *Forgotten Waltzes* of Liszt . . . Debussy. To say what he manages better is absolutely next to impossible." Even more exactly and wittily Heinrich Neuhaus said: "When Richter plays different composers it seems that different pianists are playing."

So how does Richter make up his repertory?

"We should perform a great deal more of classical music of the pre-Beethoven period—Bach, Handel, Mozart, Haydn, etc." says Sviatoslav Richter. "To my mind it deserves to comprise at least one third of our repertory. It is both a touchstone for a performer and the source of inspiration for generations of composers. It is the basis of all music."

Evidently, nowhere is the essence of Richter's attitude towards the composer's concept, his idea of the rights and duties of a performer to the text, revealed with such clarity as it is in his interpretations of Bach's compositions. In short, Richter plays Bach austerely and at the same time with striking naturalness, without romanticizing him, without making him too intellectual, or speculative.

The basis of the Bach section of Richter's repertory consists of *The Well-Tempered Clavier,* that he played in concerts more than once (for the first time in 1946) and also recorded.

Today we know the interpretations of the monumental Bach cycle by Samuel Feinberg, Edwin Fisher and Glenn Gould. Each of them is interesting, original in his own way and, what is of utmost importance, in all of them the personality of the interpreter is seen as if "through Bach" with the characteristic accents of each performer. No one will ever deny that any interpretation of Bach created by an eminent artist has the right to existence. Sviatoslav Richter's interpretation of *The Well-Tempered Clavier* is so valuable, in my opinion, because Bach appears in it before the listeners in his "pure form," not "deformed" by the strong per-

Richter's hands.

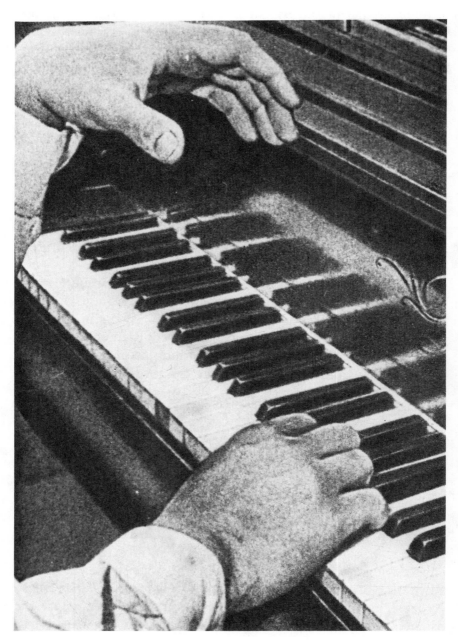

Richter's hands.

sonality of the performer. Here Richter seems to abide by Igor Stravinsky's categoric remark: "I don't want to be interpreted." The pianist himself has expressed a similar idea: "I think that the task of a true performer is to submit entirely to the composer, his style, character and outlook." However, that "detachment," objectivity in interpreting Bach is only imaginary. The genius insight of a great artist like Richter allows him to make almost imperceptible absolutely concrete principles in his reading of Bach, namely: employing all the colors of the piano without limiting them to the imitation of the harpsichord, saturating the allegro parts of his compositions with immense inner energy and revealing the entire depth of cantilena. Small-stroke phrasing of Bach is equally alien to him, as is fondness of playing non-legato.

The polyphonic line of Richter's repertory also goes through the compositions of Handel (not long ago, together with the young Soviet pianist Andrei Gavrilov, he performed all of Handel's *Suites*), late Beethoven, compositions of Franck, and, finally, Shostakovich.

We could dwell at length on Richter's execution of the compositions of Haydn, Mozart and Beethoven, Chopin, Schumann, Liszt (incidentally, the pianist played the role of Franz Liszt in the Soviet film *Mikhail Glinka*), Brahms and Franck, Rachmaninoff, Scriabin and Medtner, Ravel and Debussy and other composers; Richter has more than fulfilled his duty as a performer to each of those composers, having created interpretations that are absolutely mesmerizing by their stylistic perfection and force of expression.

But we would rather dwell only on two composers. They are Schubert and Prokofiev.

Nowadays, the name of Schubert as the author of large piano compositions is counted among the most frequently performed composers. It was different some forty or more years ago when the Schubert Sonatas, and the Fantasy *The Wanderer*, according to the figure of speech of Soviet musicologist Ivan Sollertinsky, "took a back seat in the development of world pianism."

We may say that one of the first pianists of world-wide fame who began to systematically include into his programs the Schubert *Sonatas* and the Fantasy *The Wanderer* was Sviatoslav Richter.

The naturalness, ingenuity and absolute lucidity of Richter's interpretation of Schubert's compositions more than once led the critics to the conclusion of a rare congeniality of Richter to Schubert. The nature of the pianist's disposition in the best way possible matches that of Schubert. "In Molto moderato of the *B Flat Major Sonata* it is Nature itself that bespeaks the voice of the pianist," wrote one of the reviewers of the *Soviet Music* magazine. "And at times the materiality of the piano vanishes and there remains only the boundless open horizons, the muffled roaring of faraway thunder, the commanding serenity of early morning silence—the fragrant 'poetry of quietness,' and also the melodiousness spread not even in music but in the feeling-state that engenders music. In the next to the last Variation Andante Con Moto and in the Rondo of the *A Minor Sonata* the pictures are "streaming" with such freedom that one simply ceases to notice their rhythmical pulsation. These are not just passages any longer, it is a spring; one moment it sounds tender, another it is ringing, or suddenly it turns angry, unaware of any 'questionable sounds,' any "strong or weak" beats, of the fact that somewhere on the note-paper there are groups of black circles, in fours, in sixes . . . And one can listen to it interminably, without wearying or thinking that something may seem 'monotonous.'

The main touchstone of the Schubert *Sonatas*—"the heavenly longueurs"—doesn't seem to exist for Richter at all. His ability to preserve the intensity of narration without resorting to artificial dynamic versatility, to coloring it, is amazing. Even in his long piano and pianissimo with the utmost shades of color, the feeling of monotony, of lingering, is never aroused in the listener.

It is impossible to imagine Richter without the works of Schubert or, to a greater degree, without the creations of Prokofiev.

The sketch of a portrait of Richter by R. Falck. The original portrait hangs in Sviatoslav Richter's apartment.

375

In the country house of Boris Pasternak, one of Richter's favorite poets. In this picture are Richter, Heinrich Neuhaus, Boris Pasternak and the members of his family.

It is quite characteristic that the "discovery" of Sviatoslav Richter in Moscow (the memorable concert of November 26, 1940, when he, still a student of the Conservatory at the time, played with Heinrich Neuhaus) occurred particularly with the Prokofiev *Sixth Sonata.* Many musicians found it most symbolic that with the unexpected device—a strike "con pugno" ("with a fist")—employed by the composer in "Allegro moderato," Richter proclaimed his sudden, thunderous rise to the pianistic Olympus.

Richter's first performance of Prokofiev was staggering with his large scale, colossal energy and mighty power. The impression that performance made was so great that, to a certain extent, it overshadowed the marvelous interpretations of the composer which were still remembered by musicians of the older generation. Prokofiev himself admitted indirectly that, having heard Richter for the first time soon after the memorable Moscow debut, he instantly felt him to be his best interpreter. When in May 1942 in Tbilisi Prokofiev completed the *Seventh Sonata,* its first hearing took place more than half a year later when it got into Richter's "hands." And then a miracle happened, which is understandable only if one is aware of Richter's phenomenal gift: he learned that most complicated composition in only four days.

Richter's interpretation of the Prokofiev *Seventh Sonata* is one of the peaks of his performing art. All the spiritual wealth of that man, his mighty strength of mind, his great pianism that knows no limits—all is mobilized for the re-creation of the essence of the composition. The message of the Sonata, the struggle of good and justice against cruelty, evil, violence, is realized by Richter with tremendous profundity.

The première of the *Seventh Sonata* was on January 16, 1943. And soon after Richter confirmed once again that it was difficult, if not impossible, to find his equal in the interpretation of Prokofiev. In the spring of 1946 he performed the *Sixth, Seventh* and *Eighth* Sonatas, presenting a marvelous perspective of the piano sonata creations of the composer. It was no accident when two years later Prokofiev completed his last, the *Ninth Sonata,* and dedicated it to Sviatoslav Richter.

Sviatoslav Richter giving autographs after one of his concerts abroad.

Richter continued to be the "discoverer" of Prokofiev even after the composer's death. This was vividly demonstrated during his American tour of the season of 1957-58, when the pianist offered an absolutely fresh interpretation of the Prokofiev *Fifth Concerto* playing with the Philadelphia Orchestra. Eugene Ormandy, the major conductor of the Orchestra, wrote after Richter's tour: "I only met Sviatoslav Richter here, and I was convinced that he was a most subtle, comprehensive musician and one of the greatest pianists of our time."

Sergei Prokofiev, naturally, is not the only contemporary composer in Richter's repertory. We cannot say that he strives to enrich his repertory with the newest compositions by any means. On the contrary, the pianist selects them for himself with great care. The point is that the compositions selected by such a strict judge as Richter, performed by him with the characteristic intuitive skill of a genius that makes the composition sound complete and perfect, have inevitably become part of the classical repertory. Richter himself expressed a similar idea when speaking of the cycle *Preludes and Fugues* of Shostakovich, of whom he is an inspired interpreter. "The Shostakovich *Preludes and Fugues* belong among the extremely complicated compositions for the performer (as well as for the listener). In that cycle I see the direct continuity of the traditions of the high classics. The classics are recreated in a new manner by D. Shostakovich today . . ."

But still, despite the vastness of Richter's repertory, it has its certain boundaries. And what he does not perform also in a measure characterizes him as a musician. For instance, his programs have never included transcriptions of the Bach works for the organ (Choral Preludes, Preludes and Fugues), the Songs of Schubert-Liszt, the famous Liszt's Paraphrases. This part of the piano repertory does not exist for Richter: he never plays arrangements in concerts. Evidently, the artist recognized only the originals, only compositions free from later stylistic features. There are other taboos established by him: for example, Richter has never performed publicly the *Fifth Concerto* of Beethoven, holding that after it had been interpreted by Heinrich Neuhaus he would never touch that composition.

Richter with his wife N. Dorliak, a famous Soviet chamber singer.

380

*Richter and David Oistrakh. The Richter-Oistrakh duet ap-
peared in 1968. In spite of a most intensive solo career
Sviatoslav Richter has never treated performing chamber
music as some minor field of his performing activities. On
the contrary, in performing chamber music his universality as a pianist was also apparent when he now and then
played with singers, violinists, and cellists in various mixed
chamber ensembles.*

Министерство культуры СССР
Государственный музей
изобразительных искусств
имени А. С. Пушкина

The title page of the picture exhibition catalogue held by Sviatoslav Richter in Moscow with an inscription to the family of pianist Andrei Gavrilov.

МУЗЫКАНT
и его встречи
в искусстве

Выставка портретов

Каталог

Советский художник
Москва. 1978

But even with these exceptions Richter's repertory is enormous.

Franz Liszt used to say that one should work like a miner buried in a mine, on whose labor depended whether he would live or not. That is exactly how Sviatoslav Richter has been working throughout his life. It is true that he is blessed with the phenomenal gift of sightreading; according to eyewitnesses he played from the score so perfectly the most complicated compositions he saw for the first time (sometimes from the manuscript) that his interpretations seemed to be quite ready for the concert stage. But the people who have close contacts with him know that Richter is one of the most painstaking laborers at the instrument.

Until recently there was no quota of daily practice for Richter—he would play five, seven, ten hours a day. It sometimes happened (and not infrequently) that after difficult night recitals, on his return home, he would sit at the instrument for several hours again. At present, as evidenced by his young colleague Andrei Gavrilov, the "gold" laureate of the Tchaikovsky Competition with whom he has had close creative association in recent years, Richter established for himself a daily living "subsistence minimum" and he never allows himself to practice less than that. No one knows what it is in exact figures; however, it is known that Richter (and Gavrilov now follows his example) takes accurate stock of his daily practice, marking everything in a special notebook. If because of illness or for some other reason Richter "gets into debt" he later does his utmost to work off these hours. Yet, there were such periods in his life when Richter would not go near the instrument for some five or six months.

Speaking of his approach to a new composition, of how he commences to work at it, Sviatoslav Richter pointed out at one time: "I instantaneously, from the very beginning, imagine what I'm going to do. I memorize very quickly and do not specially learn by heart. Sometimes I work separately at the most virtuoso passages—that is when it is necessary to learn a composition in a particularly short time."

Concrete examples show that it has not always been like that. Let's see how this work on the most virtuoso episodes proceeds.

Heinrich Neuhaus described such an episode. While still a student, Richter brought to a lesson one of the Prokofiev Sonatas learned in a record period of time. Neuhaus asked him how he had

Richter and Van Cliburn. Richter congratulates the American pianist, the winner of the first Tchaikovsky Competition. Evidently, the super-maximum points Richter as a member of the Jury gave Van Cliburn played a great role in the fact that the youngster from Texas got the highest award of the Moscow Competition.

Sviatoslav Richter and cellist Natalia Gutman. Natalia Gutman, as well as her husband, the famous violinist Oleg Kagan, have been among Richter's favorite partners in recent years.

managed, apart from everything else, to play so easily the passage which, though it consisted only of several bars, had been an age-long touchstone for pianists. "I had been learning it for six hours running until it came out well," answered Richter. This is what Andrei Gavrilov told the author of this book: "Richter is capable of learning one bar for an hour, or two, or three hours; more than once I witnessed him while practicing playing one page at least seventy times. Sitting in the next room listening to him, I was literally losing my senses. But he himself, whose patience in this sense has no limits, repeated the same passage again and again . . ."

Such a method of "capturing by storm" the difficult passages or a new composition on the whole without retreat, until the final result is obtained, is in general typical of Richter's practicing

Friendly sketch of Sviatoslav Richter.

habits. For instance, it is known that when he had to learn a composition, new for him, in the shortest possible time, he would do as follows: he learns by heart bar after bar several pages a day, the next day the same, and so on. It has happened that he played the whole of the composition for the first time on the concert stage. So there have been times, in spite of Richter's words, that he did have to learn a composition by heart, and purposely so.

This is of course suitable for a pianist who has the special gift of enveloping a composition on the whole, perceiving its form. And in Richter that quality is absolutely unique. The same rare sense of form was displayed by him when he played by sight, when some details, some particulars were omitted, but nevertheless, the composition appeared to those listening as if carved of stone.

The manner of "arranging" the material is unusual enough in itself. The piece that is being worked at or its fragment is played very loudly, almost hammering out the sounds in moderate or high tempo. (Incidentally, young Richter at one time was, not without reason, reproached for too much "hammering" on the stage as well.) The famous pianist Nikolai Petrov (he is often an involuntary witness of Richter's home practice, as their country houses are next door), when telling the author of this book that he often hears such playing coming from Richter's house, expresses the following supposition: "I am sure that Richter knows that that kind of practice is necessary for him. One would think, why should a musician, a great musician at that, need to "hammer out" the piece he is learning? But Richter is the wisest of pianists. And if he sits at the instrument for some six or eight or twelve hours a day and practices precisely as he does, it must be done for the sake of some certain purposes, and first of all, for the sake of music. It means that his method of "mortising" practice at home is necessary for him in order to get free of the technical things, to do away with all technical problems, in order to be able to play at the concert with that fantastic lightness, to work those miracles on the stage, which we then witness."

Richter in front of the public gathered in one of the halls of the Pushkin Art Museum in Moscow. In that hall, where only the elect can play, the pianist likes to play most of all.

Richter and technical problems? Is it possible to speak of technical hardships as applied to the pianist whom many critics hold to be the first virtuoso of our time?

In order to answer this question let's turn to the years of the pianist's youth. As he himself has said, his study of the piano began rather late, when he was about nine years old. And those were not "studies" as such in the strict sense of the word. He used to inflate the motor bellows for his father who was an organist, and play some musical games, which undoubtedly developed his imagination and fantasy and allowed him in the future to treat music and studies, playfully. But there was no system to his studies; neither was there any technical drill. Very soon his studies were left entirely to drift. It is most likely that he never played scales regularly; neither is he likely to know from his own experience what the three steps of Czerny *Etudes* are, or any other instructive literature. Certainly, Richter's Conservatory tutor Heinrich Neuhaus did not go in for perfecting his technique. True, Richter was endowed with unique technical capabilities. But that still could not allow him to forever avoid concrete technical problems which he had to solve by himself. That must be the reason this method evolved—when encountering some difficult, to take it by storm. But what hard labor it demanded! And he has become the Richter who ravished the whole world because he represents in himself an example of rare industry. That is why he succeeded in overcoming all the hurdles even when it did not come easy to him.

"Failures never dismayed me," Richter remembered of the years of his youth. "I never gave up a piece if it did not come out as I wanted it to. I went on working at it until I mastered it."

Richter has never taught at any educational institution, devoting himself instead entirely to performing. The exceptions are the rare consultations he gave some pianists at their request. Lazar Berman recalls that in the mid-50's he asked Richter to advise him on the performance of the *Eighth Sonata* of Prokofiev. "Richter is not a pedagogue. Had he been a pedagogue we would have probably met several times and worked for an hour or an hour and a half. We met only once. Our meeting lasted for five hours. And after that I played the Prokofiev *Sonata* so that it is still one of the best compositions in my repertory. He simply "bared" it to me, despite the fact that when I was going to consult him I believed it was almost ready and I understood everything in it."

Sviatoslav Richter and Andrei Gavrilov. "Richter," says Gavrilov, "is not simply a great School. It is a kind of a bio-field in which one feels absolutely different. His influence is never experienced as an overwhelming power, but rather as some guiding force. For me, associating with him proved a new step not only in the musical sense, but also in the human aspect".

No, Richter is not a pedagogue in the traditional sense of the word. But his influence on the musical youth—those hundreds of young pianists who listen to his concerts and recordings, and the "elite" who were lucky to be closely associated with him, is tremendous. Andrei Gavrilov said about it: "Richter is not simply a great School. It is a kind of a "biofield" in which one feels absolutely different. His influence is never experienced as an overwhelming power, but rather as some guiding force. For me associating with him proved to be a new step not only in the musical sense but also in the human aspect."

But apparently, nowhere is that force of Richter's "biofield" felt more acutely as when making music together with him.

Talking with many pianists of their craft and discussing the question of the ratio between solo and chamber music in their repertory—the creative "time budget"—more than once I heard the following answer: "Unfortunately, I don't have enough time for chamber music." Such a situation is absolutely unnatural for Richter. For him there is no difference between solo and chamber music performance; both aspects of the pianist-performer are considered by him as a natural demonstration of the wide range of piano repertory. Chamber music performance for him is not an exception to the rule, not a temporary distraction from the "principal"—solo performance. Because of that he is always in search of musical contacts with whom to perform.

Playing in an ensemble with many prominent musicians was exactly that higher form of making music which is so characteristic of Richter. The listeners of the older generation still retain in their memory his chamber music evenings with David Oistrakh and Daniel Shafran. A very special page of his performing activities presents his playing with the splendid Soviet singer Nina Dorliak—his wife, friend and main counselor during all his life. In the ensemble with Dorliak, Richter revived the best traditions of vocal accompaniment going back to Glinka, Mussorgsky and Medtner. Richter's performance of the Schubert *Songs* together with Fisher-Dieskau was the acme of perfection.

In recent years young musicians have become his partners. A wonderful creative result crowned the ensemble of Richter with violinist Oleg Kagan with whom he played all the Mozart *Sonatas*. Many a time Richter performed with cellist Natalia Gutman, one of the most inspired musicians of our time. The duet of Richter with violist Juri Bashmet was also a great success.

Making music . . . These words express Richter's approach to the music he executes and his emotional state when he is on the concert stage. "When Richter plays, it seems that he is in an empty hall, alone with music . . ." wrote one of the greatest authorities in the field of musical performance, Gregory Kogan. "There exists no one for the pianist at that 'lovely moment'. He does not strive to please the public . . . as if he forgot their presence altogether. The audience seems to be aware of it. In silence, holding their breath they hark to what Schumann defined by the words: 'Der Dichter spricht' (The 'Poet is speaking')."

But we know quite a different Richter, capable by his zeal, his spontaneity, almost completely to hypnotize his listeners. And the pianist is apt to be like that in Schumann and in Liszt, Rachmaninoff and Prokofiev. (The author of these lines recalls an episode that he happened to witness. Richter was performing the *B minor Sonata* of Liszt in one of the Central Moscow Concert Halls – the Tchaikovsky Hall. As soon as the sounds of the short introduction "Lento assai" died away, he "pierced" the octaves of the first page of the Sonata. He took them with such violence that the grand piano, a huge concert "Steinway" began to slide away from him. Hardly touching the chair he went on playing almost from a standing position. At the beginning of the recapitulation he attacked the instrument again and the "Steinway", unable to stand the onslaught, again began to roll forward.

Richter's spontaneity makes such a mesmerizing impression because it is not a spontaneous, uncontrolled demonstration of emotions. All his "emotional explosions" are based on accurate calculation, on his absolute knowledge of his tasks – both on the whole and in minute details.

"When I first heard Richter he startled me particularly by his spontaneity," says Lazar Berman. "I remember 1945, his performance in Moscow at the All-Union Contest, when in the light of the candle (there was no electricity that night) Richter was playing Liszt's *Wild Chase*. That onslaught cannot be described with words. Suddenly the candle falls down and goes out . . . It was a kind of an eruption of a volcano! When much later I got to his place and he worked with me for half a day I realized that no matter how spontaneous his performance could seem, he never lost his self-control and always moved forward according to a preconceived plan. Even when, as it may seem unnatural, he almost completely raises his body from the chair it is not by any means an affectation: it means that it is absolutely necessary for him to play precisely with such a movement in order to extract certain sounds."

But that is the testimony of Richter's colleague who had entered into his creative laboratory. When Richter is on stage it seems that it is especially due to that spontaneity that he electrifies the house and arouses the audience to such an extent that he makes even profession-

als completely forget the text of the familiar composition, of its details, and perceive what comes from under his fingers as pure music.

That is exactly the impression Richter's performance made, during his first concert in America, when in Chicago he played the *B Flat Major Concerto* of Brahms. According to Sol Hurok's words: "It was a truly fantastic success. The artist was encored twelve times. The ushers of the Orchestra-Hall who had been serving there for some thirty or forty years said that they had never seen anything of the kind. It is enough to say," adds Sol Hurok, "that I had to take Richter back to his hotel stealthily through the back door. Otherwise the enraptured public would not have let him pass."

Yes, Richter can be, at the piano, a dreaming poet and a raging demon. And at times, when he is playing, his appearance—his high forehead, broad cheekbones, a slightly prominent chin, his massive body with large hands—resembles that of a Master of the Middle Ages or the Renaissance, a creator who, while remaining an ordinary mortal, succeeds in infusing his art with a truly divine force.

Sviatoslav Richter.

Mikhail Pletnyov.

Mikhail Pletnyov

Mikhail Pletnyov was born April 14, 1957, in Arkhangelsk, one of the northern cities of the USSR. Soon after the birth of their son, the Pletnyovs moved to Kazan. There, at the age of seven Mischa Pletnyov began the study of the piano.

Pletnyov's parents are both musicians. His father is a teacher of the accordion, his mother is a pianist, accompanist and teacher as well. However, unlike most musical families the atmosphere in Pletnyov's family was quite different. There was absolutely no constraint in Mikhail's musical studies on the part of his parents.

His first piano teacher was Julia Shashkina under whose tutelage he studied for six years. In 1970, Pletnyov entered the Central Music School (CMS) of the Moscow Conservatory in the class of the remarkable pedagogue Yevgeny Timakin. Graduating from school with "flying colors," Pletnyov became a student of the Moscow Conservatory, where his teachers were the outstanding Soviet musician Jakov Flier and the famous pianist Lev Vlasenko.

Three times Mikhail Pletnyov participated in competitions and all three times he became the Gold medalist. In 1975, he was awarded the Grand-Prix in Paris. Two years later he won at the All-Union competition and finally he became the winner of Moscow's VI Tchaikovsky International.

Mikhail Pletnyov made his American debut in 1978. Then he became famous with music-lovers of Scandinavia, Rumania, Hungary, Japan and other countries. And whenever he played, his performance aroused the ardent enthusiasm of the public and had brilliant reviews of the press; "A Devil from Moscow . . . He uses such colors that have never been drawn out of the piano before,"—that's what the reviewers said about Mikhail Pletnyov's performance.

Being a versatile musician, Pletnyov doesn't confine himself only to piano performance. He composes music, conducts and is fond of making music at home, playing the second part violin in a quartet with his friends.

The rare natural gift, early creative maturity, surprising self-discipline and the integrity of his character allowed Mikhail Pletnyov to rise to the highest order of the most prominent and promising performers of the world.

⋆   ⋆   ⋆

Mikhail Pletnyov, now one of the world's great pianists, may have started out to be a trombonist . . . or whatever that thing is he is playing with in the photograph on the facing page.

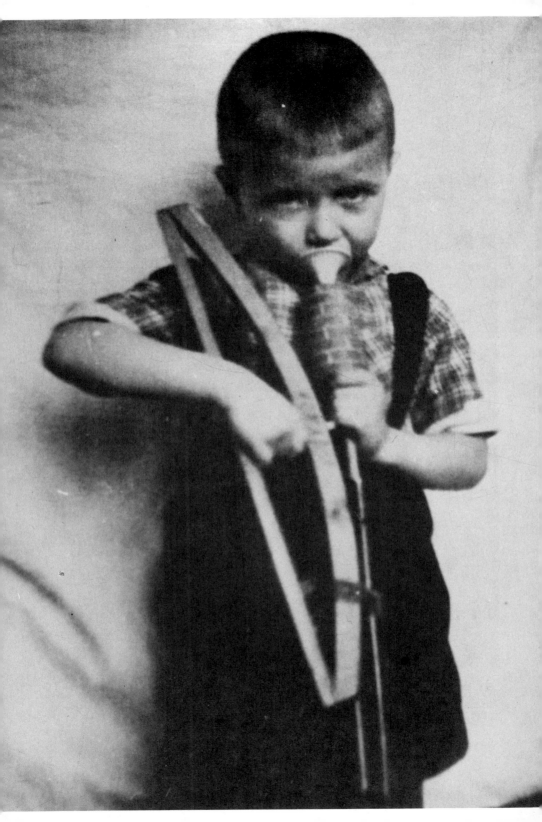

As a youngster he was intrigued by every musical instru-
ment. Here at age 4 years he is trying his skill with a violin.

One of the last days of June, 1978. It is long past midnight but the small yard of the Moscow Conservatory where the VI International Tchaikovsky Competition is held is crowded with people and is buzzing like a beehive: the contestants and their numerous fans are waiting for the results to be announced.

From time to time everyone glances at the vast lighted windows of the side wing: there the jury have been in conference for several hours . . .

And here we are together with Mikhail Pletnyov and pianist Alice Kezheradze also awaiting the decision of the jury. Pletnyov looks utterly imperturbable. He seems as calm and confident as when he appeared on the stage before the jury to play his program as well as after, when he received the thundering "bravo" from the audience and a storm of applause. Near at hand, on the steps of the entrance there sit André Laplante from Canada, pale from fatigue, and Pascal Devoyan from France, smoothing his huge shock of hair. Along with Mikhail Pletnyov, these are the major favorites of the Contest.

Suddenly one after another the cameramen spill out of the entrance of the building where the jury are in conference and elbowing their way to Pletnyov, they immediately surround him. Flashes of cameras, clicks of camera shutters, newspapermen buzzing with their cameras . . . The public exult in the success of the young pianist and he receives an ovation. But he remains as imperturbable as ever, shading his face with his hand from the blinding flashes of floodlights and cameras . . .

I remind Mikhail Pletnyov of this episode when we meet at my place and start our talks. There emerge other incidents of that memorable day. And gradually in our conversation we touch upon the role the Tchaikovsky Competition played in his fate and the problems of contests in general.

MP: It seems to me everything that could have been written about competitions has already been written. I shan't be original in saying that there is some duality in competitions. On the one hand, it is gratifying when so many musicians assemble to represent different schools of performance and it usually results in a kind of musical feast. For example, in Moscow at the time of the Tchaikovsky Competition, the halls where the auditions are held are beseiged by masses of people; a festive atmosphere reigns everywhere. That is the positive side of competitions. But participation in contests always involves appraisal. And that's where the trouble starts. It turns out that it is simply impossible to appreciate everyone objectively. That's understandable: a musician who can show himself to perfection in one style may not prove to be that good in another. A competition presupposes some kind of universality. And in connection with this a great many questions and problems crop up.

MZ: Probably such performers should participate in certain monographic competitions. There is the Chopin competition and the like.

MP: That's right. But a competition of one composer is no less difficult. Neither is it devoid of problems. For instance, among the contestants, there may be such musicians who play Chopin in a new way, differently, and perhaps in a much more interesting manner than the conventional interpretation. But can it be imagined that all or the majority of the jury members adhering to the traditional interpretation will be objective in their appraisal of the performer-innovator?

MZ: You've touched upon a very delicate question. The problem of the jury is very important and there are several aspects to it. For instance, the contestants are musicians of one generation but their performance is appraised by musicians of different generations, very experienced but still advocating different criteria, nurtured on different musical tastes.

MP: Quite right. And it all results in the fact that at competitions those who play very solidly, academically, in a sort of way universally, are acclaimed to be the best. Incidentally, while preparing for the Tchaikovsky Competition, I took this into consideration.

MZ: In other words, you tried to avoid disputable interpretations, didn't you?

MP: I've got to admit that it was really so; I tried to avoid any moot points. It does not mean that I specially adapted myself to it, but I oriented myself on tradition. I was quite conscious that at a contest audition I could not afford to do what I could "venture" at a concert.

MZ: But still, no matter what the negative sides of the competi-

Mikhail Pletnyov even played a concert on a balalaika as a child.

Can you believe this? Yes, it's Mikhail Pletnyov.

tion may be, their major advantages are too obvious to give them up. Moreover, today there is no alternative to them.

MP: Of course competitions are necessary. Only a contest can help to discover a talented person practically overnight, as a result of which he finds himself in the center of attention, and music lovers all over the world focus their attention on him. Surely, it is wonderful!

MZ: But actually at the Tchaikovsky Competition which brought you world acclaim as a Gold Medalist, you were already a mature artist. That is what the critics noted more than once. Tell us how you progressed to this point in your creative biography, tell us of the years of your studies, your childhood.

MP: Though I was born into a family of musicians and from early childhood I showed great interest in music, my parents were in no hurry to start teaching me. They often took me with them to the Conservatory, to orchestra rehearsals, thus giving me the opportunity to develop my childish inclination to music quite naturally.

MZ: Do you now think that it was good that your study of the piano did not begin as soon as your musical gift was discovered?

MP: Undoubtedly so. This "race" to set up a two or three hour practice schedule for a child of four or five years old is absolutely unnecessary. He should have the chance to enjoy music, to discover it spontaneously for himself. I really began to study the piano at the age of seven but by that time I had already known all the orchestra instruments. Though I wasn't fond of drawing in my childhood, I drew all the orchestra instruments, cut them out of paper and . . . conducted them. All that was in my pre-school years. In other words, what I want to say is that no one coerced me to study music. My way into music was absolutely natural.

MZ: Your parents are rare among musicians. Very few of our colleagues who have a gifted child could resist the temptation of launching him into professional orbit as early as possible.

MP: That is true. My parents never urged me to study music. But it was thanks to them that I was always in a good musical atmosphere. My parents have marvelous musical taste. They would not let me associate with music they considered of low standard. There has always been an appraisal of what was really fine and what was unworthy. I was nurtured on the music of the masters: Beethoven, Mozart, Tchaikovsky. I am very grateful to my parents for instilling in me a genuine love of art. It refers not only to music, but to literature and painting as well.

MZ: A few words about your first teacher. How do you evaluate her "from the heights" of your present day experience?

MP: Julia Shashkina is a very good instructor. In recent years I often happened to be in provincial towns where I was asked to audition pupils. Usually these were gifted children studying with the best pedagogues. But as a rule I came across one and the same phenomenon: either the pedal was not pure, or there were blunders of musical taste (hypertrophied accelerando or ritardando) and so on. I account for it by the provincialism of the pedagogues. But my teacher Julia Shashkina, though she lived in Kazan, a provincial town, did not by any means suffer from that pedagogical disease — provincialism.

MZ: Being aware of your unusual gift your teacher must have taken some nontraditional route with you; she probably offered rather complicated compositions to you?

MP: I wouldn't say so. Any appreciable leap in my repertoire occurred later when I became the student of my second teacher Yevgeny Timakin after our family moved to Moscow.

MZ: What urged your family to move to Moscow?

MP: Do you remember what Chekhov wrote to Gorky? Having read his first books, he persistently advised him to live in the capital. There are such notions as the "climate" of the capital, the professional "level" of the capital, and this fact must not be disregarded. In my life there also came the moment when my parents and my teacher decided that I should carry on with my studies in Moscow.

MZ: On becoming Timakin's pupil at the age of 13, did you feel the difference in the repertoire straight away or did it happen gradually?

MP: You may see for yourself. When I came to Moscow, I played the Bach suite, some not too difficult sonatas of Mozart, a sonatina of my own composition. It was my "limit." But by the end of the year, among other compositions, I played the Chopin First *Ballad* the permission for which, to tell the truth, I "got out of" Timakin with difficulty.

MZ: And did the coda come out properly?

MP: Yes, I managed to play the coda, and not badly into the

This snapshot from the family album is old and faded, but it's the first public concert Mischa Pletnyov gave on the piano.

Mikhail Pletnyov does not believe in a strict schedule of practicing. He plays as much as he feels can be productive.

bargain. The next year I was 14 and I performed the Liszt First *Concerto.*

MZ: Had you not played Chopin's and Liszt's etudes before you performed the Chopin *Ballad* and the Liszt *Concerto?*

MP: Not a single one. In fact I had not played any small pieces of these composers at all.

MZ: This really testifies not only to your enormous innate technical resources but also to the pedagogical boldness of your teacher Timakin.

MP: Right you are. I must have had some makings for a technically perfect rendition, but to reveal them, a correct pedagogical approach was needed to let the student display himself. That is what Timakin did brilliantly. He is first of all an intellectual pedagogue, one of those who recognizes the needs of each student. He is a searching, creative man and working with me he strived for some optimum method suitable particularly for me. I would say it was due to this tutelage that at the age of 14-15 I made such great progress, especially in the technical sense.

MZ: Did he as a musician inspire you?

MP: Timakin does not perform on the concert stage. He devoted himself entirely to pedagogics. But he has a marvelous command of the piano, and now, when we have spare time, we often play pieces for four hands or for two pianos, usually going through some un-familiar music. Timakin often says that it is the love of music that underlies all his work and adds that he is neither a pedagogue, nor a pianist, he is a musician.

MZ: How much did you practice daily in your school years?

MP: I've never counted . . . But I can't say that I've ever practiced too much—neither in the years of studies, nor now. I believe that one should practice as much as he feels like practicing, never forc-ing himself. Practicing can be fruitful only as long as you are in-terested in what you are doing. And at times it may last for hours on end. Sometimes it happens that because of tiredness or depres-sion the performer loses this interest altogether. When that hap-pens to me, I confine myself to short periods of practicing, that is I play no longer than is necessary to keep myself in good pianistic shape. Very often I simply improvise, play harmonies, acquaint myself with music literature. I'll give one more example. I made up my mind to learn the Liszt *Second Concerto.* I played it one day for

*Mikhail Pletnyov
and Yevgeny
Timakin, his
teacher at the
Central Music
School.*

410

about an hour and a half and another day as long as that, after which I discovered that I actually knew it. In general, in art it is the result that matters. No one is interested in how long it has taken you to learn the composition, be it ten minutes or ten years.

MZ: As the pupil of Timakin and later of Yakov Flier, you are a kind of musical "grandson" of Konstantin Igumnov, famous for his unique sound palette. Did these two pedagogues pay much attention to working at the sound?

MP: True, both my pedagogues Timakin and Flier were Igumnov's brilliant pupils. But there is almost nothing in common in the manner of their performance. For instance, what is there in common in the manner of playing of Richter and Gilels—both of them the pupils of Heinrich Neuhaus? But speaking of my teachers, I'll point out that the main thing, the principle of a very careful attitude towards the sound was, of course, characteristic of both of them. Timakin, for one, used to say that the sound should be likened to a flower. For the flower to be fragrant, all the vital powers should reach it freely, without hindrance. In other words, not a single muscle or sinew should be tense, constrained, so that the sound drawn out of the piano with the finger tips should be produced with an absolutely relaxed hand. So the main task is to provide plasticity, convenience in playing.

"Timakin (my teacher) does not perform on the concert stage. He devoted himself entirely to pedagogics. But he has a marvelous command of the piano, and now and then, when we have spare time, we often play pieces for four hands or for two pianos, usually going through some unfamiliar music."

The piano winners at the Tchaikovsky Competition were Nikolai Demidenko, Francois Devoiyon and Pletnyov.

MZ: On entering the Conservatory you entered the master class of one of the prominent Soviet musicians—Yakov Flier. What can you say about your association with that musician?

MP: All told, I studied under Flier's tutelage for three and a half years until he died. It was very interesting to study with him and I always think of him with deep gratitude. The program which I played first at the All-Union contest and then at the Tchaikovsky Competition was compiled and prepared under his guidance.

MZ: What did your lessons with Flier consist of?

MP: I'll tell you a possibly paradoxical thing: had I practiced less or had I learned a lesser number of compositions, our lessons might have been more fruitful. But I learned an enormous number of pieces and Flier simply did not always have enough time to listen to all of them. For example, during one month I learned five concertos of Beethoven. Naturally at the lessons that took place once a week I could hardly play all the five concertos for him. In fact I came to every lesson with a new concerto. And Flier could do nothing but make some general critical remarks or comments. Generally, it was a rare case when I brought one and the same composition to the lesson several times.

MZ: What you said about the years of your studies shows that you displayed creative maturity at a very early age. It became especially obvious in the Conservatory years. But still it is hardly possible to deny the influence on you of such an outstanding musician as Yakov Flier under whose tutelage you studied for three and a half years. In your opinion, what is his contribution to your musical career?

MP: It is quite natural that the mere contact with such a magnificent creative personality as Yakov Flier does a lot of good. If Flier exerted his influence on me he did it unostentatiously. Timakin said that a pedagogue was really good when his pupil did not notice his influence. The teacher is aware of his pupil's growth, of his acquiring new positive qualities, but it all comes so natural that the student does not even observe it. Incidentally, when any of Timakin's pupils would thank him he would say, "We simply worked and worked and it all came out by itself." I guess it was just that case with my studies under Flier's guidance.

The relations between Pletnyov and Flier were complicated enough. Pletnyov the student was not the one to hang on his teacher's words and follow his instructions implicitly. Flier is said to have remarked once half-jokingly that it was easier for him to give two solo concerts than one lesson to Mikhail Pletnyov. However, he was quite aware of the singularity of his pupil's talent, his great gift. Unfortunately he was not destined to witness Pletnyov's triumph.

MZ: Which of the pianists inspired you, was your idol in the years of your studies and maybe until now?

MP: Generally speaking I do not like the word "idol." But if there is a musician who is the ideal to me, it is only Rachmaninoff.

When I asked Mikhail Pletnyov that question, without having yet heard his answer, I thought he would necessarily name Rachmaninoff. And it is not the matter of my intuition. Though Rachmaninoff remains unsurpassed in the art of musical interpretation, and young Pletnyov has only recently been acclaimed as an outstanding artist, there is something in common in the nature of their gifts. Pletnyov is also discreet, reserved, outwardly restrained in showing his emotions but behind the "steel shell" there also beats the grand heart of a true artist. The unusually wide sphere of Pletnyov's musical interests also reminds us of Sergei Rachmaninoff. But who knows? Maybe in the not-too-distant future the name of Pletnyov: the conductor Pletnyov, and the composer Pletnyov (in both musical pursuits the young musician has already made successful initial steps) will become as famous as the name of pianist Pletnyov.

We returned to the period of Pletnyov's pupilage. I asked him to define what is especially agreeable to him in Rachmaninoff's manner of performance, in his creative activities.

MP: Rachmaninoff is a unique personality. First of all he was a genius who had realized his artistic potentialities both as a performer and a composer. It is a spirit, an absolute spirit of Music, he is a singular individual endowed with singular musicianship, a singular gift. Everything Rachmaninoff did pianistically or in any other sphere is Music in its absolute form.

MZ: After the death of Flier, you studied with Lev Vlasenko, didn't you?

Mikhail Pletnyov and Professor Lev Vlasenko in the class-room where they usually worked. On the wall is a portrait of the famous Yakov Flier (also spelled Flyer).

Both Mikhail Pletnyov and Prof. Lev Vlasenko are well liked. Here they are shown surrounded by students.

MP: Yes, at present I also sometimes play my new programs to him and greatly appreciate his opinion.

When our conversation turned to professor Lev Vlasenko, I remembered our recent encounter in the office of the business manager of the Great Hall of the Moscow Conservatory. It was half an hour before Pletnyov's concert was to begin. Surrounded by his numerous students and postgraduates, Vlasenko asked for the tickets for them all. "I have no tickets," Zurab Guedenidze, the manager, said and made a helpless gesture. And then he added, "You have taught him too well. The house is sold out." "There was nothing to teach him," replied Vlasenko, "he could do everything himself."

That was not a mere joke. The relations of Vlasenko and Pletnyov were not those of a teacher and a student, but rather a collaboration of two colleagues, an older and a younger one. They remain as such to this day, when Pletnyov became Vlasenko's assistant at the Conservatory.

Our conversation with Mikhail Pletnyov turned to his pedagogical activities.

MP: I teach willingly. At the same time I see distinctly the limits of what is possible in musical pedagogics. You can teach anyone the essentials. But to teach a student possessing a vivid individuality, a vivid personality is extremely difficult. Besides, there exist such things—maybe the most important at that, with which a musician is blessed—the sense of music, sense of time. Let's suppose that it is possible to develop the sense of music—possible if one constantly listens to the Great Masters. But whether it will be real perfection still remains a question. Every person displays his talent in something individual. His greatness is in his difference from others. And that absence of similarity, who knows where it comes from?

MZ: Have you a full-time schedule at the Conservatory?

MP: I don't want to take a master class of my own as yet and so I am content with my work as an assistant. Thus, I can combine teaching with concertizing. But it is not so much the matter of being busy (ideally I would prefer to have not 17, but two or three students), the point is that I would like them to be younger than the Conservatory age and level (17 years and older). Those who

*Yakov Flier's widow, deeply moved by Pletnyov's perfor-
mance, congratulates him after a concert.*

Prof. Lev Vlasenko, Mrs. Yakov Flier, and Pletnyov after his concert.

come to the Conservatory are usually almost fully-shaped musicians. Only some final touches are needed. The essentials have been already implanted in them and revealed. However what happens is that it takes the first three years for a student to forget whatever he has been taught; the next year is necessary to prepare the background for new rules and principles and when it is possible to commence the work as such, there is no time left—the Conservatory course is over. So a Conservatory student cannot in fact be regarded as a full-fledged "product" of the Conservatory pedagogue.

MZ: Then why not teach at the Central Music School (CMS)?

MP: In the Central Music School the children begin studying at an early age. And teaching such children requires specific abilities. I am not sure if I possess them. I would rather work with children who are not too young, but beginning from 10-11 years.

MZ: What do you find of utmost importance in the first stage of teaching?

MP: In the early stage one should abide by two main principles. Firstly, if a pupil studies the piano he must master everything that is necessary to know about the instrument and performing devices on his level. Secondly, he must know what orchestration is, what composition is. Let him realize that music is not confined to practicing on the piano. At seven I knew the range of all the instruments. I could write a score.

MZ: Proceeding from your experience, how would you recommend students of music to commence the work on a new piece?

MP: I begin working at every piece differently. Usually I read the composition straight through after which it is as a rule clear to me what I must do in it. As to my recommendations to students, it all depends on each individual case. The approach to a musical piece depends on the performing capabilities and potentialities of every individual. If a student does not hear the harmonic basis of the composition well enough, I would advise him to look at the composition from the point of view of harmony. I attach very much importance to it—a student who hears the harmony can comprehend a lot.

MZ: One more vital question that worries most pedagogues: in what tempo do you think it expedient to practice technically difficult episodes: in slow tempo, moderate tempo or as fast as possible?

MP: I would recommend studying a piece in the moderate tempo, avoiding too slow and too fast a tempo.

MZ: Does this also refer to the initial stage of studies?

MP: Just imagine that a child or an adult has to unwind a ball of wool. What tempo should one choose to unwind it? Perception of a new composition or mastering some technically difficult fragments is like unwinding a ball of wool. The major demand is to play in the tempo that allows you to learn the piece, the tempo that is most convenient for you, in which you feel comfortable, at ease.

MZ: If you don't mind, let's turn to the question of étude literature and the way to work at it. For every student of piano, there exists a very important borderline when he turns from strictly instructive études (Czerny, etc.) to artistic études (Chopin, Liszt). What can you say in this respect?

MP: I went through a great deal of Czerny's études. I even remember part of them till now.

MZ: Do you mean *op. 299* or *op. 740?*

MP: I am speaking about *op. 299. Op. 740* presents études of a different kind. They can be easily substituted by others. In other words, I hold that the études of Czerny *op. 299* are obligatory for every student (the more, the better). As for the études of *op. 740,* they are usually played at the stage when other études can be executed as well. There is far more interesting literature. For instance, one can already turn to the Chopin études. Of course it is useful to train certain types of technique on the études from *op. 740.* But I repeat that the études of *op. 299* are the basis of étude literature at the medium stage of studies, a vitally important stage, when the rudiments of virtuosity should be established. We spoke of WHAT études to play. But the important question is HOW to play them. I dismiss the problem of the instructive and artistic literature. One should strive to make every étude a creation of art.

MZ: You are absolutely right. It would be very useful to remind many pedagogues and students that, in her time, the famous Russian pianist Yesipova gave concerts made up entirely of Czerny's études.

MP: Joseph Lhévinne played a great deal of Czerny. But these études should be played precisely as they are written. And they are written ingeniously. They can be rendered just beautifully.

MZ: You've mentioned the Chopin études. And in this connec-

Mikhail Pletnyov giving out autographs after a concert.

Mikhail Pletnyov with his mother.

tion it occurred to me that instructors offering their pupils Chopin's and Liszt's études sometimes do it formally, not always conscious of the specific character of this material, that is, the peculiarities of the études of these particular composers.

MP: If we were to speak of the technique of piano literature of the nineteenth century on the whole, the compositions of Liszt and Chopin present two most important elements in it. But you are absolutely right in saying that the Chopin technique is quite different from that of Liszt. Utterly different! All the devices, most of the technical formulas, the attitudes to the technical realization of the musical message as such are different. Of course, roughly speaking, Liszt's technique has grown out of Czerny's in its essence, because all of Liszt's passages are positional. That is the key to understanding how to perform them perfectly. Chopin on the contrary breaks the positions. Even in his early compositions, his concertos in particular, there is no evidence of positions. Of course there may be some positions in them but Chopin has an entirely different plastic form, and the primary thing in every passage is intonation. Well, it is much more difficult for me to play Chopin than Liszt and particularly passage technique.

MZ: Have you played a lot of both?

MP: I have played practically all the Chopin and Liszt études but I have not performed them often on the stage. Nowadays Chopin's études are in general very rarely played in concerts. How can they be performed? You may either play them as an encore or devote a whole part of a concert to them.

MZ: Why so? A part of a concert may be compiled of miniatures of different genres: for instance, of études and nocturnes, or études and scherzos, polonaises . . .

MP: Probably. As for Liszt's études, it is quite a different thing, a different technique. I hold it necessary to combine the work on both types of études.

MZ: And what about the *Variations on a Theme of Paganini* of Brahms?

MP: It is specific music. It may be played and may be not played. You can just as well play *Variations on a Theme of Handel*. It is no less useful. They also involve very interesting devices. In any case I wouldn't play the whole of the notebooks. In general it is not worth the trouble to concentrate on compositions which are actually of no great importance.

427

Pletnyov during a concert.

MZ: How do you account for so unfortunate a thing that Bach, whom most of the serious pianists call their favorite composer, is performed so seldom on the concert stage?

MP: Bach is not an "advantageous" composer. To play the 24 preludes and fugues of Bach is a far cry from performing the 24 Chopin études. The "applause takings" are absolutely different. That is one side of the matter. But there is the other one, which might be more important. To perform polyphony truly well can be accomplished only by a musician who understands what polyphony is from the inside, that is a musician who can write some canon or maybe even a fugue. You get away with simply shaking your head violently or with some superficial effects. Here you've got to make music. I want you to see my point—it refers to polyphony in general, not only to Bach. Chopin is also polyphonic, and it is often that polyphonic sound that is missing when his compositions are performed. Instead, we hear just notes or well-learned parts being played.

MZ: Some words about the work on sonatas and concertos. What are the major flaws of the students in the interpretation of sonatas, concertos?

MP: One should feel the "big form." You may often hear, "I can't master the form." Such a notion does not exist for me. You must feel the form on the whole from the start. Mozart said: "I hear the whole symphony from beginning to end." I am absolutely sure that in order to play a large-scale composition one has to be himself a composer to a certain extent. A performer who does not know how the composition is composed cannot grasp the logic of the development of its form, the logic of the application of this or that expressive device; he never will understand how it should be played. He would "rush about." He may play it successfully once, but the next time he will make a complete mess of it. A musician who knows what composing music is sits down to play a new piece, takes the first chord and at once comprehends what should be done in it.

MZ: We've touched upon some particular points of piano pedagogics. They have been to a considerable degree important at all times as long as the piano has existed. But there are evidently some special demands a contemporary pianist must comply with.

MP: Undoubtedly there are such special demands. Nowadays it has become more difficult to play the piano or any other instrument. That can be accounted for by two things: firstly, by the development and spreading of gramophone recording; secondly, by the dialectic development of the pianistic art. I'll explain what I mean. In the last century, the attitude towards the piano changed dramatically. If we listen to the old Masters, celebrated performers of several decades ago, we'll see that they were not only superb musicians but above all outstanding personalities. From the professional point of view, even a Conservatory student of our days can sometimes play something better. Today the rendition must be of a very high quality. Why so? On the one hand, recording offers us a standard of performance, and there are pianists who specialize only in recording. On the other hand, there are pianists who play only on the stage, but almost as well as on a recording. For instance, there is a pianist who is of little interest as a personality but who deserves attention from the point of view of pianism and precision of execution. So at present we should look for the combination of an interesting magnificent personality with professionalism of the highest class. A good pianist must be a good composer, must know the orchestra, as well as other music apart from the piano repertory. He should strive for musicianship in the broad sense of the word. If we turn to history, we'll see that the majority of prominent pianists were composers. A pianist who does not know how modulation occurs, who fails to feel the process of the creation of a composition, for me does not exist at all.

MZ: I don't think it is possible to entirely agree with your assertion. Take, for example, the two Soviet pianists of the older generation—Gilels and Richter. They are prominent, distinctive artists. But are they composers?

MP: To a certain extent they are. Richter is known to have composed music. Incidentally, Horowitz is also a composer of a kind. He made transcriptions for the piano. He knows what it is. Sometimes Horowitz takes a small piece and writes a different end to it. And judging by how he does this, it is quite obvious that he is a gifted musician as far as composition is concerned too. In general I seldom meet truly creative personalities among pianists. As a rule, they are simply pianists who have learned the notes, have listened to a few records and are capable of playing fast, with emo-

Mikhail Pletnyov with Dr. Mark Zilberquit during the interview for this chapter.

tion and loudly enough. At the same time they may find it hard to say in what key this or that familiar melody is written.

MZ: You are quite right in saying that pianists ought to be richly, creatively gifted people. But to my mind you narrow the notion of a "true pianist" to the limit. I could name enough distinctive individuals whose creativeness finds realization not in a composer's way of thinking but in many other things . . . For example, I greatly appreciate as one of the most creative musicians the pianist and clavichordist Alexei Lhubimov. And it would be equally erroneous to assert that he is not a creative person as to claim him to be a composer. But let's get back to your example with Horowitz. What you've told me testifies to the fact that he represents perhaps the last of the pianist-improvisators. You've got to agree that there are very few contemporary pianists who would dare improvise right on the stage. Nevertheless, it does not mean that contemporary pianists do not improvise at all. In this connection I'd like to ask you what part improvisation plays in your creative work as a performer?

MP: I've been always fond of improvisation. Once or twice I happened to forget the text on the stage but I went on playing in the same style and no one noticed anything, even those who were familiar with the composition. Improvisation is a stage between com-

Pletnyov has a warm smile and even though he is basically a shy person at times, he moves easily over to the piano to demonstrate a point for the author.

position and performance. Improvisation presupposes an especial musical gift, an especial sense of music. Improvisation is essential to me both as a performer and as a person composing music.

MZ: I know you began as a composer with arrangements of fragments from Tchaikovsky's and Shchedrin's ballets which you brilliantly executed even when a student.

MP: Now I don't deal with arrangements any longer; I write original music.

MZ: For piano?

MP: On the contrary, at present I am working only at orchestra and chamber music.

When Mikhail Pletnyov mentioned chamber music, I remembered the exultant reviews of his performance in the trio with other two "gold" laureates of the VI Tchaikovsky Competition—the American violinist Elmar Oliveira and the cellist Nathaniel Rosen. They appeared together at the Festival in New York in the summer of 1979. No matter how different their temperaments, or how little they could rehearse, the concert of these three original performers was a real triumph.

When I asked Mikhail Pletnyov if he was playing chamber music I had an unexpected answer.

MP: I do not play chamber music with anyone permanently. The main problem is my busy schedule. But if I manage to gather my friends together, we play the Mozart *Quartets* with great pleasure. Usually I play the part of the second violin. It is most interesting for me. Generally speaking, any kind of musical activity is interesting for me, I would say, with the exception of theoretical things. As a matter of fact there are many more things I'd like to go in for. Very many!

MZ: Do you mean the sphere of music?

MP: What I am doing at the present time in the sphere of music is enough for me. It is first of all my practicing. Secondly, I must compose music. By the way, one usually hampers the other. If some music is "tormenting" me, ripening in me, it usually prevents mé from dealing with the performance repertoire. I told you that I had learned the Liszt *Concerto* in several hours. It is true. But at the same time it was not quite so. I left the piano and I seemed to be busy with other things but actually this music lived within me

The Gold Medal Winners of the Sixth Tchaikovsky Competition, from left to right: Elmar Oliveira, Ludmila Shemtchuk, Nathaniel Rosen and Mikhail Pletnyov.

During the interview with Dr. Mark Zilberquit, Pletnyov said "At present I read and can express myself in six foreign languages. Spanish is the next."

all the time and as with every pianist it was immediately reflected in my movements. Therefore it was enough for me to sit down at the piano and cast a glance at the score when everything came out perfectly well. So, it is piano performance, plus composition, plus sometimes conducting which I also work at when time permits. And besides there is sport; I am especially fond of badminton; there are also foreign languages. At present I read and can express myself in six foreign languages. Spanish is the next.

MZ: Your schedule is frightfully busy! I believe it is all possible only in the observance of a very well thought-out and thoroughly pre-planned regimen of the day. Isn't that so?

MP: I don't always follow a hard and fast regimen. In the morning I practice for some two or three hours. Then I go for a walk. In the daytime I work at composing music; I read. In the evening, as a rule at about eight o'clock, I sit down at the instrument once again and play till about midnight.

MZ: In other words you do not practice less than five or six hours a day.

MP: On tour I sometimes play for half an hour—as the case may be.

MZ: When you begin practicing, do you warm up?

MP: Sometimes, when I feel it necessary.

MZ: Do you warm up on scales, exercises or the current repertoire?

MP: It depends. Of exercises I still employ only one—I play different fragments (usually improvised on the spot) on coordination of the left and right hand. It is of utmost importance. For instance the right hand plays an up scale legato while the left hand plays triads (common chords) non legato, and so on.

MZ: Do you permit yourself to make long intervals in practicing in the course of the year, for instance during your vacations?

MP: No. It is awfully difficult to get "in trim" again after that. So I try to avoid any intervals.

MZ: How do you prefer to spend the day of a concert?

MP: Sometimes I simply warm up, or I play separate fragments of each composition. It depends.

MZ: During the comparatively short period of your concertizing, you've accumulated a rather substantial and varied repertoire. Do you follow any principle in choosing your repertoire?

MP: I proceed from only one consideration—I play exclusively what I appreciate.

MZ: Does it mean that in making up a program of a piano recital, a Klavierabend, there are no contraindications to be taken into account?

MP: Of course there are some. The program must be made up to meet contemporary requirements. Nowadays the audience requires that a program should have certain tendencies, a certain message, idea. Naturally, the program must reveal the strong points of the pianist, the variety of his palette. But it should also be taken into consideration that the components of the program depend on the specific audience or sometimes on the country where you are going to perform.

Mikhail Pletnyov with his mother. She has every right to be extremely proud.

MZ: When speaking of contemporary pianists, we unwittingly compare them with prominent musical interpreters of the past, though of course there are considerable differences between the contemporary style of playing and the traditions of the past. For instance, many celebrated performers of the past when playing on the stage were guided by their instinct, emotions rather than a preconceived plan, and intellect. Let's remember Heinrich Neuhaus, Vladimir Sofronitsky . . .

MP: Pianists like Sofronitsky, I mean those who play by spontaneous instinct, exist today as well. It is another matter that at present they do not quite meet contemporary requirements. In general, it is my opinion that very few pianists are really abreast of the times. Most of them do not meet these requirements.

MZ: What do you consider to be the major demands of today on a contemporary performer?

MP: The demands of the times consist of a combination of the highest possible virtuosity with correct and competent performance based on the personal attitude to the music performed. After all the only task of the performer is to gain an insight into the composer's artistic world, to somehow substitute himself for the composer, that is, to make the listener believe they are hearing the composer, the real author. He should penetrate the composer's creative process, employ certain technical devices in order to reach the composer's spiritual and emotional level and reveal it to the audience. So musical performance is a very special art—in a sense even more complicated than the art of composing music.

MZ: You are quite right in pointing out the very serious exacting demands a contemporary performer must satisfy. Because today, due to the development of gramophone and video recording, the audiences for which a performer plays are indeed enormous. I would like only to add that to my mind a musician-performer should also have a keen sense of duty to his audience, to the memory of the composer whose works he interprets, to the Great Masters of the past whose tradition he follows, and to Art.

Dmitri Bashkirov (left) with his grandmother and brother.

Dmitri Bashkirov

Dmitri Bashkirov was born November 1, 1931, in Tbilisi, in the capital of Georgia. Though his parents were not musicians he had the rudiments of musical education in his family. Dmitri's grandmother, Anna Stern, a professional pianist, a highly educated person, began to introduce her grandson to music as early as when he was four years old. At seven, Dmitri Bashkirov entered the Tbilisi Music School, into the class of professor Anastasiya Virsaladze (a former pupil of the celebrated Anna Yesipova), under whose tutelage he went through the entire ten-year course of the School. In Meisterschule, within the walls of the Moscow Conservatory and in his post-graduate course, Dmitri Bashkirov was the student of Alexander Goldenweiser. In that period covering about eight years, the artistry of the pianist was completely molded and his vivid individuality was revealed.

The 24-year-old musician scored his first great international victory at the Contest in Paris (1955). He received the Grand Prix. Margaret Long herself, whose name the Grand Prix bears, insisted that the first prize be awarded to him.

Since then, the solid artistic success of Dmitri Bashkirov has been established. "Such a dazzling original genius as Dmitri Bashkirov who, by his musicality, intelligence and technique, breaks all the habitual frames can be seen perhaps once in five years," the Finnish *Helsinki Sanomat* wrote at that time. It should be noted that when Bashkirov began to perform abroad, Soviet piano art already enjoyed the reputation of the highest possible standard, due to the breathtaking success of the musicians of the older generation—Emil Gilels and Sviatoslav Richter. Thus it was more difficult for young Bashkirov to rise to the summit of the pianistic Olympus. Yet he had managed it with "flying colors," the

Dmitri Bashkirov with his father.

reason being not only his great artistry but also the genuine originality of his gift. "Bashkirov is very different from all the rest of the musicians that the USSR has sent to the West. His profound perception of the mysterious world of pianistic colors is attended by a surprising sense of form and fiery intensity of technical reflexes," wrote the critic from the Montreal *Droits* after Bashkirov's tour in 1961. Describing the performing style of the pianist, he pointed out the following of his features: "Controlled ardor, conscious ecstasy and the superior spiritual aspirations for the actual sound of beauty in music."

Many music-lovers (Bashkirov has toured over 30 countries) were fascinated by his art not only as a soloist but also as a member of the trio (with Igor Bezrodny and Mikhail Khomitzer).

Continuing the glorious traditions of his teacher Alexander Goldenweiser, Dmitri Bashkirov, now Professor, teaches at the Moscow Conservatory. Young musicians representing the Soviet school of performance abroad have graduated from his master class.

The authority of this pianist in the music is appreciable. He was on the jury of Internationals in Leeds (England), in Uruguay, the Enesco Competition in Bucharest, the Schumann competition in Zwickau; he also had a Meisterschule in the Paris National Conservatory, in Madrid, in Finland. For the outstanding interpretation of Robert Schumann's compositions, Dmitri Bashkirov was honored with the National Prize by the East German government. Later he was awarded the Madrid University Medal (among pianists only Artur Rubinstein and A. Watts had been awarded this medal).

No matter how versatile Bashkirov's activities are, he is an artist above all. The same keen sense of the stage was inherited from Bashkirov by his daughter Elena, a pianist who in spite of her youth performs successfully as a soloist and as accompanist in many countries of the world.

Each of Bashkirov's performances is a live creation of art and perhaps the most vital thing is that each of his interpretations gives the impression of instantaneous creation being born before the eyes of the listeners. Many of his interpretations of the compositions of Mozart, Beethoven and especially Schubert, Schumann, Debussy, Prokofiev are referred to as the highest achievements in the art of

Dmitri Bashkirov (the third from left in the upper row) the student of Alexander Goldenweiser in the Moscow Conservatory. In the center of the upper row is Lazar Berman.

piano performance. It was not accidental that the West German *Suddeutsche Zeitung* wrote: "If there were a Nobel Prize for musical performance, it should be awarded to the Russian pianist Dmitri Bashkirov."

★   ★   ★

At the concert that took place on the first of November, 1981, in the Great Hall of the Moscow Conservatory despite a severe frost, the house was full. Moreover, the Great Hall regardless of its name could not accommodate all comers. Dmitri Bashkirov was to play. As sometimes happens to him, he played unevenly: the first movement of the Weber *Sonata* was performed somewhat feverishly; the second movement of the Schumann *Fantasy* a little rushed, but all was imbued with Bashkirov's sincerity, spontaneous absorption in self-expression, electrifying spirit and true artistry that immediately with the first note established an indissoluble bond between the soloist and the audience.

I was leaving the hall together with a group of Moscow musicians who were filled with impressions of the concert and were discussing it with animation. Someone pointed out a certain tempo "nervousness" of the pianist to which another, a famous Moscow pedagogue-pianist, replied: "I wouldn't exchange one of Bashkirov's concerts for three given by any other pianist of his rank, because I always know when about to listen to him, that I am to witness an exciting, fascinating performance. And I've never been disappointed. Bashkirov is a truly romantic pianist in the best sense of the word . . ."

Being described as a "romantic pianist" is by no means new for Dmitri Bashkirov. That is why it was very interesting for me to learn what he himself thought about it. That was what I intended to talk about with him when the next day we met with Bashkirov at his place.

To converse with Bashkirov is not a simple matter—the same "electrifying atmosphere" characteristic of his manner of playing is also typical of his manner of speaking; many gesticulations, and facial expressions. He sets the talk at a fast pace.

I congratulated the artist on his success at the recent concert and asked Bashkirov my first question.

MZ: That concert was not quite an ordinary one for you, was it? I believe it is not easy to remain calm on one's fiftieth birthday. You must have been very nervous yesterday?

DB: I am awfully nervous before most performances and at the beginning of a concert too. Sometimes it even tells upon the quality of my performance but I can't help it. My character is such that in the first minutes before an audience I can't help feeling uneasy. By the way, that is the reason I play so little of Bach on the concert stage but prefer to record it in the studio. Usually a recital opens with polyphony and it is simply impossible to conceal one's anxiety.

MZ: You must have come across the epithet "romantic pianist" in reviews of your performances more than once. What do you think about it?

DB: There is much confusion as to this question in both terminology and semantics. My so-called "romanticism" does not consist of the fact that I allegedly play an exclusively romantic repertory. I strive for the music of any style to breathe with freshness and vitality. The point is that pianistic flawlessness, immaculateness, "sterility" of reading the text often happen to substitute for making music "live" on the concert stage. Many pianists (especially the young ones), as if seeking to be contemporary in their performance, adopt only the outward, superficial features of the times. This finds realization in a brilliant, distinctive form, however, but is not filled with the particular charm and value of the mastery of performance – revealing the message of the composition through openheartedness, as well as originality of musical feeling.

MZ: I completely share your idea. Mastery alone, no matter how superb, if not imbued with sincerity, warmth of expression and inspiration, is of absolutely no interest from the artistic point of view. A kind of sport, perhaps . . . But the style of performance you spoke about may not be congenial to everyone. Some people think that the time of Romanticism in performance has passed, the romantic style is out of date. Is it really so? Is it right to set off one against the other?

DB: Contrasting the romantic style with the so-called contemporary style seems quite wrong to me. Of course, the pianist who tries to artificially restore on contemporary grounds the style of the performance of the past is sure to come to inevitable grief. Imitating Paderewsky, Hofmann or Cortot may turn into only a caricature today. However, many features of the masters of the past – creative freedom in the treatment of the material, of interpretation (if it does not border on arbitrariness), richness of artistic imagination, flexibility of phrasing, for our generation set by no means a less, but rather a more instructive example than performances and recordings of such contemporary "super-pianists" as Maurizio Pollini and his like.

MZ: Absolutely. Contrasting the "romantic" style with the "contemporary" style also seems wrong and one-sided to me. The more so, because when we are young we are all in a measure romantic. Besides, much in the performer's perception of the world, his creative signature stems from the mettle that was molded in his green years. In particular, don't you think that besides some definite component of your artistic talent as an artist you were to a great extent affected by the specific peculiarities of your early musical development?

DB: Undoubtedly so. For my special attitude towards music, I

Dmitri Bashkirov and Margaret Long. Paris, 1955.

am first and foremost obliged to my grandmother. It was she who was the first to introduce me to music. That introduction was purely emotional, not stereotyped. On entering the music school for instance, I was playing quite an unusual repertory: *Moments Musicaux* of Schubert, *The Wedding March* from "Lohengrin" and "The Internationale".

MZ: In what measure was that line of spontaneous introduction to music pursued at school?

DB: At school I was lucky to be for many years under the tutelage of the wonderful musician Anastasiya Virsaladze. While paying the tribute of respect and love to my second teacher Alexander Goldenweiser I've got to emphasize that, for my delicate attitude towards music, for the skill to make music on the stage, I am to a great extent obliged to Anastasiya Virsaladze. She was not only a pedagogue by calling, but also a subtle performer. She seldom played on the stage, but one of the most vivid pianistic impressions I remember is her interpretation of the Chopin *F minor (N 2) Concerto*. What wonderful subtlety, plasticity, musicality! What lovely tone! I consider it to be one of the best interpretations to this day.

Presentation of Grand Prix to Bashkirov in Paris.

***Dmitri Bashkirov during a trip with Dmitri Shostakovich
and Dmitri Kabalevsky as the members of the Soviet
delegation to England.***

MZ: She must have guided her pupils in that direction; I mean
that she regarded of paramount importance not just powerful
technical "equipment," not preparaton for "tournaments," as is
often the case nowadays.

DB: Surely. The general line of instruction of my first
pedagogue was very close to how at present I myself understand
the process of teaching and developing a musician. But do not
think that her methods were one-sided. The point is that
Anastasiya Virsaladze had also nurtured two more pianists who enjoy international popularity now—Lev Vlasenko and Eliso Virsaladze (her granddaughter), musicians of different types.

MZ: What repertory was mainly performed in the senior grades
in Anastasiya Virsaladze's class?

DB: It was mainly the traditional classical repertory. We went
through a great deal of Bach, Mozart, Beethoven, Schubert,
Schumann, Chopin. We also studied the compositions of Hummel,
Weber, Saint-Saëns. The only thing she did not teach me, because
she had not been reared on those traditons, was contemporary

Dmitri Bashkirov and Sir John Barbirolli. On the photo that Sir John presented to Dmitri Bashkirov after their concert is the following inscription: "To Dmitri Bashkirov with happy reminiscences of our co-work and amazing performance of the Mozart Concerto (C Minor) with the Munich Academy."

music. Later I did play contemporary music, but Soviet pianists of my generation did not possess as much mobility in mastering such music as do our young. For instance, sometimes a student of mine learns a contemporary piece much faster than I do, because at the time of my studies, such music was hardly ever heard either over the radio or in concerts.

MZ: What part in your studies was assigned to your technical development?

DB: My teacher was against mechanical drill. For example, her pupils never played Hanon. But we played a lot of études, especially those of Czerny, Clementi. At present these are regarded as purely instructive, auxiliary literature, but at the end of the past century Anna Yesipova gave whole concerts made up entirely of the Czerny Etudes!

MZ: Do you find it wise to divide études into "instructive" and "artistic" as is currently the practice among pedagogues?

DB: I find it harmful. The musical education of students should be complex, harmonious. A student must not be accustomed to the idea that technical aspect is one thing and musical aspect is another.

MZ: Does this mean that all exercises in general should be excluded? In particular, did your teacher offer you any exercises?

DB: In the senior grades I played the Brahms exercises though they may be dangerous for a young pianist as they may cause a severe strain of the hand. It seems to me, however paradoxical, that exercises should be played at a more mature age when they can no longer separate the pianistic form away from the image-bearing and sound message of the composition.

Dmitri Bashkirov. "Dmitri Bashkirov," wrote the Montreal 'Droits', "is different from all the other musicians that the USSR directed to the West; his profound perception of the mysterious world of pianistic colors is attended by a surprising sense of form and fiery nervousness of technical reflexes."

Dmitri Bashkirov tells highly animated musical stories.

MZ: Indeed, the practice of separating technical material from the artistic occasionally is instilled in the pupil's psychology in early childhood and in that case it is very difficult to overcome.

DB: Quite right. It often happens that many young musicians play slow pieces musically while when they turn to fast music they become robot-like. It is as if their imagination and emotions were switched off, went dead. That is why I think that it is possible to choose among the technical literature such études that would not only strengthen the fingers but also provide the opportunity to work at the tone, plasticity, and intonation.

MZ: How long did you practice daily at the instrument in your school years?

DB: I must confess that I have never practiced very much. My school years coincided with the war. It was a difficult time, to say the least. Along with the music school I also attended general school. Alas, as far as virtuosity is concerned, I haven't had solid training.

MZ: So later in the Conservatory years, did you have to make up for the lost time?

DB: It was like that only for a short period of time while I was preparing for a competition when I practiced for some four or five hours a day. It is my limit. Physically I cannot maintain it longer. My perception gets somewhat dull and I find it to be a mere waste of time.

MZ: Has your daily quota changed since then?

DB: No, it became even shorter. If I practice for three hours a day regularly I feel I'm in good shape. Don't forget that lessons with students are extremely tiring.

MZ: Do you recommend to your students that they also practice not more than three hours a day? I strongly doubt that they may be content with this regimen. I believe most serious piano students practice for five or six hours a day.

DB: I am absolutely sure that the normal regimen of practicing is four hours. In general it is not the quantity, but the quality that matters. I consider regularity of practicing to be of paramount importance; however, it does not mean that in summer one should not take a break from playing to have some rest.

MZ: To what extent did Anastasiya Virsaladze promote the development of your self-reliance? It is particularly the cultivation of the young musician's independence that is one of the major tasks of any pedagogue, isn't it? And at what age do you think you developed into a self-sufficient musician?

DB: I am convinced that the making of a musical personality occurs much earlier than it seems to many music critics and pedagogues. The young people who come to the Conservatory with nothing of their own in their background have a rough time. And it is also very hard for the teachers to work with such students. In this respect Anastasiya Virsaladze was a marvelous teacher. She had been giving full play to my aspirations since early childhood, she let her pupils, in the words of our great dramatist Alexander Griboyedov, "dare have one's own judgment." She had never been a dictator. There may have been some flaws in my development as a pianist, but I think it was in a great measure compensated by a natural, keen attitude towards music which I am striving to preserve both in pedagogics and in performance—the feature which I cherish most in myself and in my colleagues.

MZ: From Virsaladze you went to a musician of an entirely different constitution—Alexander Goldenweiser. How did your relations with him turn out?

DB: You are right in saying that Goldenweiser was a musician of quite a different mold—a subtle, intelligent pianist with a vast repertory, with austere and precise gusto and, I would say, a somewhat "dry" feeling. But the most important thing about him is that he was a man of great culture, gigantic versatile musical erudition, who represented the link between the traditions of the epoch of Rachmaninoff, Siloti, Scriabin with our days! We were on very good terms with him. I loved him dearly and he also had an affection towards me.

Alexander Goldenweiser, who paternally loved his pupils, greatly appreciated Bashkirov as an original musician. As early as 1956 he wrote about him: "He has a quality that cannot be taught: a performer's talent, the ability to captivate the audience with his performance. On stage Bashkirov does the best things he is capable of. His makings of a virtuoso, his ear for music are superb . . . In his student years his playing often lacked a sense of measure; there used to be exaggerations . . . Persistent work and constant self-control helped Bashkirov in his quest for simplicity of expression

Professor of the Moscow Conservatory Bashkirov with his students.

and perfection of the pianistic apparatus."

It is quite possible that the flaws pointed out by Goldenweiser were really characteristic of young Bashkirov. However, in spite of the fact that the teacher and the student liked each other immensely, their creative views did not always coincide. And Bashkirov speaks openly about it himself.

DB: Creative conflicts arose and sometimes my professor was indignant with me, would not approve of my interpretation. It was not without reason that people used to say that by nature and cast of mind I had a propensity for the Neuhaus school.

MZ: In what do you see the influence of your Conservatory tutor, Professor Goldenweiser, on your creative development?

DB: My unbridled nature badly needed a counterpoise. And though I complained desperately and at times set my face against Goldenweiser, many of the things he taught me eventually became part of my flesh and blood. And especially with the years I am

Bashkirov with one of his pupils, Finnish pianist Eero Heinonnen.

more and more imbued with these feelings. Still, his influence on me as a performer was to my mind not so great as that of a pedagogue.

MZ: As we very well know, the times when a pianist could win over the public and critics with his emotions only have long passed. Today musical performance is inconceivable without a blending of the emotional and the rational, the instinct and the intellect, spontaneous feeling and accurate reckoning. It is not by chance that in today's musical pedagogics such great importance is attached to the development of the musical thinking of a future performer. Don't you think that your acquiring the logical component in your performance is connected particularly with Goldenweiser's influence on you?

DB: Really, I am much obliged to Goldenweiser. He stimulated my own aspirations for clear thinking in music. With my nature that always seeks spontaneity of expression on the stage, it was extremely important — it was necessary that behind that spontaneity there should be a distinct, clear-cut design. However, the presence of this pre-conceived idea is not always perceived by the audience or by the critics as well, who are sure that my performance is one hundred percent spontaneous. Nothing of the kind! Everything is thought out and through in advance. I teach the same thing to my pupils—a precise design of the construction, accuracy and purity of style, but only as the foundation for creating on the stage.

MZ: Your "service record" of participation in International Competitions is much more modest than that of many a young pianist. If I'm not mistaken you participated in only one competition in Paris in 1955, didn't you?

DB: Yes, only in one. Generally speaking I belong to the so-called "non-competition" performers. For even that competition I had misadventures. I learned the "wrong" Sonata of Beethoven and only a week before going to Paris I had to prepare the one that was on the program of the competition. I went there without the slightest idea of which musicians were on the jury. Recently in the USA I've met the musicians who participated in that competition together with me. They remembered how amazed they were when I was relating anecdotes and making jokes while everybody was nervous waiting for the jury's decision to be announced.

Dmitri Bashkirov during rehearsal.

MZ: Did you have personal contact with Margaret Long during the competition? What was her attitude towards your performance?

DB: It was particularly thanks to Margaret Long that I was awarded the Grand Prix. The point is that after summing-up it turned out that the jury had not awarded the first prize to anyone at all. When the ceremony of awarding prizes began, Margaret Long got up and said something and mentioned my name and there arose an awful hubbub in the hall. Everyone began to applaud. She had announced that as long as the Grand Prix bore her name she had the right to deal with it and she awarded it to me . . . That was how I became the winner of the M. Long Grand Prix.

MZ: More than a quarter of a century has elapsed since then. In the meantime your own pupils Dmitri Alexeyev, Nikolai Demidenko, Alexander Bonduriansky and others became laureates of International competitions. You have been on the jury of Internationals more than once yourself. In this connection I'd like to discuss with you the problem of appraisal at competitions of the so-called "non-competition" pianists among whom in your opinion you yourself belong. Is it possible to come to such criteria, to such estimation, that a "non-competition" musician should be appreciated according to his talent, his potential that may not be fully revealed at a competition?

DB: Unfortunately, I don't think it possible. As far as I am concerned, when I am sitting at the jury's table, it is of utmost importance for me to comprehend and see in a young musician whether he is simply a "race horse," a one-day figure in music or whether his intentions are serious, if the vividness and originality of his gift will allow him even in 10 or 20 years to have his say in the art of performance. Those of my pupils whom you've named—and I'd like to add to this list the name of another of my pupils,—Finnish pianist Eero Heinonnen—I hope, will remain a "constant" in the pianistic firmament.

MZ: As long as you've mentioned your pupils, I'd like to ask you to speak of your pedagogical activities. Having begun as Professor Goldenweiser's assistant you have had your own master class for a long time already. During this quarter of a century that you've been teaching you must have formed your own pedagogical views and principles . . .

DB: When asked: "Speak of your pedagogical and performance

Dmitri Bashkirov during rehearsal.

principles," I usually answer that I've got none. Why so? Because if I had any completely formed principles I would be finished as a performer and as a pedagogue. When I am 80, when I stop teaching and performing, I'd rather give it a thought and formulate my "principles." In the very notion of a "principle" there is something still, fixed. And now everything in me is in motion, in development. I've got some considerations rather than principles.

MZ: All right. Let's call it "considerations." What are your general considerations on piano technique? Very "strong," technically well-developed young musicians enter your Conservatory class. Nevertheless you are sure to confront one or another problem of technique in your work with them.

DB: I have no special liking for the word "technique." I always prefer to use the word "pianism" instead. Many of our young have brilliant technique, but it is not pianism. For them technique itself is the end. But for me the word "pianism" implies culture of tone and diversity of articulation, intonational subtlety.

MZ: What types of technique presented the greatest difficulty for you?

Bashkirov rehearsing with conductor Pavel Kogan.

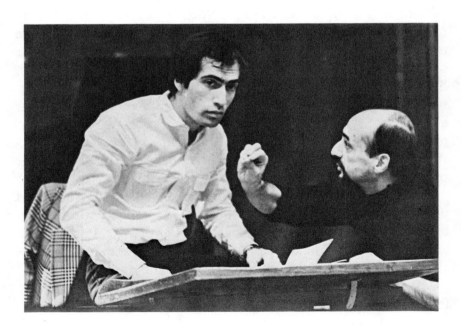

DB: Just as many instrumentalists, in particular, even many famous violinists, do not possess innate staccato, I don't have a light enough repetition hand. Perhaps if this had been developed in me from early childhood, I would have been much better off. But I am a fatalist in these matters. If you are not endowed with something by nature . . . An experienced ear can always tell a born virtuoso from a pianist who has developed his virtuosity. Even when we are carried away by the virtuoso perfection of Sviatoslav Richter which excels the innate virtuosity of many other outstanding artists, it is still obvious that it has not sprung up by itself, but is the result of titanic labor and the work of intellect.

MZ: We all know the advantages a student has by virtue of possessing innate virtuosity. At the same time it is common knowledge that acquired virtuosity also allows the achievement of great results. Evidently, you have pupils of both kinds. What do you see is the difference between them?

DB: The "congenital" technique has one paradoxical quality: sometimes it degrades easier than the acquired, "intelligent" technique. However, that is explicable: people lacking innate virtuosity must employ the means which are rational to the utmost. They mobilize not only their physical but also spiritual, intellectual resources and achieve brilliant results. Physiology (in this case the inborn mobility of the fingers) does not always provide an optimum artistic result anyway. At times the result is quite the reverse. Yet, inborn physical predisposition to playing the piano is an enviable thing!

MZ: I absolutely agree with you. I think that judging by the lightness of repetitions in the hand it is possible to a certain extent to diagnose the pupil from the point of view of his potential dexterity.

DB: It was just such a case with my pupil, now a famous pianist and a profound musician, Dmitri Alexeyev. He entered the Conservatory as a rather mediocre student. But when he asked me to take him into my master class I paid attention to the natural lightness of rebound of his fingers and hand from the keys. (By the way, he plays table tennis with equal dexterity.) These are all interdependent things—swift reaction, springiness of muscles. These qualities furthered the development of his pithy virtuosity.

MZ: As we've touched upon different aspects of piano techni-

Yelena Bashkirov Kremer, Gidon Kremer and Herbert Ax-elrod after the Kremers' concert with the N.J. State Orchestra.

Dmitri Bashkirov, Igor Bezrodny and Mikhail Khomitzer.

que, we cannot bypass the question of fingering. Incidentally, do you mark the fingering in your students' scores?

DB: I do, when the fingering offered in the scores does not correspond to the artistic task. We often come across such a thing. Some prominent musicians have edited classical pieces, marking fingering scrupulously. At first sight it seems quite logical, especially in instances when it is based on the traditional Czerny principles. But when the composition is performed in a concert variant (by an artist or a student) these fingering principles often do not prove their value. Why? Because they are based on dogma rather than proceeding from the artistic image that should be created by a certain passage. As to the fingering, I believe that even in the most lucid passage there may and must be different variants of fingering depending on the hand structure of the performer and on whether it is played articulato, legato or staccato . . .

MZ: And first of all on the contents of music . . .

Dmitri Bashkirov with Dr. Herbert R. Axelrod. Axelrod presented Bashkirov's daughter, Yelena Kremer, as a guest artist with the New Jersey State Orchestra.

MZ: Absolutely. In one case the passage should be played as if it were glissando, another time almost melodiously, "chopinizing" the texture, etc. Then the sketchiness, the formality vanish.

MZ: It is well-known that the thumb gives a lot of trouble to students of the piano . . .

DB: I call the thumb a "churl," a "martinet."

MZ: Then how do you make it "cultured"?

DB: First of all by being attentive, realizing that it is quite agile. Second, it is essential that the player pay special attention to it lest it "overload" the entire hand. Third, every time, when it is necessary to put the thumb under, it should hardly touch the key, that is, it should be the lightest of all fingers.

MZ: In other words, you suggest not putting the thumb under, but shifting it; that is, you find it necessary to strive for positional playing, don't you?

DB: Yes, in general I am all for positional playing. It is indubitable. Of course, there are pianists born with God's blessing, to whom it makes no difference whether they play positionally or not. As far as ordinary mortals are concerned, I am an advocate of the positional approach to solving technical problems, because on contemporary instruments and with the contemporary repertory, the positional approach provides more convenience, and less tension.

MZ: How can constraint and lack of agility in the fourth finger be overcome?

DB: Unfortunately, we've got to develop our fourth finger all our life, though with time we come to the conclusion that if it does not acquire utter freedom and independence of motion, we'd rather do without it wherever possible. At least that's what I am doing.

MZ: There are many exercises for the fourth finger. I persistently advise my students to play the chromatic scale upwards and downwards with the third, fourth, fifth fingers among other exercises. It is very useful.

DB: I agree with you that it is a wonderful drill. But one shouldn't at the same time forget to relax the tension coming from the first finger!

MZ: Let's turn now to the question of polyphony. There is a traditional recipe for mastering a polyphonic piece: playing it in parts, in "horizontals." Is that necessary for an advanced student?

Bashkirov in his study.

DB: I don't find it necessary for gifted pianists. It is much more useful to play the whole texture in a three- or four-part fugue switching attention from one part to another alternately. Then there remains the feeling not only of the "horizontal" but also of the "vertical". Otherwise, hearing the horizontal separately, one has to "assemble" the vertical. It is a kind of double work. Our consciousness is polysemantic: it seems to us we are listening only to one part, but in the background we unconsciously perceive all the rest. And only by way of exceptions I advise (mostly to less talented students) learning separately some very complicated lines, intricate, concealed for our ear. I am still of the opinion that it is better to accustom oneself to the texture on the whole but with a differentiated approach.

MZ: Do you prefer your students to come to the lesson with a new composition to be played from memory?

DB: I simply don't permit it otherwise. I hold that in the process of studying, we must train the student's memory to the utmost, that it provide him with a durable stock of memory. Another of my methods – barbarous and tormenting for the pupils in class but

Bashkirov in his study.

Dmitri Bashkirov with his daughter Yelena—a marvelous pianist, the former wife and partner of Gidon Kremer.

which builds great confidence on the stage later, is the requirement that a student should play from memory the piece he is learning, beginning at any phrase. And in this I am merciless.

MZ: Students often dream of studying in the class of a concertizing pedagogue who can explain things not only by means of words but can also illustrate them on the instrument. So, I wonder if you often resort to the help of the piano at the lessons?

DB: I try to do it as little as possible. My aim is to turn exclusively to verbal explanation by the end of our studies. The more talented the student, the less he needs to be shown; and for the pedagogue himself to play provokes imitating. The point is that by showing something on the piano, I am doing nothing but offering some definite sounds and emotions he must re-create. Therefore I try to explain to the student what he should be striving for. If he comprehends and carries out what is necessary, next time he will be able to do everything by himself, without my prompting him.

MZ: How do you commence your work at a piece?

DB: I do my best to grasp its general idea at once, its emotional tone, mood. Generally speaking, if I undertake a piece, it is not haphazardly. It means I am looking forward to working at it and consequently I have a rough idea of what I've got to work at.

MZ: Do you use the recordings of other performers in the process of your work?

DB: I allow myself to listen to a recording only after I have sized up my own intentions in connection with the composition I'm working on. If I am sure of what I want to achieve, I may listen to anyone I choose and as much as I choose. I may derive some details from that but I will never turn my own interpretation into a copy, an imitation. For instance, at one time I played an encore of the Gluck *Melody* in Sgambati's arrangement. Then I heard it performed by Rachmaninoff. His interpretation was not congenial to me, but it was so impressive that I suddenly lost my own attitude to this piece. There was nothing left for me to do but to put this piece aside, so to say, until I forgot Rachmaninoff's interpretation in order to recover that of my own once again.

MZ: All children beginning to study the piano are taught to sit at the instrument almost always in the same manner. But it is common knowledge that every pianist finds his own most convenient position at the instrument. What can you say about the position at the piano, particularly that of your own?

DB: Many people are puzzled by my manner of sitting at the piano. I'm fond of sitting on the entire seat while playing and leaning upon its back. It is against the rules. But it is convenient for me; this position allows me to relax; it releases physical tension from the body. When I sit comfortably, I relax my body and then it is easy for me to play. So as to the question of the position at the instrument, there doesn't exist any laws for me. All my life I used to sit rather high. At present, closely watching over my students and listening to their considerations as to why it is convenient for some to sit high or for another to sit low, I arrive at the conclusion that I should sit lower and in recent years I've changed my position at the piano. I would say that for classical repertory a "low" position is recommended, for romantic and contemporary, — a higher position. But it can't be changed during a concert, can it? So one has to make his choice once and for all!

MZ: One of the most important periods in your life is connected with your performing in a chamber ensemble, in particular in the trio with Igor Bezrodny and Mikhail Khomitzer. What in your

Dmitri Bashkirov and Dr. Mark Zilberquit.

opinion is the benefit of playing chamber music for a musician?

DB: Playing in an ensemble does a lot of good and brings great delight. It disciplines, cultivates mutual compliance, confirms the necessity for making some compromise for the sake of the whole. It is also beneficial for one's solo work.

The trio of Dmitri Bashkirov, Igor Bezrodny, Mikhail Khomitzer was formed when the trio of the older generation (Lev Oborin, David Oistrakh, Sviatoslav Knushevitsky) ceased to exist. Some people have said that in the Soviet Union making music in trio was dying away. But it turned out that the new trio was successfully continuing the wonderful traditions of the older generation. It was a tremendous success. For seven years it has been one of the best trios in the world. And today the recordings of the Trio of Dmitri Bashkirov and his comrades are thoroughly studied by the young. They are considered to be almost a primer for students. Unfortunately, only two records were made: the Trios of Mozart, Tchaikovsky and Shostakovich. Shostakovich himself in a letter to D. Bashkirov called that recording of his Trio "a marvelous, precious present."

MZ: Did you have any creative disagreements with your partners?

DB: Surely, there were differences of opinion of all kinds: repertory, phrasing, and others. And maybe the most important were those of a psychological character. But in spite of all the difficulties and even conflicts (I still keep the tape of our stormy and even abusive dispute during the recording of the Tchaikovsky Trio), we did have a creative alliance and that alliance produced a very good final result.

The creative "result" of the Trio was great indeed. That was ascertained by the press as well as the most authoritative musicians. One of them, the famous Finnish pianist and pedagogue Eric Tawaststjerna wrote: "For famous artists, performing in chamber ensembles is always a psychological problem. Very often some partners shade the brilliance of the others or lose something in their own personality. The Moscow Trio belongs among the exceptions. It is like a separate small state of the Renaissance—in spite of the individual features of each of its participant, it presents one indivisible spiritual value."

Dmitri Bashkirov and Dr. Mark Zilberquit.

Further on, characterizing each participant of the Trio, he wrote of Dmitri Bashkirov: "The fiery intellectualism of D. Bashkirov reminds one of the description of how Hans von Bülow used to play. Bashkirov is an analyst of genius, but at the same time he is demonic, charging every note with an unremitting latent force."

In our talk with Dmitry Bashkirov we turned back to some urgent problems of contemporary piano art. We touched upon the subject of the piano literature of the last decades.

MZ: If we analyzed every two or three decades of this century we'd easily discover that the last decades, in comparison with the previous ones, are quite poor in significant compositions for the piano.

DB: Unfortunately, that is quite correct.

MZ: What do you think are the reasons for that?

DB: I am not going to undertake the analysis of all the reasons, but probably the matter is that the reflection of world problems that are today worrying mankind, including the foremost artists, seems more possible to them on some other instrument other than the piano. Perhaps our beloved piano has proved too static for expressing all the "elaborate" processes and problems of our days. It seems to me that many composers in their creative imagination fail to see any objective possibility of using the piano as a solo instrument to represent, so to say, the "noise" of the universe, the sounds of the contemporary world.

MZ: But if the pianistic creative abilities of composers are running short, doesn't it threaten to turn the army of contemporary pianists into kind of "museum workers"?

DB: This is partly true, but even so is of no small importance. We have in our possession such a vast repertory (I still do not give up hope that it will be increased) that to be a contemporary pianist is a great honor anyway. And to be a truly contemporary performer is in general not easy. Besides, the future will show if this is perhaps simply a temporary tendency. I do hope that is just the case.

MZ: Then the last question: what do you mean by a "contemporary" pianist?

DB: We may sometimes hear in an appraisal of one or another artist: "He won't allow himself to completely display his soul; he is reserved in self-expression, precise in performance, lucid in his in-

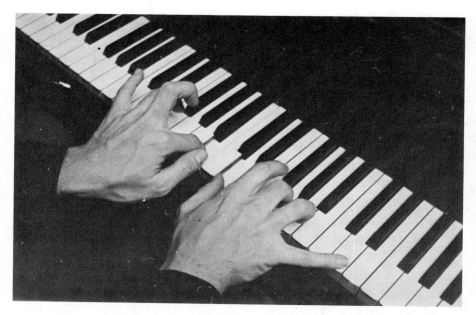

Dmitri Bashkirov's hands. Comparatively small but very soft, elastic hands of the pianist according to his own words have never given him much trouble and did not necessitate many hours of practicing at the instrument.

tentions—he is very contemporary!" But for me an appraisal like that entails something negative as well. In such cases I always recall my talk with Heinrich Neuhaus, and his words that "perfection is not always with the "plus" sign. Our contemporary is not devoid of passions and doubts, of inner struggles, of ardor—so to say, all the emotions so vividly expressed in romantic art.

MZ: Obviously, it is no accident that you returned to the problem with which we began our talk. It means that the role of romanticism in the creative work of a contemporary performer is the subject you are constantly concerned with. I share your idea that the contemporariness of an artist is represented not in the outward attributes, but in the deeply embedded process occurring within himself.

DB: Yes, for a true artist it is important to reflect not the superficial, outward features of the time. It is his attitude that is of utmost importance. We performers are invested with the supreme right to bring to life our own values, to enrich it spiritually sometimes even ahead of time, or to remind us of what has been partially lost, and what is most important: to give birth to live music with its enormously rich spectre of feelings, moods, emotions.

Our discussion was drawing to a close. We were parting with Dmitri Bashkirov, that outstanding artist whose art has one enviable and rare characteristic—the ability to reach his listeners' hearts, to speak with them in the language of candor.

Rodion Shchedrin

Rodion Shchedrin was born in Moscow on December 16, 1932. His father was a composer and instructor in subjects pertaining to musical theory.

When the boy was seven he began to learn the piano. However, the lessons were broken off by the Great World War II. His musical training gained a regular footing in the Moscow Choral Singing School (1945-1950); on finishing he went on to the Moscow Conservatoire, where, under the guidance of prominent musicians, he attended two departments (the composer's, under Yuri Shaporin, and the pianist's, under Yakov Fliyer) at a time.

As a composer and pianist Shchedrin first won recognition by creating—back in his Conservatoire years—his *First Piano Concerto* (1954).

On graduation and the subsequent completion of a post-graduate course Shchedrin fruitfully worked in a variety of genres. A notable success fell to the share of what he wrote for opera theatres and the ballet. World renown was brought to him by his ballets *The Little Humpbacked Horse, Carmen Suite, Anna Karenina* and *The Seagull* and his opera, *Dead Souls*.

Incontestable originality and mastery mark his choral and orchestral works. Critics all over the world insist that Shchedrin is one of the leading creators of modern choral and orchestral music.

The piano claims a special place in the multifaceted endeavor of the composer, who has to his credit three piano concertos, a sonata and the cycles of *Twenty-Four Preludes and Fugues, A Polyphonic Notebook and Notebook for Youth.* Shchedrin's miniatures, *Humoresque, Basso ostinato* and *An Imitation of Albeniz* are among the best specimens of modern piano music.

Rodion Shchedrin in concert.

Practically all Shchedrin's piano works are extensively performed by concert pianists and the less complex ones have formed an organic part of the musical training repertoire.

Shchedrin is a truly Russian composer. Appropriate evidence is furnished by the subjects of his program and stage works and by the fact that practically all he has written obviously suggests his distinct nexus with composers such as Lyadov, Stravinsky and Prokofiev. However, his compositional media are modern in the best sense of the word. Imaginatively re-creating many techniques of modern music writing, Shchedrin has evolved a style which is all his own.

In addition, Shchedrin is an extremely interesting pianist, his playing standing out for its subtlety of taste, bold phrasing, spectacular sweep and imaginative grasp of the instrument. Finally, far from being a cloistered artist, Shchedrin is a major public personality—Chairman of the Board of the Union of Composers of the Russian Federation and a jury member of many international competitions, including those of pianists. In 1976 the composer was elected member of the Bavarian Academy of Fine Arts (FRG).

I met Shchedrin in his spacious flat, in which he lives with his wife, the queen of ballet Maya Plisetskaya. Our conversation began in the drawing-room, adorned by portraits of this great ballerina, and was concluded in the composer's huge workroom, all its simple and strict furnishings indicating that it is *his* study.

In the corridor which leads to his room I could see paraphernalia which bespoke its master's passion—a host of rods, skeins of line, sets of hooks and other fishing tackle.

It is a pleasure to associate with Shchedrin. His easy, natural deportment immediately makes his interlocutor disposed towards him. As he talks he invariably smiles never losing the chance of enlivening what he says with a fine joke and an ironic observation.

However, never once during our interview did he exhibit an ounce of posturing or show-off. Equal simplicity pervaded Shchedrin's glimpses of his maiden steps in music, which he made at my request.

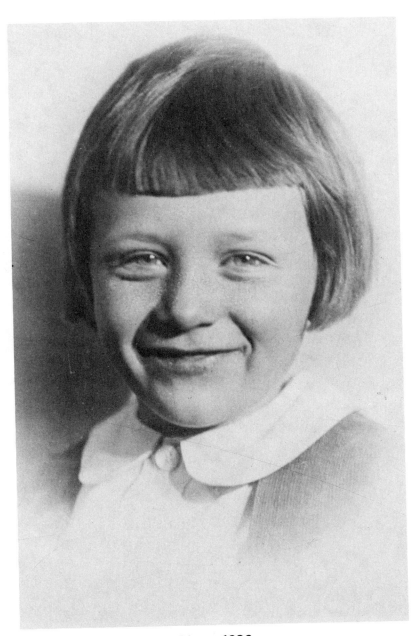

Rodion Shchedrin. Circa 1936.

Rodion Shchedrin. Circa 1941.

RS: Born into the family of a musician—my father was a composer—in my childhood I was, naturally, introduced to the ABC's of music. I remember my mother, an economist of the Bolshoi Theatre, taking me to a piano teacher, Maria Lazarevna Hechtman, who diligently explained to me what staff the note C belonged to and that a whole note consisted of two halves. True, her lessons failed to leave a deep mark on my musical career. My discovery of the world of music came later, when I joined a choir. That was what gave me my first minutes of delight in music.

MZ: And when did you develop intimacy with the piano?

RS: In the closing months of the war, more exactly, on January 1, 1945, I entered the Moscow Choral Singing School. In those years its principal, our outstanding musician Alexander Sveshnikov, had brought together a good teaching body. My piano master was Grigori Dinor, an excellent teacher whose remarkable skill largely explains my absorption in piano music.

MZ: Since you became a serious piano student while an adolescent your teacher must have set you a fairly fast working pace?

RS: I should say Dinor was right in his choice of a policy towards his pupils: he offered us pieces of obviously insurmountable difficulty. With our modest pianistic grounding we could cope with them only by exploiting our enthusiasm, with which we bubbled over. In spite of our formidable workload we tried to spend whatever free minute we had at the instrument. I remember rushing to the piano during the intervals in order to snatch at least another 10 minutes' training scarcely had the teacher closed the door. Our ardor brought remarkable results: a fascinating world opened up before our youthful minds and hearts awakening our interest and, I should say, instilling in us a hunger for learning and for plunging into some hidden recesses of music.

MZ: Could you recall a program you played at your school finals?

RS: My piano program would have looked spectacular even if it had been played by a professional pianist, let alone a graduate of a choral singing school. It included, for instance, several fugues from Bach's *Well-Tempered Klavier* (of which I could take my own pick!), pieces by Liszt, *Rhapsody on a Theme of Paganini* by Rachmaninoff. It is another matter that, as I now realize, my performance was far from flawless. But then, it was quite natural.

479

However great was my enthusiasm for the piano, it was not my key school subject. Besides, I did only six years in the school.

MZ: What factors, in addition to the atmosphere which prevailed in the school, kindled your piano fire?

RS: In those years the school maintained the fine tradition of holding concerts by remarkable musicians. We played host to Dmitri Shostakovich, Aram Kachaturian, the brilliant virtuoso pianist Grigori Ginzburg. Within the school walls I also heard another pianist, Yakov Fliyer, who became my lifelong idol. I keep an unfading impression of his performance. He must have deliberately selected a program for a young audience. Among the pieces he chose for us were Skriabin's *D Sharp Minor* study and *Campanella* by Liszt. His playing and his entire make-up simply overwhelmed us. It seemed to us that a god had come down to our school enabling us to watch his hands, his profile and his carriage from just a few meters away. We were captivated by the startling sensation of the fantastic musical feast which befell us on that night.

When Rodion Shchedrin begins to recall Yakov Fliyer the slightly ironic smile which lends its typical expression to his face momentarily disappears. He grows absolutely serious. Of Fliyer Shchedrin speaks exclusively as he would of his idol, his god. And, as I understood in the course of our interview, this should be attributed to something greater than the fact that Fliyer had become his piano professor at the Conservatoire. Association with a powerful personality such as Fliyer — artist, educator and man — was a factor of inestimable importance in Shchedrin's life.

Asked to recall how he met Fliyer, the composer had this to say.

RS: Once, all of a sudden, Dinor said: *Today you and I will go to the Conservatoire. I want to introduce you to Fliyer.* Shortly, I found myself sitting at a piano in Fliyer's classroom. I played some pieces by Chopin, which I had no right to play. After each piece the professor's emphatically "polite" face showed the absence of delight. Feeling that my chances had sunk to zero point, Dinor said: *Besides playing, he writes his own music!* Out of the same politeness and tolerance, Fliyer agreed to listen to a few samples of my self-expression. *Well, let him play something.* I began with one of the piano studies I had written. When I finished I saw an entirely different expression on Fliyer's face. It showed some spark of interest.

The mother of Rodion Shchedrin.

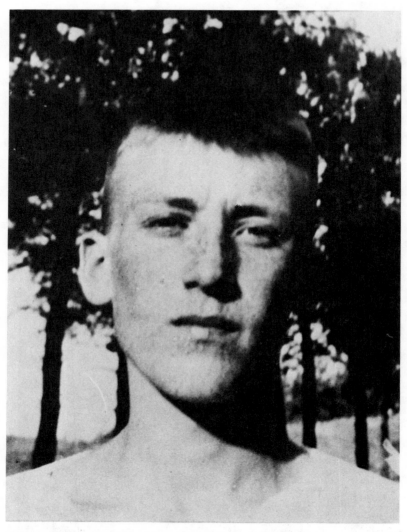

Rodion Shchedrin. Circa 1946.

Well, have you written anything else? he asked. After the third or perhaps the fourth piece Fliyer announced: *I will take him to my class.* That settled my fate. In the autumn of 1950 I entered the Conservatoire as a student of Yakov Fliyer.

MZ: How did Fliyer construct his classes? Was his preferred method that of practical demonstration on the piano or that of verbal explanation?

RS: Yakov Vladimirovich always sat at the second piano: there were two Bechsteins in the classroom. His students had a boundless repertoire. Fliyer had an inherent quickness of wit and could draw curious parallels from painting or literature. But, far more important, he could immediately play for his student. And play exhibiting such brilliance of perfection that the student would be overcome with colossal amazement: how can this be possible at all? At times Fliyer's lessons developed into his solo concerts. Perhaps these were the best minutes I spent in his class.

MZ: What were the repertoire-forming principles and stylistic attachments of Fliyer the educator? In particular, what place in his work with the students was claimed by 20th Century music?

RS: The repertoire policy of Fliyer the educator was both emotional and subtly thought out. How skillfully he brought to me specific works within my reach! For example, it was precisely Fliyer who introduced to me the impressionists, who in those days were unfamiliar and whose works were scarcely ever played in our country. I have in mind *Fetes* by Debussy (a piano transcription of the nocturne brought by Yakov Vladimirovich from Brussels before the Second World War) and his *Suite Bergamasque* as well as Ravel's *Le Tombeau de Couperin* and *Ondine*. Fliyer frequently made me play Bach. Suffice it to say that in the Conservatoire I did the majority of the preludes and fugues from the *Well-Tempered Klavier*. He had particular fondness for transcriptions of Bach's organ works amazingly performing them himself. I have mentioned just a few composers. However, Fliyer steered his pupils through the reefs of all styles.

MZ: In the Conservatoire you attended two departments simultaneously—that of composers and that of pianists. How much did your piano classes, in particular, your association with Fliyer, mold you as a composer?

RS: I owe Fliyer a great deal as a composer as well. In my first year I wrote several piano works—a *Suite* and some other pieces. Naturally, my first listener was Fliyer. On several occasions he gave me good counsel as a pianist. However, I found his advice to reveal the skills of a professional composer being of utmost relevance in the recording of some specific fragments, to say nothing of form development. Thus, Fliyer provided answers to some of my questions with regard to compositional technique. Besides, it should be borne in mind that I wrote my *First Piano Concerto,* to which I owe my renown as a composer, when I was in the fourth year at the Conservatoire, in other words, when I studied under Fliyer.

Shchedrin's *First Piano Concerto,* written in 1954, created nothing short of a sensation. In addition to being the maiden triumph of this young composer, it became a landmark in the history of Soviet piano music.

Shchedrin's performance of the *Concerto* had other important welcome results for him. Soviet professional composers form the USSR Union of Composers—a creative organization entry to which is a sufficiently complex and time-consuming process. Shchedrin's case, however, exhibited a different pattern. Here is what he recalls in this connection:

RS: It so happened that my *First Concerto,* written, as I said earlier, back in my student days, was included in the program of a plenary session of the Composers' Union. Shortly after I played it in the Grand Hall of the Conservatoire I suddenly received at my home address an envelope with a letterhead saying: USSR Union of Composers. Enclosed was an extract from the minutes of a session (date indicated, 1954) which listed who had been present and what had been decided. I read: ". . . to extend to R.K. Shchedrin membership of the USSR Union of Composers." Without receiving an appropriate application from me and without having me present any documents and fill in any questionnaires, simply on somebody's initiative, I, a fourth-year student, was made member of the Union! My concerto must have made a favorable impression at the plenary session. I was the more surprised since during the discussion of my work the professors had expressed different views. Someone had even proposed giving me a satisfactory mark, not more.

Rodion Shchedrin. Circa 1949.

MZ: Since you have told me the story of your *First Piano Concerto* I would like to discuss with you the other two you have created. Your *First Concerto* and your *Third*, written in 1973, are 20 years apart—undoubtedly an immense period. However, your evolution is astounding. It has taken in literally all aspects of a composer's endeavor: the idiom, and the form, and the notation, and, of course, the imagery. I assume that the critics who claimed that the *First* and *Third Concertos* appeared to have been authored by different composers had serious grounds for their statement. What do you say?

RS: I have heard statements that my *First* and my *Third Concertos* appear to have been written by different authors. However, I find it strange to hear it. My own perception of the music of both works suggests to me that they belong to one composer with one view of the world and creation. As regards the evolution which is disclosed by a comparison of these two works, to my way of thinking, it is natural. The many long years which divide my two concertos made me wiser, including lots of experience. The world around me changed and I changed in the process. On the contrary, what I always find strange is how an artist can write, think and create as he did decades ago.

MZ: I will take a brief look at the form of your *Third Concerto*. It has thirty-three variations and a theme. This involuntarily suggests an analogy with Beethoven's *Thirty-Three Variations on a Diabelli Theme*.

RS: You are quite right. The analogy is there but it is fairly conventional. The history of my *Third Concerto*, which I wrote in the 1970's, goes back to the period when, a student of the Conservatoire, I played Beethoven's *Variations*. But I should say the analogy does not go beyond the number thirty-three. Take, for instance, the fact that in my work the theme follows the variations. Further, in some fragments the piano plays one variation while the orchestra does an entirely different one. However, I don't think this is an expression of chaos or the result of an extravagance of the design. Each note is thought out and weighed in the work.

MZ: Since you have raised the question of your compositional techniques I would like to know, at least in brief outline, how you compose music.

Rodion Shchedrin. Circa 1952.

Rodion Shchedrin applauding the orchestra after they performed one of his pieces. "I hold that music writing is as individual a process as, for instance, the manifestation of love."

RS: I hold that music writing is as individual a process as, for instance, the manifestation of love. I for one begin to compose music by a momentary grasp of the whole in a special state which I conventionally define as aural vision, in other words, the inner sensation of the opening of a work, not in terms of sounds, but conventionally. More exactly, I feel the mood which attends the opening, of how it mounts, ebbs and necessarily draws to a close. I emphasize that the process does not begin by some theme coming to my mind and prompting me to develop it in some appropriate form. Far from it. The entire work presents itself before my inner ear as a whole.

MZ: This brings back to my mind Mozart, who, on completing one of his symphonies, said that at some moment he suddenly had heard the whole of his creation from the first note to the last. However, his older contemporary, Haydn, attached crucial importance to melody as the grain from which grows the entire work.

RS: No doubt Haydn was right in his own way as well because at times, when a composer gets down to writing a new work, already the opening theme, if not the opening line, dictates the rest. It is precisely this theme that determines the path which will be followed by the thought and spans a bridge to the culminations, certain dramatic key points and, finally, the conclusion. If the beginning is formed by another line the composer is led in an entirely different direction. Already the first bars of the future work contain the conception, the material gripping the composer: it stands behind the general dramatic pattern of the work, and its design, and its intonational aspect, in short, its entire magnetic field.

MZ: Do you compose at the piano?

RS: Never. I write orchestral and operatic music in partitura form. Even when I write piano music I use the instrument as a means of checking what I hear rather than a tool of direct composing.

MZ: Your works show a remarkable diversity of genres embracing operas, ballets, choral and instrumental pieces. However, it is precisely your instrumental music that reveals your attachment to the piano to the detriment of, for instance, the violin or the cello.

RS: This is true. My gravitation towards the piano is due to my Conservatoire grounding. I graduated as a composer and a pianist. Besides, the piano is my vehicle of self-expression as a performer. At times this becomes absolutely imperative! A composer becomes

Tikhon Khrennikov and Rodion Shchedrin.

swept by an entirely specific feeling when he plays for a living audience! In instances like these I experience a particular satisfaction both in the rare cases when I play works by other authors, especially Chopin, and of course, when I play my own pieces.

Following a remarkable tradition which goes back to Bach, Scarlatti, Mozart and Beethoven and maintained by Chopin, Liszt, Skriabin, Rachmaninoff, Prokofiev and Shostakovich, musical composers have been interpreting their own piano works. A composer's desire to perform his music for audiences is so natural that at times I ask myself why do not all composers strive to appear before listeners as interpreters of their own works? After all, the

Rodion Shchedrin. Circa 1967.

Rodion Shchedrin is a complete sportsman spending all his free time in fishing, swimming, skiing and other sport activities. He maintains himself in splendid physical condition.

composer's performance of his own music before a living audience is a mutually beneficial and no doubt mutually interesting process. The public becomes introduced to perhaps the most authoritative and convincing presentation of the work while the composer, by re-creating his own work before the listeners, gains a specific impulse for creative endeavor.

Regrettably, by the time Shchedrin started on his career as a musician in his own right Prokofiev had no longer been among the living and Shostakovich had been giving exceedingly few performances. In fact since then Shchedrin has been the only Soviet composer to give piano recitals made up exclusively of his own works.

Shchedrin's extensive activity as a performing pianist began in the mid-1950s, after he had written his *First Piano Concerto*. His presentation of the work at the 1955 World Festival of Youth and Students in Warsaw made music history. Later, the author played it before a variety of audiences revealing the originality of compositional thinking as well as artistic mastery. Following one of his own performances of his *Second Concerto* — a work which sparked off extensive debates — offered in Italy in 1968 the newspaper El Secolo wrote: *A pupil of Shaporin in composition and of Fliyer in the piano, Shchedrin has shown himself to be not only an ideal performer of his own work, but also a talented virtuoso in general.* Shchedrin's performance of his *Third Piano Concerto* was a triumph in Switzerland, Austria, Sweden, the Federal Republic of Germany and Italy.

The composer fairly frequently plays his *Twenty-Four Preludes and Fugues and Polyphonic Notebook* — works intensely complex in all respects.

Shchedrin's fairly intensive if erratic work as a pianist led me to ask him how regularly he practices on the piano.

Replying, the composer said:

RS: Regrettably, for many long years I have been having no chance to do regular piano practice having to exploit the skills formed by attending Fliyer's classes. If I could avoid exhausting regular exercises I would gladly play the piano. Alas, this is impossible. Frankly, when I think of the young pianists who enthusiastically spend many hours a day at the instrument I involuntarily ask myself what they will feel like after they are past 40. After all, piano exercises are comparable to galley slavery!

Rodion Shchedrin with his wife, the world famous balle-rina Maya Plisetskaya.

MZ: How then do you regain the appropriate shape without regular practice, your concert following a prolonged break in the exercises?

RS: Our friends refuse to believe my wife, Maya Plisetskaya, when after my concert as a pianist she tells them that I scarcely ever play the piano. However, this is almost the truth. Several days before I am to make my stage appearance I proceed to work myself back into shape. My customary stamping ground is Brahms's *Variations on a Theme of Paganini*, studies by Chopin and Liszt, some works by Rachmaninoff and Skriabin. However, even the few hours I have to spend at the instrument appear to me to drag incredibly slowly—so much I have become oppressed by this vital part of piano "application."

MZ: You perform mainly your own piano compositions. However, I have happened to hear you (at a concert held in memory of your teacher, Yakov Fliyer, in the Grand Hall of the Moscow Conservatoire) play Chopin. And although you did short pieces—several preludes and mazurkas—you exhibited tempting subtlety and a highly unorthodox approach to the material. I wonder if you have ever felt like giving a concert of your own works alongside those of other composers?

RS: Of course. I have on many occasions been tempted to prepare a program of works by, for instance, Chopin and Skriabin. However, my preoccupation with music writing has always stood in the way. I already doubt if I will ever be able to carry my design into execution. Now that I have turned fifty I have been prizing every minute of my time. Of course, if I could stretch the twenty-four hours of my day into thirty-six and work, instead of erratically, with calculated assiduity, I would exhibit greater output. However, I cannot say "no" to winter fishing, water skiing, windsurfing, one of my newly developed hobbies, or other pleasures of life.

MZ: You have mentioned Chopin and Skriabin. Apparently, they are your two favorite piano composers?

RS: To me piano compositions do not stand apart from the rest of music. This is why the list of my favorite composers includes Bach, Rossini and Mozart as well. I frequently listen to the last quartets by Beethoven. Of course, I also love Russian music. I am simply nurtured on its life-giving juices. However, of the piano

In the Shchedrins' apartment, from left to right: Rodion Shchedrin, Mrs. Mark Zilberquit, Maya Plisetskaya and Dr. Herbert Axelrod.

Rodion Shchedrin with Andrei Voznesensky.

composers Chopin and Skriabin are the most important for me.
Perhaps this also trails from Fliyer, and, no doubt, my other youth
idol, Vladimir Sofronitsky.

MZ: Regrettably, Sofronitsky, who has been deified by several
generations of Soviet musicians and music lovers, is scarcely
known in the West. And, of course, his recordings fall short of offering an ample concept about this unique master of the keyboard.
This is why it would be particularly interesting to have your impressions about his art—impressions of a present-day instrumen-
talist—in a book addressed to American audiences.

RS: Sofronitsky graced the Soviet musical stage in that prolonged and amazingly fruitful period in the history of our pianistic

art which was dominated by Konstantin Igumnov, Heinrich Neuhaus, Maria Yudina, Sviatoslav Richter, Emil Gilels—all of them outstanding pianists. However, of this brilliant galaxy my preferences go to Sofronitsky. I remember minute details of many of his performances—great, and unfelicitous, and even scandalous, when, forgetting the text, he left the stage, came back and erred again. However, during his unmatched peaks he attained an exceptionally rare impact, as, for instance, in his rendition of works by Schumann and especially Skriabin: in interpreting Skriabin's pieces he had no equal.

MZ: You have mentioned the failures which occurred to Sofronitsky, as, incidentally, they did to another amazing keyboard

Rodion Shchedrin with Yuri Temirkanov.

artist, Heinrich Neuhaus. I involuntarily feel like comparing them with dozens of present-day pianists, who are impeccably stable and fail-safe but in artistic terms are dwarfed by the towering figures of the past you have named.

RS: I am convinced that modern instrumentalism, in particular pianism, is in crisis. It is due to many factors, which, of course, warrant comprehensive research. I will confine myself to saying that what is practically the only currently adopted form of stage contact between the piano soloist and the public—the piano recital—has largely outlived its day. It is not even the minor point such as clothes that matters. These "tails" concerts, as I call them, which create a certain barrier (more often than not, insurmountable) between the tailcoated artist and the audience appear to me to be anachronistic. Recently invited to a piano music festival in Munich, I asked its organizers: *Tails or dinner-jackets?* And I was immensely pleased to hear an answer from which I realized that the festival would not resemble the traditional stiff-style concerts which have bored the public to death. It can reasonably be asked: *What do you propose instead?* The question is by no means simple. I will only say that I stand for a diversity of the forms of pianist-listener communication, the directness of its forms and the naturalness of its atmosphere. I vote for playing before audiences, for the art of improvisation rather than devitalized art. Having attended many competitions and festivals, to which I had been invited at different times, I discovered particular congenialness to. concerts in which the playing was at times unrehearsed or in which young musicians improvised before the public.

MZ: Which of the pianists of the middle and younger generations do you hold to be the best interpreters of your works?

RS: I am happy to know that my music is being played both by concert pianists and by students. During my recent stay in Saratov, for instance, I was incredibly amazed to hear a girl student of the local conservatoire play all my *Twenty-Four Preludes and Fugues.* My *Humoresque, An Imitation of Albeniz* and *Basso ostinato* enjoy major popularity. I have heard many superb renditions of these miniatures. As regards my concertos and other large pieces pride of place goes to our well-known artist Nikolai Petrov—in my opinion, a pianist with a boundless potential, who, although he looms large on our pianistic horizon, remains to be appraised at his true merit.

As a souvenir of his visit, Maya Plisetskaya presented Dr. Axelrod with two biographies of her life . . . one in Russian and one in English.

A very short while ago I discovered for myself a young pianist who also gave a rarely perfect treatment to my *Polyphonic Notebook*—Alexander Malkus, a winner of international competitions.

MZ: Your compositions really have an enviable fate, being played by professional musicians and amateurs alike. A piano instructor myself, I can state—and this is by no means a fresh discovery—that some of them have struck deep roots in the training repertoire. This is what lent such great interest to your last piano work, *Notebook for Youth,* whose very name indicates the category to which it is addressed. How was its design born and executed?

RS: Classical piano cycles for children and adolescents such as *Album für die Jugend* by Schumann, *Children's Album* by Tchaikovsky or *Music for Children* by Prokofiev are commonly familiar. Remarkable specimens of a similar genre have been created by Shostakovich and Kabalevsky. This is why the concept of my *Notebook* floated in the air until it finally matured in the summer of 1981. Its realization was touched off by purely external circumstances. I was then holidaying in Sukhumi. In the room above mine taking turns stayed two young men who diligently practiced on the piano, exhibiting a surprising similarity of repertoire—so much so that I was amazed to discover that one young pianist had yielded place to the other. Then I thought: why not write pieces based in character and content on Russian material? That was how *Cross Psalm Melody, Russian Joy-Bells, Village Mourner* and *Petrine Canticle* came into being. I would also like to extend this cycle by pieces which could introduce young pianists to some techniques of modern notation. And, of course, it would be fine if young musicians, practicing this material, again felt the remarkable potential of the piano—an instrument for which I have great fondness and in whose future I place great faith.

MZ: It is a great pleasure to hear this from you: far from all modern musicians take this attitude. And still, hasn't the piano become an obsolete instrument? Doesn't it look old-fashioned against the background of its newly-invented electronic counterparts, including synthesizers?

Rodion Shchedrin in concert.

RS: A synthesizer is really a remarkable addition to the family of musical instruments. Having recently received one of the latest models from Japan, I must confess that I admire its potential. However, as before, I assume that preaching requires a high "pulpit." Hence, I prefer music sources which have already withstood the test of centuries—the symphony orchestra, the human voice, the violin, the cello, the organ, the winds and, naturally, the piano—the musical media which best express elevated ideas. Perhaps my attachments make me sound slightly old-fashioned but take a look at—and listen to—this miracle of a piano.

Taking me to a piano which stood in the middle of his room, the host opened its lid, inscribed **Steinway**. Then he sat down at his instrument and, his fingers on the keyboard, said: *This is what it sounds like.*

The very first bars enabled me to recognize the piece. It was his remarkable *Russian Joy-Bells*. The composer played simply but, at the same time, with a wonderful, truly monumental sweep, his piano sounding like some huge belfry with many bells—big, medium, small . . .

The piece finished, the composer and I discussed some abstract concepts. Shortly, however, I left. As I walked down the street the sounds of Shchedrin's Steinway kept ringing in my ears.

Rodion Shchedrin in concert.

INDEX

Page numbers set in *italics* refer to illustrations